THE JEFFERSONIAN TRADITION
IN AMERICAN DEMOCRACY

THE JEFFERSONIAN TRADITION IN AMERICAN DEMOCRACY

By

CHARLES MAURICE WILTSE

 HILL AND WANG, INC.

NEW YORK

To

My Grandmother

PREFACE

WHEN THIS STUDY first appeared, the principal concern of most Americans was how best to overcome the forces of world-wide depression. In Europe people were trading their birthright of freedom for glib promises of speedy recovery, and dictatorships of the left and of the right were supplanting constitutional governments. In America, where individual liberty had deeper roots, people turned to a re-examination of their own past, seeking for faith and hope in their own heritage of greatness. The name that recurred most frequently in those depression days was that of Thomas Jefferson. It was under this stimulus that I undertook to find out just what this first great American liberal stood for, and why.

In the process of reconstructing a coherent body of doctrine out of actions, letters, and public utterances covering more than half a century of time, two main conclusions emerged. The first was that Jefferson's influence was out of all proportion to his intellectual contributions. He was not an original thinker but his unique position in time and place and the special quality of his mind made him the instrument for giving practical application to the ideas of others. It was through Jefferson that the political liberalism of accumulated centuries passed into the democratic tradition, where it helped to mold the American way of life and to offer hope and comfort to all those peoples who were still enslaved. The second conclusion was that Jefferson's appeal, both for his own time and for ours, lies less in doctrine than in point of view; it lies in his premise that whatever they may be led to do in moments of stress or passion or fear, people have in the long run enough intelligence, enough morality, enough wisdom to govern themselves, not merely passably but well.

The decades of swift, dynamic change that have followed

the age of Roosevelt have not shaken my faith in the validity of either conclusion. We have participated in one global and in one limited war. We have watched a revolutionary ferment like that of Jefferson's time reappear in Europe and spread to Asia, to Africa, to South America. We have seen old empires die and new republics come into being around the world, inspired as our own revolution was inspired by the will to be free. We have seen the powers of government immeasurably strengthened; the areas of governmental control extended; our right to speak and even to think challenged in the very halls of Congress. Yet in the long run we have not lost but rather have reinforced our freedoms; for the courts, the bulwark of reaction in Jefferson's time and still the stronghold of conservatism in Roosevelt's, have stepped in to uphold the worth and dignity of all men where President and Congress alike have failed. In a more physical sphere, we have discovered new ways to combat disease as well as new ways to kill. We have found sources of propulsion that have shrunk this withered apple of a world to the proportions of a neighborhood, and are now permitting us to probe far beyond the limits of our planet. We have learned to use the vast energy imprisoned in matter itself, to the eternal glory, or perhaps to the destruction, of mankind.

It is there, I think, that the true secret of Jefferson's hold over the minds and hearts of men is to be found. Never for one moment would he have entertained the thought of destruction. The collective wisdom of mankind would not permit it. Deep in the innermost core of his being he believed that man, and the world he lived in, were alike ordered, rational, and ultimately good. So he could counsel tolerance even of error, as long as reason remained free to combat it, because he could not doubt that reason, unshackled, would triumph over every obstacle. So we may live as we must with folly, with bigotry, with evil, as long as we hold fast to our belief in ourselves and to our faith in man.

A multitude of books and articles have dealt directly or indirectly with Jefferson's life and thought since the *Jeffersonian Tradition* was first published, but though they have added richly to the literature they have not altered the basic conclusions here expressed. Most important of the new publications is, of course, the Princeton edition of Jefferson's papers, edited by Julian P. Boyd and still in process. Hardly less important, and also still in process, is Dumas Malone's splendid multivolume *Jefferson and His Times*. There have been excellent biographies of many of Jefferson's contemporaries, new editions of personal and public papers, and specialized histories by the score. There is also new and rich literature, biographical, historical, and analytical, covering the years of individualistic emphasis and the later years of social responsibility, both stemming from the Jeffersonian heritage. The reader who wishes to explore more widely will find no dearth of material for his choosing.

As for personal acknowledgments, I can only repeat from the first edition the expression of my indebtedness to those who then constituted the faculty of the Sage School of Philosophy at Cornell University, and most especially to Professor George H. Sabine, whose influence has been enduring. Acknowledgments are also due to the editors of the *American Political Science Review*, and of the *American Journal of International Law* for permission to reprint material that first appeared in their pages; and to the John Day Company, the *New Outlook,* and the University of Minnesota Press for permission to use copyrighted matter.

C. M. W.

Washington, D. C.
January 1960

TABLE OF CONTENTS

[xi]

Have you thought there could be but a single Supreme?
There can be any number of Supremes—one does not countervail
  another, any more than one eyesight countervails another, or one
  life countervails another.
                                                    —WALT WHITMAN

BOOK I

THE INTELLECTUAL HERITAGE

Equality consists in the same treatment of similar persons, and no government can stand which is not founded upon justice.

—ARISTOTLE

CHAPTER I

WINDS OF DOCTRINE

I

POLITICAL THEORIES and economic doctrines are never clean-cut, standing each by itself and apart from all others. Even in the speculative sphere they tend to merge, and in the world of practical affairs they slide easily into one another. Each succeeding political thinker, too, owes an ineffaceable, if sometimes intangible, debt to the thought and to the history of the past. The catholic principles on which new governmental structures are upreared become part of the consciousness of a people by such gradual steps, through the broad sweep of daily existence, that no man can say whence they arose; and when some reforming spirit formulates them in words the masses understand, they are looked upon as having been always a part of a sacred heritage.

But though the underlying principles are of slow and scarcely noticeable growth, the varied fabrics woven from them are the creatures of a given time and place. For political theories arise when old institutions crumble, or when new forces enter into the social life of a people. They are not motivated by mere speculative curiosity, but are consciously created to justify the destruction of an existing order, or to defend the status quo against the attacks of the radical and the disgruntled. Interest in politics lags when things are running smoothly; but when some institution seems no longer to fulfill its appointed function, the whole system of which it is a part is questioned. New theories spring up in periods of unrest, and ages of civil war and revolution have been ages of active political speculation.

Yet those theories which leave an enduring mark on the course of practical affairs are theories based on ideas which the ordinary course of historical and economic growth has predisposed the people to accept. Governments are not thought out in abstraction, but spring from practical needs, and must meet the requirements of practice. However rational our principles, and however logical the consequences we deduce from them, they will have value only if they work. The final test of good government is a pragmatic test. No philosophy of the state, therefore, can be made intelligible without some comprehension of the social, economic, and intellectual forces out of which it arose. Political thinking is an integral part of man's eternal quest for truth. It belongs, with religion, with science, with philosophy, to his attempt to understand and adjust himself to the world in which he lives. And the success or failure of each adjustment, together with those visionary proposals, too advanced, perhaps, for the day in which they are offered, or impossible to carry out, which therefore never gained a hearing in the councils of state—all these things pass into history, to become the groundwork for a new generation of theorists in a new period of change.

The materials of which political doctrines are formed are drawn from the inexhaustible storehouse of the past; for to be received they must have about them the ring of familiar speech and the odor of the commonplace. The originality of any theorist depends on his giving to these old and settled truths new applications, or new interpretations: on his bringing the experience and the intellectual achievements of the past within the compass of a present point of view. If he departs too radically from the main channels worn by the thought of his time, he will be put by, for later generations to discover and make use of. So must history be rewritten in every age; for we learn from the past only as we are able to bring it into the focus of the day in which we live, and read into it the terms with which we are familiar.

It is thus in a sense true that every political creed is already outgrown by the time it becomes practically effective. Developed to meet a given emergency or to solve a given problem, the need will generally have passed by the time the principle evolved to deal with it has gained popular acceptance. Conditions of the moment are met by the give and take of practical politics; by compromise and adjustment within a fixed framework of accepted ideas. It is the speculative thinkers, like Hobbes or Marx, who formulate these principles, within which more practical men, like Locke or Lenin, work out the solutions demanded by the times.

Thomas Jefferson is preëminently of this latter type, approaching his problem from the side of practice and immediate needs. His theory of the state is built up around practical solutions to practical problems, yet set within the framework of a conscious intellectual heritage, from which he chose as he saw fit. It is on the wisdom of his choice among the conflicting principles accepted by his generation that his claim to immortality rests; but for this very reason it is the more necessary to understand what these principles were, and what the problems to which they were applied. To understand Jefferson we must appreciate what preceded him; to evaluate, we must consider what has followed.

II

The period of political unrest and readjustment which culminated in the American revolution had its roots in the Reformation. Throughout the middle ages, church and state had been coequal powers, symbolized by the allegory of the two swords; but with the division into many sects, the church could no longer stand alone. Luther had been forced back into the arms of the temporal power for protection and support; and Calvin had sought to absorb the functions of the state within the church. In the one case the church depended on the state, in the other the state upon the church; and as they developed side by side, conflict was inevitable, for neither could tolerate the other. On one hand stood the established church, Lutheran in Germany, Anglican in England, with the victory in France in doubt; and on the other stood the nonconforming sects, which refused to submit in spiritual matters to any temporal power whatever.

Calvin had retained in Geneva the outward form of the republican institutions he found there, but altered their substance to conform to his own exalted notion of the function of the state. In a kingdom of the saints, the saints themselves should have both political and ecclesiastical control; and the state must necessarily regulate the morals of its citizens. In theory Calvin seems to have intended no change from the mediaeval doctrine of the dual power. If the result was different, it was not so by design. But different it certainly was; for church and state came into far closer union than the middle ages could have conceived, with the whip hand always that of the church. In theory, the congregation was represented in the consistory, but actually the lay members were nominated by the clergy.[1]

Luther had denied the right to resist, even on grounds of conscience, the temporal authority of the state; and Calvin had in his turn upheld the doctrine of passive obedience. Circumstances, however, forced differences of another sort between the two. Luther, if his reforms were to abide, had to depend on the support of the German princes who had accepted Protestantism, just as the reformed Church of England was dependent on the crown; but Calvin owed no such obligation. It was therefore possible to modify the Calvinist thesis to the extent of condoning resistance on the part of any special body created for the sole purpose of limiting the power of the king; but this was excuse enough for John Knox. It was Knox rather than Calvin who made the right of resistance a part of Presbyterian dogma; for with the church synods behind him, he was supported by a body more genuinely representative than the Scottish Parliament. Raising the issue against the "monstrous regiment of women," he triumphed over the Catholic court of Mary Stuart, only to lose the support he should have received from Elizabeth. To allay her suspicions, Knox modified his position. In

[1] Calvin's *Institutes of the Christian Religion*, Bk. IV, chap. 20; also Preserved Smith, *Life and Letters of Martin Luther* (Boston and New York, 1911); Ernst Troeltsch, *Protestantism and Progress* (London and New York, 1912); G. P. Gooch, *English Democratic Ideas in the Seventeenth Century* (Cambridge, 1917), Introduction.

behalf of true religion a sovereign may be resisted, but a woman, otherwise qualified, may rule. The gesture came too late, and the English Presbyterians were left to work out their own salvation without aid or comfort from the crown.

Calvinist theory comes to include a defense of the rights of minorities, because the Calvinists were generally in the minority. But there are other reasons for the fact that the revolutionary movements of the seventeenth and eighteenth centuries have a close connection with the Genevan theology. Its first premise is the absolute sovereignty of God, leaving man powerless in the hands of his maker. Salvation is a free act of grace, depending neither on merit nor on works; and evil is disobedience to the inscrutable will of God. The Calvinist believes, therefore, in self-abnegation and devotion to duty: an overwhelming sense of obligation. The stress, since the ways of the Lord are beyond the comprehension of man, is on activity, labor, individual initiative, backed by a sense of saintliness which refines and hallows the pursuits of daily life. This individualism lends itself both to the denial of political absolutism and to the growth of a capitalistic system; for the purposes of the state are subordinated to the will of God, and what better evidence of divine approval than material success![2]

Calvinism leads also to a looser and more democratic form of church organization because of the ambiguity it contains as to the elect. If all church members are of the chosen few, then new communicants may be admitted only with the greatest care. Although Calvin himself had regarded the church as universal in the mediaeval sense, the kingdom of the saints presupposes a small and select body: a presupposition irreconcilable with a national church. The more saintliness is emphasized, the more the church tends to become a limited group, held together by agreement among its members. Presbyterianism, with its divisions into synods and presbyteries, was of state-wide scope; but it could be held together only by leaning on the temporal

[2] Max Weber, *The Protestant Ethic and the Spirit of Capitalism* (London, 1930); R. H. Tawney, *Religion and the Rise of Capitalism* (London and New York, 1926), especially pp. 175 ff.

power. When political support is withdrawn, it tends to break up into independent congregations. By 1600 Congregationalism seems to have been well known, and its founder, Robert Brown, had commenced his activities some twenty years earlier. It was not a separatist movement, but denied theological finality and the consequent authority of a centralized church, which led to ungentle treatment from Presbyterian and Anglican alike. It was episcopal persecution which drove Robinson to remove his congregation to Leyden, whence the younger members of the group embarked on the Mayflower in 1620.[3]

After St. Bartholomew, the right of resistance becomes general in Protestant literature. The injunction is to obey God rather than man, and, if necessary, to resist the earthly monarch; for God wills what is best for the people, and if the sovereign does something obviously subversive of the popular good, he is acting contrary to the will of God. The best representative of this body of literature is the *Vindiciae contra Tyrannos* in 1579, the work of a French Huguenot, probably Duplessis-Mornay, arguing for the religious liberty of a minority. Arising out of sectarian dispute, it is the forerunner of a long train of controversial tracts designed to show that governments are set up by agreement between ruler and ruled, to carry out a definite purpose; and that when this purpose fails to be achieved—when the king defaults—the contract stands dissolved. This is one of the two lines of argument on which the English civil wars, and ultimately the American and French revolutions were based. The contract theory itself is, of course, much older; but in the *Vindiciae* it receives its revolutionary form in that it is for the first time consciously aimed at the ruler. The second of the two revolutionary arguments goes back to the same period, and is also a product of the French religious wars, finding its early expression in Hotman's *Franco-Gallia* in 1573. Here the appeal is to certain constitutional rights inherent in the history of a given people. Hotman argues that the Frankish kings had

[3] See T. H. Green, *Four Lectures on the English Revolution*, I, in *Works* (ed. by R. L. Nettleship, 2nd ed. 3 vols. London and New York, 1889-1890), 277 ff.

never been absolute monarchs, and that the people were justified on historical grounds in demanding representation.[4]

There is yet another theory which sprang from the disorders of the French religious wars: the nationalism of Jean Bodin, whose *Republic* (1577) was one of the books in Elder Brewster's Massachusetts library.[5] Rising above factional strife, Bodin saw the only way out in a strong monarchy, supported by religious toleration. He takes this position on purely realistic grounds. Two religions, with the king allied to either, must be fatal, but many sects, with the king a member of none, could be safely played off against each other. He would secure the unity of the state through political nationalism rather than religious universalism, and bind its citizens, not in the name of any church, but in the name of France. The means to this end was to strengthen the central power, by making the fundamental principle in the state the relation of submission which makes the king sovereign and the people subject. The mark of the sovereign is his legislative power, the only absolutely necessary thing in the state; and even this is limited by the law of nature, by the constitutional rights of the subjects, and by the explosive principle that taxes cannot be levied without the consent of a representative body.[6] As if to hurl his admonition in his teeth, Bodin sat in the last estates-general that was to meet for two hundred years.

All three of these theories found their way across the channel in the seventeenth century, where they were adapted to serve the needs of English institutional development, and assumed the various forms in which they passed on into the American heritage.

[4] See H. J. Laski (ed.), *A Defense of Liberty Against Tyrants:* A Translation of the *Vindiciae Contra Tyrannos,* Introduction, 1-60; and review of the above by G. L. Burr, in *Philosophical Review,* XXXIV (January, 1925), 76-79.

[5] Edward Channing, *History of the United States* (6 vols. New York, 1905-1925), I, 295.

[6] Jean Bodin, *Of the Lawes and Customes of a Common-wealth* (English translation by R. Knolles, London, 1605), especially Bk. I, chap. 8; Henri Baudrillart, *J. Bodin et son Temps* (Paris, 1853), pp. 222 ff.; J. N. Figgis, *Studies of Political Thought from Gerson to Grotius* (Cambridge, 1907), pp. 110 ff.

III

In opposition to the contract theory stands the dogma of the divine right of kings, with its chief support an established church. Its classic English formulation is that given it by James I, in his *Trew Law of Free Monarchies*.[7] Like all the political writers of the period, James couches his argument in theological and legalistic terms, justifying the monarchy on three grounds: from scripture, from the history of Scotland and England, and from the law of nature. Monarchy is assuredly the "trew paterne of Divinitie," for it is related in the eighth chapter of the first book of Samuel how the people asked for a king, persisting in their demand even after the prophet had foretold the scourge he would be. The king holds his power, therefore, by the grace of God, and to resist him is to resist the divine will. Still more shaky is the historical argument; for James contends that the kings of Scotland and of England took their kingdoms by conquest, which gave them in their own persons title to all the land in the realm. Law was made by the king before there was any Parliament, and Parliament itself is a creation of the king. It is the royal signature, and not the approval of peers or commons which gives the law its sanction. The king is above the law, but the good monarch voluntarily rules by it and places himself under it for the common weal. The argument from natural law follows the analogy that as the "head cares for the body, so doeth the king for his people." The body may be chastised by the head, or a diseased member may be cut off, but the body cannot lop away the head.

Answering the objections to his theory, probably with the *Vindiciae* in mind, James goes on to assert that no matter how wicked the king may be, the state is still better off with him than without him. He is indeed a scourge sent by God, but God alone may remove him. The people can only suffer in silence the duration of the divine displeasure. There is no contract, because the people, if they were not already subjects,

---

[7] C. H. McIlwain (ed.), *The Political Works of James I* (Cambridge, 1918), pp. 53-70; cf. Figgis, *The Theory of the Divine Right of Kings* (Cambridge, 1907).

would not be a corporate body, and hence would be unable to make a contract; but even if there were, neither party to it could judge of its infraction. It would remain for God to judge, and to punish; and in so far as the king is above his people, he is the more liable in the sight of God.

The duty of the subject is passive obedience to the commands of the king, who may be advised by Parliament, but is in no way bound to take that advice. The king has also a very wide and flexible prerogative, which is beyond the power of courts or Parliament to abridge. He can himself give up some portion of his power, but if he does so, or even if he obeys the law at all, it is an act of grace rather than a right on the part of someone else.

Under the Tudors the power of the Parliament had been implicit rather than manifest, and although it had grown to as yet undiscovered proportions, it had not reached the point of challenging the crown. It was hardly likely that the issue raised by James's exercise of the prerogative would be drawn in Parliament; but the common law tradition was more firmly rooted, and fully able to stand its ground. So we have the assertion by the common law courts of a constitutional doctrine which is superior to the crown, and which the prerogative of the king cannot overstep. It was the first move in drawing the lines for the coming conflict; and in the foreground of the controversy stands the stubborn figure of Sir Edward Coke, chief justice of the King's Bench.[8]

Coke conceives the constitution of England to rest on the common law, which is fundamental, and not to be overruled or modified. The rôle of the judge is passive, to speak the law rather than to make it. The law itself is fixed, and is superior to the king, who has no prerogative but that which the law concedes him. No royal proclamation can make a crime what was not a crime before. The common law is constitutive, assigning

---

[8] Gooch, *op. cit.*, pp. 63-65; see especially Bonham's case, 8 Co. Rep. 107-18; and John Campbell, *Lives of the Chief Justices of England* (3 vols. London, 1858); also T. F. T. Plucknett, "Bonham's Case and Judicial Review," *Harvard Law Review*, XL, 30-70.

to the various parts of the government their proper place in relation to the whole. So when James issued writs of assistance to the ecclesiastical courts, Coke held it the intention of the common law to restrain these courts, and denied the king's authority to interfere. It is the familiar doctrine of judicial review, foreshadowed in Magna Charta, which has grown with the growth of sentiment for the written constitution. The very incident which provoked Sir Edward's resistance, too, was not without its later parallel; for it was the issuance of writs of assistance in defiance of the common law which led James Otis in 1761 to deny the supremacy of Parliament, even as Coke denied the supremacy of the crown.

The notion of a fundamental law did not, of course, depend on the English background. It could be duplicated in any country in Europe at that date, as law of reason, or law of nature. But whatever name it goes by, it was conceived as a law in some sense constitutive of a social order, beside which kings and Parliaments were transitory and feeble things. Coke's significance lies, not in originality, but in the fact that he was the one man best qualified to say, and in the best position to say effectively, what a great number of people believed.

Roman law, depending on a clean-cut legal sovereignty, gave rise, when projected over into the complex organization of the middle ages, to numerous anomalies, most striking of which was just this subjection of the sovereign to the law. For the notion of sovereignty involves both the power to make law and immunity from its operation. For Coke, the fundamental law is above sovereignty, and there are many things the sovereign cannot legally do. Bodin, half a century earlier, had advanced further, but even for him there were bounds, albeit wider ones, which the sovereign could not overstep. To take the final position the logic of the concept demanded remained for the logician, Thomas Hobbes.

Political theories from the English Civil War down to the French Revolution were highly individualistic. They were philosophies of political disintegration, which rendered obsolete older institutions, such as the churches and the guilds. The movement tended to break up the older complex unity into autonomous political groups, based on voluntary coöperation—a type of theorizing into which the legal formula of contract fitted admirably. Whether by insight or by accident, Hobbes grasped this disintegrating movement, and set forth its philosophy more clearly than any other writer.

Hobbes begins by distinguishing between right of nature *(jus naturale)*, and law of nature *(lex naturalis)*.[9] The former is identified with self-preservation; the latter is a prohibition, which forbids man to do anything destructive of his life. Right is liberty to do; law is obligation not to do. He has thus redefined the older terminology to strip it of all ethical significance. The aim of life is self-preservation, and laws of nature are simply commands or prohibitions conducive to this end. From rules of right, inherent in the nature of the world, laws of nature have become, for Hobbes, analogous to the laws of mechanistic science, and of logic. They are neither moral nor immoral; they are simply there: principles of explanation rather than rules of conduct. Man is motivated by self-interest and the desire for self-preservation; these then are the laws of nature, and the axioms from which a science of politics must be deduced.

Hobbes's system is a thoroughgoing individualism, in which all social values are reduced to individual self-interest. Men have not, to be sure, individual rights; but they have individual motives, or springs of action, and these are the primary facts of group life. The human organism is so constructed that it will perpetuate itself; and all action is motivated by organic needs. Action can therefore be neither good nor bad; it is simply human, and assumes ethical significance only by convention. Society itself is only an aggregate of individuals, and there is no justification for social organization unless it can be shown to be advantageous to the individual.

Hobbes did not doubt that it was so: security alone is enough

[9] *Leviathan* (Oxford, 1881), chap. 13.

to make the organized state not only justifiable but necessary. And following the accepted dogma of the day, he bases it upon a contract. It is, however, a contract between individuals, to which the sovereign is not a party. He is therefore absolute; and he maintains his power, not by consent of his subjects, but by force. The sovereign could not be bound by an agreement even if he could enter into one; for the only sanction of any contract is force, and to assume a force binding upon the sovereign would be to destroy his sovereignty. Every form of social organization is included under Hobbes's contract; morality, property, law, justice—all are creatures of the state. Outside of organized society, right can have no other meaning than power. Hobbes is not writing history; he is trying to erect a logical substructure on which to build a political society. His contract is wholly unhistorical, and he probably would have been quite willing to admit as much; but it is more than a fiction: it is a logical construction, like the lines and points of geometry. It is not fact, but a means of explanation.

The essential point in Hobbes is the notion of sovereignty,[10] which had been imperfectly grasped by Bodin. He insists that there must be some single power in the state which is ultimate and final, and from which there is no appeal. The sovereign must, from the very nature of the concept, be absolute. But although Hobbes himself defended the cause of monarchy, his system does not, as the royalists quickly discovered, logically presuppose a king. The sovereign may be a person, or group of persons; one is as logical as the other. And in fact the revolution of 1688, when it shelved the king, simply passed on the sovereignty to Parliament.

IV

Hobbes was anathema to Cavalier and to Puritan alike, for his theory served neither to support the monarchy nor to justify the substitution of the commonwealth. From the point of view of the political development in America, it is the revolutionary theories which are most significant; and these are nowhere bet-

[10] *Ibid.*, chap. 8.

ter presented than in the doctrine of the short-lived but far-reaching leveller movement, which ran its course between 1647 and 1652. The English civil wars were conducted by a religious minority, which lacked doctrinal unity even within its own ranks; and it was the more radical element in Cromwell's new model army which gave formulation to the political views which, from the standpoint of later achievement, were the most important of the period. With the power of the army established, differences soon arose between officers and men as to how that power was to be used in reorganizing the government. These differences were thrashed out in conference in 1647, and reported in the Clarke papers.[11] Reappearing in civilian dress in 1649, the movement was quickly overshadowed by the trial and execution of the king.

Perhaps the most startling thing about the men who took part in the army discussions is their freedom from their own theology. But for terminology, they are quite as rationalistic as the natural rights school of the following century, on which they exerted some measure of influence; for the general lines of the leveller movement were followed out by the nonconformist elements in America, where the atmosphere was more favorable to democratic individualism. Both parties to the debate—the conservatives, represented by Cromwell and Ireton, his son-in-law, and the radicals, for whom Wildman spoke most effectively—both sides seem agreed that the basis of government is a contract; but the left wing gave it a special twist of their own: the individual has no duty to a government until he has put himself under it. All men are equal, and universal manhood suffrage is a natural right.

The first move toward clarifying the issues involved was a document put forward in August, 1647, by the officers, and known as the *Heads of Proposals*,[12] which aims at limiting the

[11] C. H. Firth (ed.), *The Clarke Papers* (4 vols. London, 1891-1901), especially preface. See also T. C. Pease, *The Leveller Movement* (Washington, 1916); Eduard Bernstein, *Cromwell and Communism* (London, 1930), chaps. VI-IX, XI, XII; Gooch, *op. cit.*, pp. 139-65, 195-206.

[12] S. R. Gardiner, *Constitutional Documents of the Puritan Revolution* (2nd ed. Oxford, 1899), pp. 316-26.

power of the king rather than actually altering the structure of the government. Both houses of Parliament are retained, but representation is to be equalized by equalizing constituencies. All coercive power is taken from the clergy, and the army is to be placed under control of Parliament for a period of ten years; but the question of electors is passed over in silence. The whole program, embodied in concrete legislative proposals to be carried into effect by the law-making body, resembles the reform bill of 1832, save that it is more drastic.

The *Heads of Proposals* was answered about a month later by the first *Agreement of the People*,[13] in which certain liberties regarded as fundamental were exempted from the control of Parliament, foremost among these being religion. It is the first demand for a written bill of rights, depending on a distinction drawn between rights of property and natural rights. The latter are purely individual, attaching to man simply because he is man. They are his birthright, of which no law can deprive him. All men may not have property, but all men have, none the less, certain inalienable political rights. With regard to Parliament, the *Agreement* proposes to raise the commons to the dominant position, giving them full governing powers but for the noted exceptions, and removing the veto of the house of lords. The levellers wanted also representation on the council, and a guarantee of trial by jury. The right to universal manhood suffrage is not expressly asserted, but is clearly implied; for no man can be justly subject to a government he has had no voice in choosing. All these things are the familiar provisions of the American constitutions, which added to them only the experience of a century of interpreting colonial charters.

It is the question of the suffrage which is the greatest point of difference between the opposing groups, Ireton arguing that any system which allows all men, irrespective of property, to vote, can be nothing but anarchy. It is the man who owns property, understood as property in land, who has a definite stake in the society and a visible interest in preserving the government. The man with no property, or property in easily movable form, can take care of himself; but the man who is rooted in the land is wholly dependent on the government. Thus the suffrage is claimed by the levellers as a natural right, on the principle that government is a matter of consent, while the conservatives look upon it as inhering in property.

In the second *Agreement of the People*,[14] brought forward early in 1649 by a civilian group, of which Lilburne was the leading spirit, this difference has been compromised, with paupers definitely excluded and the suffrage confined to householders. It is proposed, also, that members of the Parliament be forbidden to sit in the council, or cabinet as it came to be called—a proposal which would have made the ministerial system impossible in advance. Here is the same jealousy of the executive which bulks so large in American institutions, and which was abandoned in England only after the Act of Succession was rewritten under Anne, too late to affect the course of development in the colonies. The exemptions from legislative control are divided by the second *Agreement* into two groups, civil and ecclesiastical. The former includes a denial of the right of Parliament to pass any law menacing to public security, discriminating against birth, or destructive of property rights; while on the side of religion a general scheme of toleration is presented, from which only Catholics are excluded.

The doctrine of the levellers, shorn of its theological terminology, is strikingly like the position of the philosophical radicals of the Benthamite era; and has also much in common with the contemporary beliefs of the Quakers. Tradition has it that Lilburne died a member of that sect; and the documents of the movement resemble closely William Penn's constitutions for Pennsylvania and West Jersey.

There also emerges at this period a definitely socialistic movement, the followers of which are known to history by the picturesque title of the "Diggers." The levellers take it for granted that politics is one thing and economics another: that

[14] *Ibid.*, pp. 359-71.

people of all varieties of political belief may come from any
sort of economic background. It is the typical English and
American argument for the two-party system. Quite different,
however, is the utopian socialism of Gerard Winstanley, who
gives to his doctrine a decidedly economic cast.[15] Winstanley
argues, as had James I, that all kings of England have been
successors of the Conqueror, and all ownership of land is in
succession from his gift. But with the execution of Charles,
the line ended; and with it the artificial property rights it
created. Land tenure in pre-Conquest England being not much
improvement on the Norman regime, Winstanley proposes to
go clear back to the fall of man, and build on the "law of creation." Commonly accepted Christian doctrine attributed
private property to sin; but the "digger" theorist modifies this
notion somewhat, contending that all other evils arise from the
covetousness which begets private property. He sees society as
divided into two classes: those who have property, and those
who have not. To the former belong the gentry, the lawyers
and the preachers; and law and government are their means of
exploiting the masses. Taxes and tithes go hand in hand. Winstanley's solution is to abolish all buying and selling of the
land and its products, which are to be held in common. There
should be neither wages nor servitude, but each should receive
his keep, and the fruits of his own labor. It is the first of a
long line of theories protesting against the exploitation of the
dispossessed, and one which had its echo in nineteenth-century
America.

v

The levellers had been influenced by the independent movement; and although their own particular doctrine was crushed
out by the restoration, the claim of the larger group to a right
of life, liberty, and property found practical expression in the
colony of Rhode Island, organized by Roger Williams in 1647,
and theoretical expression in the political writings of John Milton. Natural law, from this time forward, means natural indi-

[15] Bernstein, *op. cit.*, pp. 116-33; Gooch, *op. cit.*, pp. 206-26.

vidual rights; rights no longer restricted to groups wielding economic power, but inhering also in John Smith and his neighbors.

Milton combines with great learning and rare literary skill, a magnificent idealism of the sort that makes revolutions possible. He has nothing original to contribute, and everything he wrote on political questions was called forth by specific circumstances; sometimes even made to order. But he had wide influence because he was widely read, and he put into enduring form many of the current opinions of his day. He enters the lists with a plea for complete separation of church and state, holding that a man's relation to his God is no concern of the temporal power. Liberty is the birthright of man as well as nations, and toleration is essential to its preservation. So, too, is unrestricted freedom of the press, for reason is supreme, and truth must ultimately prevail over error if allowed to present its case. The same principle which dictates his denunciation of censorship leads him to deny also the power of the state to interfere with the concerns of the individual in any field—in dress, in morals, in manners. Uniformity is abhorrent under any circumstances to one who conceives society as made up of discrete beings rather than as an aggregate or mass.[16]

In his pamphlet on the *Tenure of Kings and Magistrates,* written in defense of the regicides, Milton is on the familiar ground of the American declarations. All men were born free, and governments are founded upon agreement of individuals with one another, choosing kings and magistrates to exercise for them a delegated power. Sovereignty belongs to the people, and they may revoke at any time the commissions entrusted to their rulers; for their rulers are never more than agents of the people, wielding their authority in trust during faithful performance. Thus Milton justifies the execution of Charles in the same language Locke was to use a few decades later in extenuation of the claims of Parliament against the second James.

[16] Milton's *Prose Works* (5 vols. London, Bohn, 1848-1881), especially II, 1-138.

By 1776 these arguments had been hallowed by the authority of the years.

Also important in the background of American theory is James Harrington. Although in form a utopia, the *Oceana* is a piece of political realism of a high order.[17] The state has, for Harrington, a definite economic basis, which must be preserved if the government is to endure. Dominion follows property; from which he reasons that the state will be monarchical, aristocratic or democratic, according as the bulk of the land is held by one, by a few, or by many. The preservation of a commonwealth, by which term he designates the republican form of government, will therefore depend on the distribution of the land among a majority of the citizens. So he fixes a property limitation, providing that all property over a certain value be forfeited to the state. He assumes without much question that the best government is one in which all the people share; and by identifying political and economic power, he is forced to see that all his citizens are possessed of land. This is the "equal agrarian," and is one of the two great principles of government.

The second principle is the "equal rotarian," by which he means such frequent rotation in office, and elections so conducted, that all qualified individuals will have an equal chance to hold public office. The structure of the government is very simple, and is dictated by the division of society into two groups —the principle of natural aristocracy, which so impressed John Adams. In any body of men, says Harrington, if they set about discussing any question, it will be seen that the smaller number, perhaps a third, will make suggestions, and the rest will pass judgment on these. There should be, then, an upper house, or senate, to propose laws, and a second somewhat larger branch to choose among the proposals offered. A body of magistrates to carry the laws into execution completes the constitution. The scheme then provides that members of the two legislative chambers shall serve for three years, with one third of the number retiring at the end of each year—the system later put into practice in the American legislatures.

---

[17] *The Commonwealth of Oceana* (London, 1656), especially Part I.

Many of Harrington's views had passed into popularly accepted doctrine by the eighteenth century, among them the idea we have already met with of government by consent of the governed, and the notion of a written constitution to fix rigidly the bounds of governmental authority. William Penn was influenced by the *Oceana* in his Pennsylvania and West Jersey plans of government, and the book left its mark, also, on the "fundamental constitutions" of Carolina. The economic interpretation of politics which Harrington advances found its echo in the *Federalist* papers, and as late as the nineteenth century in the writings of Daniel Webster.[18]

It was in John Locke, however, that the contract theory, and the natural rights doctrine, received what was, from the point of view of the American revolution, their definitive form. Locke's law of nature is a body of rules for the guidance of men in a state of nature, which is prepolitical rather than pre-social. Every man has an individual right to life, liberty, and property; and self-preservation is the primary motive of human action. But liberty is circumscribed by the law of nature, and each man is enjoined to respect the rights of others, even in the prepolitical state.[19] The only difference between civil society and the natural state is that in the former there is a common organ for interpreting and enforcing the law of nature, while in the latter each man must be his own judge and executioner. It is the difficulty in enforcing the law which leads men to enter into the social contract, whereby each yields to the whole group —not to any single individual or body of individuals—his power in this respect.[20] The group then appoints a specific organ to interpret and administer the law of nature. This is the sole purpose of government. The individual retains his rights to life, liberty, and property, agreeing to be guided by the voice of the majority in all matters committed to the community as a whole, and to support with his personal power the executive, legislative, and judicial organs set up by the group.

[18] See H. F. Russell-Smith, *Harrington and his Oceana* (Cambridge, 1914), pp. 154 ff., *et passim*.

[19] *Of Civil Government* (London, 1924), Treatise II, sec. 6.

[20] *Ibid.*, sec. 87; chap. 8, *passim*.

Locke too is an individualist; and membership in the society is voluntary.[21] By placing himself and his goods under a government, the individual gives tacit consent to its authority, but he may withdraw from it whenever he chooses. The final power remains in the hands of the people themselves, who have delegated to their chosen rulers, not their sovereignty, but only its exercise. It follows that they may change their government whenever they deem it no longer to fulfill its function of protecting them in their natural rights. The main features of Locke's doctrine go back through various writers into the preceding century; but the significance of his formulation lies in the definiteness and clarity with which he brings it to a focus, in its emphasis on individualism, and in its widespread influence in the course of the next hundred years. It stands out in sharp contrast to the doctrine of Hobbes, and although less logical and less penetrating, it wielded the greater influence.

Where Hobbes sought to establish the necessity for an absolute state, Locke labored to limit governmental authority. For Hobbes morality, law, justice, are conventions, created by the state; for Locke, on the other hand, natural right is equivalent to natural rights, and justice obtains even in a prepolitical state, rights carrying with them correlative duties. From Hobbes's theory it follows that the end of the state is force, the power to maintain order; and revolution, accordingly, is always wrong. Locke holds, on the contrary, that men enter into society for the protection of property, and have consequently a right to change their government, by force if necessary, when it no longer fulfills this purpose. Locke's argument justified the American Revolution; but when it came to establishing a government for the thirteen United States, there were those who placed greater confidence in the opposing view. Outstanding among the champions of Hobbes was Alexander Hamilton, while Locke's basic position was espoused by Jefferson, who added to it certain modifications and distinctions of his own.

[21] *Ibid.*, secs. 116-20.

CHAPTER II

THE AMERICAN SCENE

I

WITH THE BREAKUP of the unified church came the collapse of the mediaeval order. Commerce took on new importance, bringing in its wake increasing congestion in the cities, and an increasingly bitter rivalry for sea power and the control of trade routes. Slowly a capitalistic class emerged, and as the rich became richer, the poor sank into a deeper and more hopeless poverty. Ships sailed to distant lands in search of gold and other commodities, while trading posts sprang up in remote places, on the edge of the wilderness. But ships must be manned, and trading posts must be garrisoned. If the rise of capitalism supplied the means and the incentive for exploration, it supplied also the human jetsam of which colonies were made. Numbers multiplied, while growing economic pressure combined with religious intolerance and civil war to fan the embers of discontent, and to fill with miserable but eternally hopeful humanity the reeking hold of every vessel outward bound for the new world.

Throughout the seventeenth and eighteenth centuries the burden of European overpopulation was relieved by a steady exodus of religious and political nonconformists. Calvinist and Quaker fled from England in search of toleration and economic independence; and with them came detached groups of Catholics and Episcopalians and loyalists of the Stuart dynasty, followed by French Huguenot and German Lutheran, Scotch Presbyterian and Irish malcontent, Dutch trader and Jewish merchant. All these sects and peoples ultimately found refuge in America, where they were joined by ever increasing numbers of the discontented and the dispossessed, who hoped for better fortunes in the new country. It was, in fact, discontent rather than dissent which drove most of the colonists across the sea, the religious factor being in general a secondary one. And in the new world they built a new society, its institutions molded by the motives which had led them to leave their homelands, by the inherited traditions they brought with them, and by the conditions with which they were faced in the American wilderness.

The institutional development of the colonies was based on the seventeenth-century English models, but from this common starting point diverged considerably under the influence of local conditions. In England the notion of a fundamental law which was above both king and Parliament went back to Bracton, and had been pointedly reaffirmed by Coke and the theorists of the commonwealth period. But this fundamental law was unwritten, existing only as a mass of precedents in the hands of the common law judges. The English colonists took over the common law; but in their charters they had another fundamental canon, couched in precise terms, and no longer the exclusive possession of the initiated. The colonial charter was in form a contract between king or proprietor on the one hand and the people of a given colony on the other, and was the lineal ancestor of the written constitution.

The colonies were provided with legislative assemblies, standing in relation to the royal governor as Parliament stood to the crown. But the Americans were unhampered by an hereditary aristocracy, and were too remote from the mother country to be greatly affected by the direction of her institutional development. Men were few enough in the early years, and the dangers and hardships of a wild and thinly settled land demanded that they pull together. Where the members of the British Parliament represented classes, the colonial assemblymen acted for distinct constituencies. Representation was fairly evenly distributed, and the sovereignty was actually delegated by the voters of a given region to one of their number, who sat for them in the assembly.[1] Both apportionment and franchise were regulated by general rules, and there was nothing in America even remotely corresponding to the English "rotten borough."

An example of the determining influence of local conditions on political institutions is furnished by the growth of the ballot system in Massachusetts, where the governor was elected by this method as early as 1634. It was dangerous and difficult for the freemen to assemble in any given place to vote in person, and so proxies came to be widely used, one man carrying with him to the designated place the votes of his neighbors. To avoid dishonesty, the votes soon came to be written down, and the proxy merely delivered them to be counted.[2]

There were other factors also which served to render the colonial assemblies far more democratic than the British Parliament. For the great demand for labor in clearing and cultivating land gave the worker a substantial position in the community, while the ease with which a dissatisfied laborer could acquire land of his own, together with the small property qualification, gave great political power to the lower classes.

Just as colonial institutions tended to develop in isolation from their English models, political and social reforms in England were introduced with no thought of extending them to America. However the "glorious revolution" may have limited the power of the king in England, royal authority long remained supreme in the colonies; while such liberal legislation as the Triennial and Habeas Corpus Acts did not apply to the far-flung outposts of the Empire. The Act of Settlement, which did include the colonies, served only to emphasize their divergence from the main stream of British constitutional evolution. In addition to establishing the Hanoverian succession, the Act provided that no officeholder could sit in the House of Commons. The ministerial system, uniting legislative and executive functions, was already firmly rooted in England, so this pro-

---

[1] Channing, *History of the United States*, III, 75 ff.
[2] *Ibid.*, I, 349 ff.

vision was disregarded, and in time annulled; but in America the two branches were at opposite poles, and the Act tended to maintain them so.[3]

Even the less important among colonial institutions tended to be democratizing forces in the life of the people, in sharp contrast to the inbred caste system of the homeland. New England had her town meetings, where citizens met as equals to discuss matters of public concern; and outside New England the vote for members of the various legislatures was conducted in open meetings, where the rude and untutored could gather and weigh the arguments of the educated and intellectual. The abundance of land, and the absence of a fixed landed gentry, made for equality; while in New England, at least, there was a system of universal public education as early as the middle of the seventeenth century.[4]

II

Gradually, thriving communities replaced crude frontier settlements, their forms still determined by the character and environment of their people. In New England, theocracy dominated for a generation, yielding at last to the assaults of religious schism and of rapid commercial expansion. The Dutch trading post of New Amsterdam grew at length into the wealthy port of New York; while Quaker Pennsylvania prospered in agriculture, manufactures, and commerce. Virginia grew from an unsuccessful commercial venture into a planter aristocracy, where tobacco ruled, and the possession of broad acres was the open sesame to power; and the Carolinas developed along the same general lines as their northern neighbor. The early sufferings and strenuous labor of the colonists had been amply rewarded by material gain, which brought with it confidence and aggressive independence: a self-sufficient sense of separation from the Old World and its traditions.[5]

[3] *Ibid.*, II, 220-21.
[4] *Ibid.*, pp. 462 ff.
[5] Cf. Carl Becker, *Beginnings of the American People* (Boston and New York, 1915), p. 161.

For although they still clung to the customs of their fathers, the Americans refused to be molded by them into the old-world pattern. Where the common law protected them against arbitrary government and despotic officials, they loudly proclaimed their birthright; but where it interfered with their development, they ignored it, or passed statutes contradicting it.[6] Even before the civil wars—as early, in fact, as 1642—Massachusetts seems to have regarded herself as independent of the British Parliament; and by 1664 she had so far progressed towards political independence that his majesty's commissioners experienced insuperable difficulties in the way of any investigation of the colonial government. It was in fact for some time in doubt whether Massachusetts would proclaim the Stuart triumph after the Restoration.[7]

In Virginia the same independent temper led to a popular uprising in 1676 under the leadership of Nathaniel Bacon, which succeeded in forcing various reforms against the will of the royal governor; while in New York some four years later the colonists refused to pay certain duties levied by the Duke of York, proprietor of the province, on the ground that their imposition was contrary to traditional constitutional rights.[8] Early in the following century the South Carolinians also rebelled against their proprietors, forcing the transfer of the province to the crown; while the North Carolina planters refused to pay quit-rents to the governor, and made good their case.[9] In 1746 the northern counties of the same colony refused to pay taxes voted by an assembly in which they deemed themselves inadequately represented, in much the same spirit as the stamp tax agitators of two decades later.

After the beginning of the eighteenth century it was perfectly obvious to Englishmen that the sovereignty actually rested with Parliament, its exercise in the colonies being determined by expediency. The colonists, however, were inclined

[6] Channing, op. cit., I, 529. [7] Ibid., I, 448-49; II, 74 ff.
[8] Ibid., p. 60; for Bacon's rebellion, see ibid., pp. 85 ff.
[9] Ibid., pp. 350 ff., pp. 359 ff.

to make their own legislative bodies supreme. The century opened in America on a scene of remarkable material achievement, for which the colonists claimed entire credit. Their sense of accomplishment bred a sense of common destiny, which in turn fostered a disposition stubbornly to maintain their "rights" in the face of all opposition: an attitude which the colonial governments were designed to encourage. For Great Britain had followed the negative policy of spending as little trouble and as little money as possible on her American settlements. While in most of the colonies governor and council were appointed by the crown, legislation was universally in the hands of the elected assemblies, and these were the real sources of power. It was the duty of the royal governor to look upon the colony as part of a larger empire; but the assembly was concerned only with local needs and problems, and the assembly controlled the purse strings. Thus the governor's salary could be made conditional on his surrender to the legislative will; and by specific appropriations, minutely detailed as to their use and manner of administration, the governor was reduced to the level of a figurehead.[10]

Nor did they stop here; for when the king exercised his power of disallowance, which he not infrequently did, by voiding statutes of the colonial legislatures, the assemblies found ways of their own to nullify the royal will. The objectionable law might be reënacted in slightly different phrases; it might be passed subject to a time limitation, falling just within the period allowed for presenting it to the king; or it might, still more brazenly, be called a "resolve" instead of a law, and be never submitted to the king at all.[11]

It must be remembered that the American colonies were already well developed before the course of events in England settled the issue between king and Parliament, once and for all. The final emergence of Parliament in 1688 as the actual seat of British sovereignty found the colonies engrossed in their own

[10] *Ibid.*, pp. 248-49; cf. Becker, *op. cit.*, pp. 162 ff.
[11] Channing, *op. cit.*, II, 240 ff.

affairs, and willing to remain so as long as they were let alone. They had waged their own battle between elected assembly and crown governor, with results not unlike those in England; but with this signal difference: that it happened under their own eyes, and they were directly concerned in the outcome. When the colonists thought about sovereignty at all, they thought in terms of their own legislative bodies, which were directly responsible to the people. They thought of themselves, not as parts of an empire, but as independent states, connected with the homeland only by the accidental allegiance to a single executive head, who had no power to make laws for them.

They clung also to their belief in a fundamental law, guaranteeing them certain rights which were beyond the power of even their legislatures to abridge. This was no doubt due in part to the example of their charters, and in part to the training of their lawyers, who had learned the common law largely from the *Institutes* of Coke. This it was which led them to resist to the last all attempts at taxation by anyone other than their own representative assemblies. No taxation except by representatives of the people taxed is asserted as a fundamental right of Englishmen in the Virginia Resolves of 1765, pushed through the assembly by Patrick Henry in protest against the Stamp Act. It was reaffirmed in the same year by the Stamp Act Congress, even while acknowledging subordination to Parliament, with the additional assertion of a right to trial by jury against the encroachments of the admiralty jurisdiction. And the right to be taxed only by representative legislative bodies was finally proclaimed in the Virginia Resolutions of 1769, written by George Mason, introduced in the chamber by Washington, and signed by Jefferson and Henry.[12]

III

It was perhaps inevitable that some form of aristocracy should spring up in America, even though it was not quite so "natural" as those of its members who had read Harrington would have liked to believe. For the lines of distinction were

[12] *Ibid.*, III, 55 ff., 103-4.

mainly economic, and the colonial elect were the well-to-do merchants of Boston, New York, and Philadelphia, and the wealthy planters of the Deep South. Colonial culture reflected that of Europe in the eighteenth century, and the American aristocrat could claim, with his English cousin, a polite deism, a belief that Englishmen could be free without being equal, and a sophisticated radicalism which shrank from contact with realities.[13] Like his English cousin, too, he read Pope and Shaftesbury; and sent his son to Harvard or to Yale rather than to Oxford or Cambridge.

But of a far different sort were the streams of immigrants steadily moving westward from the coast. On the extreme frontier in the shadow of the Appalachians the Scotch-Irish pioneers, martial and independent, fought back the Indians, making the fertile valleys between their outposts and an already effete East a safe haven for German and Celtic farmers. These were men who had scant use for England and knew little of English tradition; who brought with them the ideals of Wittenberg and Geneva; and who believed in the right of men to labor the earth and enjoy the fruits of their toil. Theirs was an instinctive belief in the equality of men, backed by deep-seated religious convictions.[14] The result was a sharp division between the old and the new America; between the freedom and equality of the frontier, and the wealth and aristocracy of the coastal cities and plantations. Yet class and sectional conflict within the colonies before the revolution was not incompatible with a growing sense of solidarity against the outside world, a growing feeling of nationalism.

The earliest expression of an intercolonial unity grew into the New England Confederation of 1643, embracing Massachusetts, Plymouth, Connecticut, and New Haven. The Confederation was organized primarily with an eye to defense against the Indian tribes, who made no distinction between colonies; but it went on to provide a loose federal structure, in no way infringing individual sovereignty, but arranging for extradition of

<hr>

[13] Becker, *op. cit.*, pp. 170 ff.   [14] *Ibid.*, pp. 179 ff.

criminals and arbitration of disputes. The union lasted for a generation, doing yeoman service in King Phillip's war, and furnishing empirical data in a local setting for the controversialists of a century later. The sense of common destiny, if not the actual idea of political coöperation, soon spread to other colonies, and we find Massachusetts magistrates issuing a proclamation for the apprehension of Virginia's rebel, Nathaniel Bacon. Then, too, New York's Jacob Leisler in 1689 had called upon the other colonies to join him in seizing the governments for King William and Queen Mary; and while it is not recorded that his more distant brethren risked their necks in the venture, they did at least show gratifying interest in a matter of common concern.

The back country made little distinction between the religious sects which had divided the older colonies; and when differences did arise, they served only to unite those of the same persuasion in different localities. The establishment in 1710 of a General Post Office rendered communications relatively easy; and the feeling of unity was greatly enhanced by the dissemination of intelligence through the newspapers, which flooded the colonies from Boston, from New York, from Philadelphia, and later from leading southern cities. The importance of the press in fusing into a nation what Pitt in exasperation was to call a "map," cannot be overemphasized. From the Zenger trial in 1735, which established the American tradition of a free press, until the appearance of the Federalist papers, the newspapers were a vehicle for controversy and for agitation whose influence in giving direction to the movements for intercolonial unity and for independence was of immeasurable importance.

"What a strange doctrine it is," declared the octogenarian Andrew Hamilton in his masterly defense of John Peter Zenger, "to press everything for law here which is so in England!"[15] Zenger was charged with libel for printing in his *New*

---

[15] Peleg W. Chandler, *American Criminal Trials* (2 vols. Boston and London, 1841-1844), I, 151-209; cf. Channing, *op. cit.*, II, 483 ff.; G. H. Payne, *History of Journalism in the United States* (New York and London, 1920), 1-100.

York Weekly Journal articles criticizing the official conduct of Governor Cosby, urging among other things that Chief Justice Lewis Moriss had been illegally removed from office. Tried before Moriss's successor, Zenger's case was hopeless, for not only the judge but the English law as well was against him. Hamilton, however, was equal to the emergency, and persuading the jury to return a verdict as to both law and fact, secured the acquittal of his client in the sacred name of liberty and the rights of Englishmen. From that time on all attempts to muzzle the press in the colonies failed. Under the editorial guidance of the Franklins and the Bradfords, the newspapers achieved a power and an influence not to be denied, and the thirty-four journals in the colonies in 1775 were the real vehicles for proclaiming liberty throughout the land and to all the inhabitants thereof.

It was not until the necessity for action together in the French and Indian war became pressing, however, that an actual scheme for a federative union was drawn up, although it was not to become a reality. The plan adopted by the Albany Congress in 1754 was drafted by Franklin, and provided for an executive appointed by the crown, with a legislative body chosen by the assemblies of the several colonies. It had its good points, perhaps chief among them being the approval of the king; but the colonies were as yet jealous of their sovereignty. The time was not ripe, but it was coming, soon enough; and the Albany Plan was destined after three or four decades to be called reverently from limbo by another group of federalists, chastened by experience and more willing to agree. With the close of the war, the work of uniting the far-flung colonial settlements in a sense of spiritual kinship was virtually complete. The provincials, brought together in large numbers for the first time, found their religious and social differences with each other of little consequence in comparison to the arrogant condescension of the British troops. Finding themselves despised for their provincialism, they soothed their wounded pride by uniting to condemn the virtues they might once have sought to emulate;

and in the stupid incompetence of the British for the frontier warfare at hand, they found visible ground for resentment.[16]

Religious feeling, strong in the colonies from the start, and fanned by traveling evangelists in the earlier seventeen-hundreds, was directed after the middle of the century into political channels, under the skillful guidance of such men as John Witherspoon, Scotch-Presbyterian president of Princeton. The Puritan theocracy in New England had already given way to a Puritan democracy, and as early as 1717 John Wise had asserted the equality of men and the sovereignty of the people in his *Vindication of the Government of the New England Churches*. Too radical for its own day, the book passed through two editions in 1772.[17] The soil was already prepared, and the stamp tax served as the incentive for Sons of Liberty to form in various colonies. The New York and Connecticut organizations united, and were about to be joined by those of Massachusetts and New Hampshire when news came that the odious act had been repealed. The final scene in the unification of the colonies was also a British invention; for the Boston Port Act, punishing the city for the tea party, served a purpose quite other than that for which it was designed. Instead of starving the rebels into submission, it brought shiploads of supplies and pledges of support from Virginia and the Carolinas, as well as from the more northern provinces.[18]

Perhaps the most significant notion of the age was its belief in the intimate union of morals and government. The aim of the state, like that of the church, was to breed good men. It was this which led the colonists to reject legal precedent for the right of Parliament to tax unrepresented subjects, and to demand in its stead moral justification. Since positive law would not support their case, they appealed to the law of nature.[19]

[16] Cf. Becker, *op. cit.*, pp. 191 ff.

[17] Cf. V. L. Parrington, *The Colonial Mind* (vol. I of *Main Currents in American Thoughts*, 3 vols., New York, 1927-1930), pp. 118 ff.

[18] Channing, *op. cit.*, III, 136.

[19] Becker, *op. cit.*, p. 233. The case for positive law is ably made out by C. H. McIlwain, *The American Revolution* (New York, 1923); see also R. G. Adams,

Precedent having failed them, they fell back upon philosophy. And it was no doubt fitting that they should. For in eighteenth-century America the ideal society of the philosophers came nearer to realization than was possible anywhere else. Here, for a time, equality was a substantial fact, the reward of labor was sure, and the age of reason seemed near to taking tangible form.[20]

IV

Parallel with the rapid economic and political growth of the American colonies was a growing interest in speculative thought, and a disposition to improve rather than blindly to accept the intellectual heritage carried over from Europe. The two centuries between 1620 and 1820 saw five distinct philosophical movements run their course,[21] each measurably enriching American culture and each succeeding doctrine preparing more surely for the birth of an American philosophy of the state.

The first phase is Calvinism, as brought over by the Puritans and established in the early theocratic governments of New England. Here God is all-powerful and remote; yet is at the same time concerned with the most minute details of daily living, and interferes arbitrarily in the course of human events. His decrees are inscrutable and beyond the understanding of man, who can know the divine will only through revelation. All that comes to pass has been foreordained by God. Thus men are predestined from all eternity to be saved or to be damned, and life on earth is but a prelude to an everlasting life of torment or of bliss. The social routine of the New England pioneer was accordingly austere and hard, as befitted one whose hope was fixed upon another world; and the government of state and church were indistinguishable. There is a curious parallel between the position of God in the colonial theocracy

---

Political Ideas of the American Revolution (Durham, 1922); and chap. 3, sec. IV, below.

[20] Becker, *op. cit.*, pp. 196 ff.

[21] I. Woodbridge Riley, *American Philosophy: The Early Schools* (New York, 1907), *passim*.

and that of the divinely anointed king in the Stuart monarchy. Both were absolute, both were set off apart from and above their subjects, both were omnipotent with respect to the most insignificant happenings; and both were destined to yield to the challenge of deism.

The deistic phase in American thought begins in a reaction against Calvinism, and culminates in the importation of French skepticism. The difficulty of the Puritan creed had been the impossibility of reconciling determinism with a transcendent God; and deism sought to solve the problem by introducing the conception of natural law, which allowed freedom within the limits of reason. The solution was made possible only by pushing God outside the universe; the Creator of the world ceased to be its ruler, and the law of nature took His place in the guidance of human affairs. The deistic revolt was first expressed in a substitution of theodicy for theology, ultimately in a substitution of ethics for religion. The early deism rejected the notion of divine interference in the events of this world; but it was unprepared to dispense entirely with revelation, which was still deemed necessary to support natural religion. It was this partially developed form of the doctrine, gradually gaining possession of the colleges, that undermined the roots of the older theology, rather than the later, more vigorous blows of men like Ethan Allen and Thomas Paine. As it became more widespread, however, deism was more sharply in opposition to revealed religion; and the later assumption of a natural religion, discoverable by reason alone, is basal to the logical argument of the revolutionary period. From the premises of natural religion, men like Samuel Adams and James Otis arrived at the conception of a law of nature independent of God, and by which God himself is bound; and it was to this law of nature that the supporters of independence appealed for justification.

A third stream of American speculative thought was towards idealism: a conviction that behind perceived phenomena lay something more fundamental, and an effort to explain objects of sense in terms of this nonsensuous essence. Idealism sprang up spontaneously with Jonathan Edwards,[22] in whom it took the form of a mysticism colored by Calvinistic theology; while in Samuel Johnson, first president of King's College and greatest disciple of Berkeley, it followed the principles advanced by the Irish philosopher. When Berkeley left Rhode Island to become Bishop of Cloyne, Johnson assumed the task of disseminating his teaching; but everywhere he met cold response from men who had already fallen under the sway of Anglo-French materialism, or of the Scottish philosophy of common sense, enthroned at Princeton. It was these two latter schools of thought which made most rapid headway in the period immediately preceding, and that following, the Revolution. Both could be reconciled with deism, and often enough all three were combined in an uncritical eclecticism of which Jefferson himself is an excellent example.

The attempts of the materialists to explain the universe in terms of the interaction of particles of matter, follow in general the lines laid down by European thinkers, such as Hobbes and Hartley, Condillac and Cabanis, and D'Holbach. Exponents of the doctrine in this country during the formative period of American institutions were Cadwallader Colden, for a time governor of New York, and the more original Joseph Buchanan of Kentucky. Franklin's experiments with electricity furnished grist for the materialist's mill;[23] and the removal of the English chemist, Joseph Priestley, to Pennsylvania added measurably to the influence of the school in America, as did the ingenious arguments of Dr. Benjamin Rush of the Philadelphia medical college. But most influential of all, in the early years of the republic, was the Scottish realism, proceeding by observation and induction, and offering an explanation of the world in terms of common sense. Brought to Princeton in 1768 by John Witherspoon, the doctrine spread rapidly throughout the northern and middle states, penetrating the back country with the hordes of Scotch immigrants, and making progress at last even

---

[22] *Ibid.*, pp. 126 ff.; cf. Parrington, *op. cit.*, pp. 152 ff.
[23] Riley, *op. cit.*, p. 262.

in the materialistic south. In the Virginia of the Revolution, however, only Jefferson appears to have been influenced by it, and in him it was combined with other doctrines.

Perhaps the most significant point in connection with all these early efforts at speculative thinking in America is their effect on the movement for independence, and their influence in the creation of the new state. For all fostered a spirit of inquiry, and of independent evaluation of facts; and the stimulus to friendly interchange of ideas through the different colonies, and the recognition of a spiritual solidarity, was considerable. Having boldly questioned the nature of the world and the authority of God, it was but a step for the colonists to question the nature of the state and the authority of kings.

v

When they had achieved an economic self-sufficiency and an intellectual maturity, the Americans turned their attention to politics; and they found in Locke a champion ready to their hands. For in the eighteenth century, nature had "stepped in between man and God," so that one could know God's will only by discovering the laws of nature;[24] and Locke had shown that the laws of nature were operative in the world of human affairs no less than in the physical world. It followed, of course, that kings and priests, if they were out of harmony with nature, were no better than rebels against God. So in the Cambridge of 1746, Jonathan Mayhew could charge that ecclesiastics "who preach the divine right of titles and the equity of sinecures, are not ministers of God but pirates and highwaymen."[25]

Locke had argued also for the sovereignty of the people, and had shown that governments "derive their just powers from the consent of the governed." All of which appealed to the colonists as indisputable; for the governments under which they lived were of precisely this type, and what they most wanted to believe was that their popular assemblies were ordained by the

[24] Carl Becker, *The Declaration of Independence* (New York, 1922), pp. 37, 57 ff.
[25] Riley, *op. cit.*, p. 27.

law of nature. And they could accordingly conclude, as they earnestly desired to conclude, that "taxation without representation" was opposed to the will of God.[26]

The appeal to the law of nature by men whose consciences or political aspirations could not be reconciled with the positive laws of their country is as old as the Sophists and Cynics of ancient Greece. The Americans inherited the notion along with the English common law, and its lineage may be traced back indefinitely. For if Jefferson copied Locke in the *Declaration of Independence*, Locke in his turn had quoted Hooker, Hooker had followed Aquinas, and the Angelic Doctor had borrowed freely from Cicero and from Aristotle. It was with St. Thomas that the law of nature was broadened into a more or less definite code of rules which could be ascertained and formulated by reason; while Grotius and Pufendorf, both of whom influenced Locke, had derived from it the law of nations.

The real significance of the appeal to nature is its negative element. It is not so much calling the changeless universe to witness and justify a given line of action, as it is a convenient lever for upsetting the status quo. The conception of a law of nature was already old when it became a revolutionary rallying cry in the eighteenth century; and it had already been used, upon occasion, for the same purpose. Each of the three great authorities of the mediaeval period—Aristotle, Justinian and the Bible—had contributed something. From the Bible alone it had been possible for the Levellers to argue for a natural equality of man; for were not all men sons of Adam? and might they not become by adoption sons of God? Surely distinctions of birth, of wealth, of power, would be cast aside in the kingdom of the saints.[27]

In the American colonies, where the Protestant influence was dominant, the doctrine of natural rights was an almost inevitable consequence, bound up as it is with deism. For the natural rights theory is Protestantism shorn of its otherworldli-

---

[26] Becker, *The Declaration of Independence*, pp. 71 ff.
[27] Cf. David G. Ritchie, *Natural Rights* (New York and London, 1895), pp. 7-8.

ness and stripped of its traditionalism.[28] The Middle Ages accepted a law of nature discoverable by reason, but subject to the interpretative guidance of Church and Holy Writ. The Protestant, having renounced the authority of the church, was left with natural law and the Bible, standing in no very clearly defined relation; but the logical development of Protestantism settled the issue between them. Either there must be one Church, whose authority is final, or every man must be his own authority in interpreting the sacred texts. Many churches is a contradiction in terms. Since Protestantism took the road to individualism, the intellectual descendants of Luther appear as deists and rationalists in the eighteenth century. It should not be forgotten that Rousseau was bred in Calvin's Geneva, while Massachusetts produced Samuel Adams.

The appeal to a social contract was also old long before it passed from mouth to mouth in the heated days preceding the American Revolution. Glaucon expounds a contract theory of the state in the second book of Plato's *Republic;* the feudal system was for the most part contractual; and by 1579 in the *Vindiciae contra Tyrannos,* the theory was effectively used to deny the power of a king to command his subjects where obedience might be detrimental to their welfare. Hotman's *Franco-Gallia* in 1573 reaches much the same conclusion, arguing on the basis of traditional constitutional rights. Thus the revolutionary argument takes two forms, both of which look backward into the past: an appeal to rights historically exercised or claimed; and an appeal to a law of nature, argued on the basis of a social contract. These doctrines were crystallized in France in the last quarter of the sixteenth century, found their way across the channel in the next half-century, and served in due course the leaders of American independence.

[28] *Ibid.,* pp. 13 ff.; see also Ernst Troeltsch, *Protestantism and Progress* (London and New York, 1912), pp. 117-27.

CHAPTER III

MEN AND BOOKS

I

It is seldom indeed that a political theorist has been successful in politics; seldom also that a successful statesman has written a philosophy of the state. Jefferson's achievement in this regard, like that of Cicero before him, was due in part to the circumstances in which he found himself, in part to a rare combination of talents. It was because he was by nature and inclination a scholar no less than a leader of men that to him it was given, perhaps more than to any other man, to synthesize the liberal thought of his age, to fuse it into a concrete unity, tempered at the forge of experience, to make it actual in the councils of a government. He shared also with Cicero a belief in the worth and dignity of the public service, which led him, in spite of his repeatedly expressed desire for retirement, to devote more than forty years to the administration of affairs of state.

Jefferson combined with the rugged independence of the pioneer American, who had wrested from the wilderness a potential empire, the intellectual independence of the best in eighteenth-century thought, which had cast authoritarianism to the winds. An aristocrat by birth, by temper and by culture, he yet denied all but the natural aristocracy of talent, and based his state on the equality of men. The political theorist, with whom this study is primarily concerned, is but one aspect of a many-sided personality. He was the most widely read American of his generation,[1] a lover of music and literature, keenly interested in nature and natural science. He stands out as educator and as

[1] *Literary Bible of Thomas Jefferson* (with an Introduction by Gilbert Chinard. Baltimore, 1928), Introduction, p. 2.

agriculturalist; and in his later years was the wise and beloved patriarch of a model plantation. That his life was devoted mainly to politics was rather an accident of the times than of his own seeking; but the choice once made, he brought into the public service scholarship, sympathy, and understanding.

Yet Jefferson's humanity is always of the head rather than of the heart. Although ever the champion of the common man, he remains always aloof from the masses; and if he claims equality for all men, it is not because he feels that men are equal, but because he reasons that they must be so. He had not risen from the people, as Lincoln did; he had never felt, as Lincoln felt, the poignant suffering of the human soul; he could never have made his own the sorrows of mankind. His is rather a rational world in which emotion must give place to logic. Not that he was cold or passionless: he was intensely human; but he could not suffer vicariously because others suffered; and he could not doubt that the world order was rational, and therefore ultimately good.

He found in reason a sufficient source of all we need to know, and beyond the limits of reason he had no desire to penetrate; or if for a time, as a very young man, he dallied with abstract speculation, he soon gave it up as fruitless. Even in old age, when active minds inevitably turn to the enigma of death, he refused to relinquish his belief that the business of life was living, and the rest would take care of itself. It is to make the business of living more pleasant and life more secure that the state exists.

Jefferson lived in an age of political unrest, and his life covers an historical span of tremendous significance. He helped to establish the independence of the American colonies, and for eight years directed the destiny of the new republic. In Paris, he saw the storming of the Bastille; and with the perspective of distance, he watched the progress of the French Revolution, and the political upheavals that followed: the partition of Poland and the Napoleonic wars, Waterloo and St. Helena, and the restoration of the Bourbons; from all of which he drew empirical data for the testing of his own philosophy of the state. To profit by the mistakes of others is the essential lesson of history.

It is impossible to consider Jefferson's political philosophy apart from the institutions in which he sought to actualize it. Before the American government was formed, he was motivated by the necessity for justifying a separation from Britain; during the formation period he was concerned with the principles on which political authority should rest, and with historical precedent for various conflicting views; and after the adoption of the American constitution in 1789, he thought always in terms of the problems and policies of his government, modifying or expanding as occasion required. That his country did not always follow the policy Jefferson advocated for it is true enough, but his views were always such as could have been followed, consistently with the principles on which its order rested. And Jefferson would never have held that his way was the only way to a desired end. For him, government was essentially a pragmatic process.

Jefferson possessed, in the words of John Adams, a "happy talent of composition," and expressed himself with a "peculiar felicity of phrase."[2] His voluminous writings, covering as they do a chronological period of more than sixty years, range over a series of topics as broad as the interests of men; and his views are always clearly, sometimes brilliantly expressed. His touch is never more deft, his ideas never marshalled with greater force or logic, than when adding throughout the course of a long and varied life, detail after detail to the broad theory of the state of which the *Declaration of Independence* was the first systematic expression. He is not, to be sure, always consistent— but there is an inevitable inconsistency between word and act, between theory and practice. What system of political ideas can withstand unmodified the test of forty years' experience in governing? It is high endorsement of the soundness of Jefferson's philosophy that its broad outlines were only confirmed by

[2] *The Works of John Adams* (10 vols. Boston, 1850-1856), II, 513-14.

experience, and to his own credit as a thinker that he himself saw so many of its weaknesses, and modified his views as he realized their inadequacy.

II

Living in the comparative isolation of the American colonies, Jefferson was prevented by limited contacts with books and men from joining any particular school of thought; and he cannot be judged by the standards of European theorists.[3]   Like most men of affairs, he was more inclined to find in the books of others justification for an already determined course of action than determination for future acts, and he was primarily influenced by books which tended in the direction of his own thinking.[4] He took progress as a matter of course, and is impatient with those who "look backwards instead of forwards for the improvement of the human mind, and . . . recur to the annals of our ancestors for what is most perfect in government, in religion and in learning."[5] He knew the annals of the past, however, well enough; and if he is unsparing in his condemnation of some of the works of antiquity, he is as outspoken in his praise of others.

It is the moralists and historians who most impress him among ancient writers, with metaphysics holding practically no place in his classical heritage. Though his commonplace books reveal wide reading in the drama and poetry of Greece and Rome, the passages which appealed to him sufficiently to be copied out were in the main political and ethical maxims.[6] Historians like Thucydides and Tacitus he rates highly;[7] even going so far as to say of the latter that he is the "first writer in the world without a single exception. His book is a compound

[3] Cf. Gilbert Chinard, *Thomas Jefferson, The Apostle of Americanism* (Boston, 1929), p. 32.

[4] Becker, *The Declaration of Independence*, p. 28.

[5] To Priestley, Jan. 27, 1800: *The Writings of Thomas Jefferson* (Memorial Edition, 20 vols. Washington, 1903-1904), X, 148. All subsequent references to Jefferson's works will be to this edition unless otherwise noted.

[6] *Literary Bible*, Introduction, pp. 5 ff., *et passim*.

[7] To Wilkinson, Mar. 10, 1811, *Writings*, XIII, 23.

of history and morality of which we have no other example."[8]
A true philosopher like Plato, however, does not fare so well
at his hands. "Speaking of Plato, I will add, that no writer,
ancient or modern, has bewildered the world with more *ignis
fatui,* than this renowned philosopher, in Ethics, in Politics, and
Physics. . . ."[9] And in another passage, he charges that "Plato
. . . dealing out mysticisms incomprehensible to the human
mind, has been deified by certain sects usurping the name of
Christian."[10]

In answer to an inquiry as to the relative merits of Gillies's
translation of Aristotle's *Politics,* Jefferson explains that he has
not seen the book, but adds that "so different was the style of
society then, and with those people, from what it is now and
with us, that I think little edification can be obtained from their
writings on the subject of government. They had just ideas of
the value of personal liberty, but none at all of the structure of
government best calculated to preser7e it. They knew no
medium between a democracy (the only pure republic, but impracticable beyond the limits of a town) and an abandonment
of themselves to an aristocracy, or a tyranny independent of the
people. It seems not to have occurred that where the citizens
cannot meet to transact their business in person, they alone have
the right to choose agents who shall transact it; and that in this
way a republican, or popular government, of the second grade
of purity, may be exercised over any extent of country. . . .
The introduction of this new principle of representative democracy has rendered useless almost everything written before on
the structure of government; and, in a great measure, relieves
our regret, if the political writings of Aristotle, or of any other
ancient, have been lost, or are unfaithfully rendered or explained to us."[11] This is in general his point of view in regard
to historical systems, and he is seemingly unaware of how much

[8] To Anne Cary Bankhead, Dec. 8, 1808, *ibid.,* XVIII, 255.

[9] To Short, Aug. 4, 1820, *ibid.,* XV, 258.

[10] To Short, Oct. 31, 1819, *ibid.,* p. 219; Cf. to Adams, July 5, 1814, *ibid.,* XIV, 147 ff.

[11] To I. H. Tiffany, Aug. 26, 1816, *ibid.,* XV, 65-66.

this new principle of representative democracy owes to the ancient world.

Among classic moralists, he singles out in 1785 to recommend to his nephew the Socratic writings of Xenophon and Plato, and the works of Epictetus, of Cicero, Seneca, and Antoninus.[12] In general his preference at this period is for the Stoic doctrine. Some time later, however, his point of view has changed considerably. Seneca, he still regards in 1819 as "indeed a fine moralist, disfiguring his work at times with some Stoicisms . . . yet giving us on the whole a great deal of sound and practical morality."[13] But he now reserves his highest praise for Epicurus: "I consider the genuine (not the imputed) doctrines of Epicurus as containing everything rational in moral philosophy which Greece and Rome have left us."[14] His system, "notwithstanding the calumnies of the Stoics and caricatures of Cicero, is . . . as frugal of vicious indulgence, and fruitful of virtue as the hyperbolical extravagances of his rival sects."[15] Epictetus includes for Jefferson at this later date all that is worth preserving of the Stoics.[16] The period at which he changed his allegiance from the Stoic to the Epicurean doctrine cannot be precisely determined, but it is probable that it dates from his contact with the Helvetius group in France.[17]

Finally among ancient writings by which Jefferson was influenced, the Bible must be named. He advises his nephew to read it as he would Livy or Tacitus,[18] and he seems to have read it himself with even greater care. "He that shall collect all the moral rules of the philosophers," wrote John Locke, "and compare them with those contained in the New Testament, will find them to come short of the morality delivered by our Savior."[19] Whether acting on Locke's suggestion, or on his own

---

[12] To Peter Carr, Aug. 19, 1785, *ibid.*, V, 85.

[13] To Short, Oct. 31, 1819, *ibid.*, XV, 220.

[14] *Ibid.*, p. 219.

[15] To Charles Thompson, Jan. 9, 1816, *ibid.*, XIV, 386.

[16] To Short, *ibid.*, XV, 220.   [17] *Literary Bible*, Introduction, p. 16.

[18] To Peter Carr, Aug. 10, 1787, *Writings*, VI, 258.

[19] "Reasonableness of Christianity," *Works of John Locke* (3 vols. London, 1740), II, 576.

initiative, Jefferson prepared a syllabus of the doctrines of Jesus compared with those of others, from which he concludes that the moral system of the Nazarene is the most sublime and benevolent code ever presented to man.[20]   He insists, however, on confining this unqualified praise to the words of Jesus himself, and that he might not err he prepared the famous "Jefferson Bible," clipping from the Gospels and compiling into a volume the sayings of the founder of Christianity.[21]

In the field of politics proper it is not easy to determine which among ancient writers Jefferson most fully endorsed. For Cicero he found an early admiration, but seems to have cooled toward the Roman statesman later in life, and objects to the use of Cicero's orations as parliamentary models.[22]   He nevertheless couples the works of Cicero and Aristotle with those of Locke and Sydney as the "elementary books of public right" scarcely a year before his death.[23]   Jefferson's whole point of view, and many of his ideas, are also to be found clearly expressed in Thucydides, notably in the funeral speech put by the historian into the mouth of Pericles.

III

With the thought of his own, and of the immediately preceding age, Jefferson was on better terms.   Hobbes he knew, but found unpalatable;[24] Descartes, Leibniz and Spinoza he names,[25] but late in his life, and without reference to their work, which was probably imperfectly known to him, if at all. Milton he admired, both as poet and as political pamphleteer, and seems to have been familiar with his controversial writings early in the Revolution;[26] and his copy of Harrington's *Oceana* is still preserved in the Library of Congress, although there is

---

[20] *Writings*, XIII, 390; for the syllabus, see *ibid.*, X, 381 ff.

[21] See *ibid.*, XX, for facsimile.

[22] *Literary Bible*, Introduction, pp. 14 ff.; 72 ff.

[23] To Henry Lee, May 8, 1825, *Writings*, XVI, 118-19.

[24] To F. W. Gilmer, June 7, 1816, *ibid.*, XV, 24 ff.

[25] To Adams, Apr. 11, 1823, *ibid.*, p. 426.

[26] *Literary Bible*, Introduction, pp. 21 ff., 134 ff., 164 ff.; *The Commonplace Book of Thomas Jefferson* (ed. by G. Chinard. The Johns Hopkins Studies in Romance Literatures and Languages, Extra Volume II. Baltimore, 1926), pp. 384 ff., 388.

no evidence that he was greatly influenced by it.[27]   The deism
of Bolingbroke also impressed him, and he copied long extracts
into his literary commonplace book from this "Alcibiades of his
time."[28]   But it is to Locke, whose "little book on government
is perfect as far as it goes,"[29] that we must turn for the ultimate
source of the ideas which most influenced Jefferson during his
formative years.

He knew Locke so well that the very phrasing of the second
Treatise recurs in the *Declaration of Independence,* although
Jefferson protests that he "turned neither to book nor pamphlet"
while writing it;[30] and in answer to Lee's charge that it was
copied from Locke, he replied that it had been no part of his
task to "invent new ideas altogether, and to offer no sentiment
which had ever been expressed before."   It is impossible not to
conclude from this that he was thoroughly familiar with Locke's
argument at the time the *Declaration* was written, and although
his extracts from the philosopher bear no date, it is probable he
had read the books some time earlier.   To minimize the direct
influence of Locke, as Chinard seems inclined to do,[31] because
mention is made of him only once in the *Commonplace Book,*
is surely a questionable interpretation.   The *Commonplace Book*
was undoubtedly prepared while Jefferson was studying law,
and the entries in it are, almost without exception, such as would
be made by a student interested in tracing the historical development of legal institutions and processes.   It is no more remarkable that political theorists as such should be omitted, than that
any other field of thought aside from the law should find no
place.   Neither does he abstract from Sydney in the *Commonplace Book,* yet Sydney's *Discourses* are named along with
Locke's second *Treatise* as sources in government for the Uni-

[27] See Russell-Smith, *Harrington and his Oceana,* p. 179, *et passim.*
[28] *Literary Bible,* pp. 40 ff.
[29] To T. M. Randolph, May 30, 1790, *Writings,* VIII, 31.
[30] To Madison, Aug. 30, 1823, *ibid.,* XV, 462; cf. to Henry Lee, May 8, 1825, *ibid.,* XVI, 118-19.   Cf. also John Locke, *Of Civil Government,* Treatise II, sec. 225, and *Declaration of Independence,* par. 2.
[31] *Commonplace Book,* Introduction, p. 54; *ibid.,* Appendix, pp. 377 ff.

versity of Virginia.[32]   In the few instances in which he does
quote from other than legal writings, as in the case of extracts
from Helvetius's *De l'Homme*,[33] it is probable that it was done
after he had ceased to be an active student of the law.   The
absence of quotations from Locke, if it indicates anything at all,
probably implies simply that he had read the *Treatises* before
he began the *Commonplace Book;* and it should surely not
weigh as evidence that he was little influenced by Locke.

It is, on the other hand, perfectly true that Locke's ideas on
government had, by the latter half of the eighteenth century,
become almost axiomatic with many other writers, especially in
America; and there can be no doubt that Jefferson imbibed
Locke's principles from Lord Kames, whose *Historical Law
Tracts* receive considerable attention in the *Commonplace Book,*
and from Dalrymple, as well as from Locke himself.[34]   That
these principles should have appealed to him as being unquestionably true was inevitable; for the inspiration of the American
Revolution was the British parliamentary struggle of the preceding century, and the justification of 1688 could as well be
made the apology for 1776.[35]

Of Locke's successors in the English empirical tradition,
Jefferson seems not to have known Berkeley; and for Hume he
had scant respect, although he is fair enough to admit that several of his *Political Essays* "are good."[36]   His criticism of the
great skeptic is based primarily on his *History of England,* the
language of which Jefferson charges "seems intended to disguise
and discredit the good principles of the government," although
there is an extract from Hume's political writings appended at a
very late date to the *Commonplace Book,* with ironical comments by Jefferson.[37]   If he knew the *Treatise of Human Na-*

---

[32] Minutes, etc., Mar. 4, 1825, *Writings,* XIX, 460-61.

[33] *Commonplace Book,* arts. 849-51.

[34] See arts. 557-569; 569-585; Introduction, pp. 16 ff.

[35] Becker, *op. cit.,* p. 79.

[36] To T. M. Randolph, May 30, 1790, *Writings,* VIII, 32.

[37] Art. 905.   A quotation from an 1824 newspaper fixes the date within two years
of Jefferson's death.   See also letters to Norvell, June 11, 1807, *Writings,* XI, 222;
to Duane, Aug. 12, 1810, *ibid.,* XII, 404; to Spafford, Mar. 17, 1814, *ibid.,* XIV,

ture, he does not mention it; so it is safe to assume that it did not impress him.

With Hume's critics, Jefferson had more in common. The Scottish School, having its historical origin in an attempt to answer Hume's skeptical attack on causation, set forth a metaphysics with which he could not fail to agree. If the appeal to "common sense" was a new departure in English philosophy,[38] it was no new principle to Thomas Jefferson. He did not need Reid to tell him that there "are ways of reasoning with regard to first principles by which those that are truly such may be distinguished from vulgar errors or prejudices," or that to judge of those principles "requires no more than a sound mind free from prejudice, and a distinct conception of the question;"[39] and when he learned the doctrine from Dugald Stewart, with whom he became acquainted in Paris, he was fully prepared to accept it. It is significant that it was to Stewart he turned for assistance in selecting the first occupant of the chair of moral philosophy at the newly established University of Virginia.[40] Among other philosophers of the Scottish group, Lord Kames has already been mentioned as one of Jefferson's early influences, and he knew also both the moral and economic writings of Adàm Smith.[41]

Jefferson's background was predominantly English, and his debt to French thought is small. Montesquieu he read between 1774 and 1776[42] with evident approval, and devotes twenty-seven articles to *l'Esprit des Lois* in the *Commonplace Book—* more than he gives to any other writer. Yet he writes of the book in 1790, that it "contains, indeed, a great number of political truths; but also an equal number of heresies: so that the

120; to Adams, Nov. 25, 1816, *ibid.,* XV, 86; to Cartwright, June 5, 1824, *ibid.,* XVI, 44; to ———, Oct. 25, 1825, *ibid.,* p. 125.

[38] James Seth, *English Philosophers and Schools of Philosophy* (London and New York, 1912), p. 230.

[39] Quoted in *ibid.,* p. 235.

[40] To Dugald Stewart, Apr. 26, 1824, *Writings,* XVIII, 331 ff.

[41] To Norvell, June 11, 1807, *ibid.,* XI, 223.

[42] *Commonplace Book,* Introduction, pp. 8 ff. See also *ibid.,* pp. 31 ff., and arts. 775-803.

reader must be constantly on his guard;"[43] and this distrust is even more pronounced twenty years later: "I had, with the world, deemed Montesquieu's work of much merit; but saw in it, with every thinking man, so much of paradox, of false principle and misapplied fact, as to render its value equivocal on the whole."[44] There is little in Jefferson which can even remotely be traced to Montesquieu, the principal exceptions being his belief in the influence of geographic factors in the development of law, and his use of the historical method in dealing with laws and institutions. And it is impossible to give full credit to the French jurist for this: Jefferson might have taken the method from Aristotle, or more probably, from Lord Kames.

Rousseau he seems not to have known at all. The *Contrat Social*, had he read it, must have impressed him strongly, agreeing as it does with many of his own ideas, and he would not have failed to make note of the fact; but he does not mention the work, and it does not appear in the catalogue of his library.[45] Helvetius he read, and quoted in his *Commonplace Book*, one of the extracts in particular describing a federative system similar to that advocated by Jefferson himself;[46] but it is probable that it appealed to him, not as something new, but as additional precedent for his own theory. He made extracts, also, from Voltaire's *Essai sur les Mœurs*, but seems to have regarded the work more as a mine of curious information than as a source of new ideas.[47]

While American minister in Paris, Jefferson met at the house of Madame d'Houdetot a distinguished group of thinkers, including Destutt de Tracy, principle theorist of the Ideologist group, Abbé Morellet, and Cabanis, then a young man; and with de Tracy and Morellet he kept up an intermittent cor-

---

[43] To T. M. Randolph, May 30, 1790, *Writings*, VIII, 31.

[44] To Destutt de Tracy, Jan. 26, 1811, *ibid.*, XIII, 13; cf. to Duane, Sept. 16, 1810, *ibid.*, XII, 413-14.

[45] Becker, *op. cit.*, p. 28; *Commonplace Book*, Introduction, p. 44.

[46] Art. 851; Introduction, pp. 47 ff.

[47] *Commonplace Book*, arts. 852-62; Introduction, pp. 48 ff.

respondence throughout his life. There is, however, no evidence in the letters written during his stay in France that he endorsed, or even took serious notice of the political views prevalent there at the time.[48]

If he helped to spread in America the doctrines of the Ideologists,[49] it was because they were ideas which accorded, or at least did not conflict with, his own. For example, he writes of de Tracy's commentary on Montesquieu, a book which he sponsored in an English version, that it is "a most valuable work, one which I think will form an epoch in the science of government, and which I wish to see in the hands of every American student, as the elementary and fundamental institute of that important branch of human science."[50] Jefferson endorses the book because it states so precisely his own views, just as he endorses works on political economy by de Tracy and by Jean Baptiste Say.[51] In other instances, notably in de Tracy's advocacy of a plural executive, and of Hobbes's view of the presocial state, he does not hesitate to take his friend to task.

On the whole, we must conclude that Jefferson was only very slightly influenced by French thought;[52] and he himself took pains to uncover the source of the charge, familiar in his own day, that he was a theorist under French influence: "After I retired from that office [Secretary of State], great and malignant pains were taken by our federal monarchists, and not entirely without effect, to make him [Washington] view me as a theorist, holding French principles of government, which would lead infallibly to licentiousness and anarchy."[53] It was rather Jefferson who exerted some measure of influence on French political thought. The esteem in which he was held in France is evidenced by the fact that Auguste Comte, on the threshold

[48] Chinard, *Thomas Jefferson*, pp. 161, 215.

[49] Chinard, *Jefferson et les Idéologues* (Baltimore, 1925), p. i.

[50] To Dr. Thomas Cooper, Jan. 16, 1814, *Writings*, XIV, 63.

[51] To Duane, Apr. 4, 1813, *ibid.*, XIII, 231.

[52] Sir Henry Maine is alone in maintaining a contrary view. See *Ancient Law* (London, 1861; New York, 1864), p. 91.

[53] To Dr. Walter Jones, Jan. 2, 1814, *Writings*, XIV, 52.

of own brilliant career in 1824, wrote to the aged sage of Monticello to offer his respect and homage.[54]

IV

To understand the relation of Jefferson's political ideas to those of his own contemporaries, it will be necessary to review briefly the main line of the prerevolutionary argument. The appeal to natural rights was the final and irrevocable step. As late as 1774, with the Boston Port Act already in force, the keenest of colonial thinkers were arguing from the British constitution itself, with no thought of withdrawing from the empire. The point of attack was the authority of Parliament, which Blackstone had declared to be the seat of the *jura summi imperii*. But the celebrated *Commentaries* did not appear in print until the years between 1765 and 1769. John Adams was admitted to the bar in 1758, Jefferson and James Wilson in 1767, while Sir Edward Coke still dominated the American law schools; and my lord Coke had flatly asserted that king, lords, and commons were under the law. James Otis, first American to deny the supremacy of Parliament, in his argument against the granting of writs of assistance, based his denial on the declaration of Coke that the common law controlled acts of Parliament when such acts were against common right and reason.[55] Similar, too, was the position of Richard Bland, burgess of Virginia, who denied in *The Colonel Dismounted* (1763) the right of Parliament to legislate with regard to the "internal polity" of a colony, a term which includes taxation; and expanded his thesis in 1766 with an *Inquiry into the Rights of the British Colonies*.[56] Though friend of Jefferson and Henry, Bland belonged to an older generation, for which Parliaments and kings were overshadowed by the common law.

It was on this fundamental law, conceived as binding on the

---

[54] Chinard, *Jefferson et les Idéologues*, pp. 285-86.

[55] Channing, *History of the United States*, III, 9; cf. R. G. Adams, *Political Ideas of the American Revolution*, p. 124.

[56] Richard Bland, *Inquiry into the Rights of the British Colonies* (ed. by E. G. Swem, Richmond, 1922); and L. G. Tyler, "Bland's Constitutional Argument in 'The Colonel Dismounted'," *William and Mary Quarterly*, XIX, 31-41.

Parliament itself, that the constitutional argument was based, and it was ably fortified by legal precedent drawn from the English courts. The clearest statement of the American position is that set forth in James Wilson's pamphlet, entitled *Considerations on the Nature and Extent of the Legislative Authority of the British Parliament*.[57] The pamphlet was not published until 1774, although probably written some three years earlier, and is remarkable for its anticipation of the present theory of the British empire as a commonwealth of nations.

Wilson argues, citing Burlamaqui, that the happiness of the society is the first law of every government. It is founded in the law of nature, and must control the acts of the legislature. And he finds the possession on the part of the British Parliament of "supreme, irresistible, uncontrolled authority" over the colonies not calculated to insure and increase the happiness of the latter. Sovereignty is legitimate only when it serves to procure the felicity of the people over whom it is exercised. Now Parliament, as sovereign, consists of king, lords, and commons; but from the American point of view, the authority must ultimately rest in the commons alone. For the king has no power under the British constitution to bind his subjects, and the peers sit as a collective rather than as a representative body. Acts of the commons, however, cannot be binding on America; for the commons derive their authority solely by delegation from the people, whose representatives they are, and the colonies are not represented in that house. The power of the commons resides originally in the English people, those in America no less than those in the homeland.

This general argument Wilson then proceeds to fortify by citing decisions of the English courts. It was held in Calvin's case that statutes of Parliament do not bind Ireland, because Ireland has a parliament of her own and sends no representatives to Westminster. An unanimous ruling of the justices of the King's Bench declared that English statutes were not in force in Jamaica; and, argues Wilson, "whatever was resolved

<hr>

[57] *Works of James Wilson* (3 vols. Philadelphia, 1804), III, 199-246.

concerning Jamaica is equally applicable to every American colony." While in still another case Lord Chief Justice Holt held that the laws of England did not extend to Virginia. When Blackstone speaks of the dependence of the colonies on Great Britain, therefore, he can mean only one thing: that the people of the colonies are subjects of the crown. A parliament has no subjects. The new lands were settled with the king's consent, and in his name, while charters and grants were from the king alone. It was not until the interregnum, when the king was in exile, that there was any thought of interference by the legislative branch.

The connection between Britain and the colonies is for the interest of both to preserve, but it "will be better preserved by the operation of the legal prerogatives of the crown, than by the exertion of an unlimited authority by the parliament." And in a lengthy note at the end of his pamphlet, Wilson goes on to clarify the theory of the empire, the various members of which are conceived as distinct states, each making its own laws and developing in its own way, with a common allegiance to the crown as the sole bond of union, and the crown itself as the sole regulating power in the empire. Although Wilson makes numerous references to Blackstone, whose *Commentaries* were then the last word in English law, the argument clearly rests on the jurisprudence of an earlier period. In effect, it is a denial of parliamentary sovereignty and a reassertion of the older belief in a fundamental law.

In this general position, as well as in the theory of the empire, Jefferson and Adams concurred, although how far there was any reciprocal influence between them is doubtful. There is one abstract in the *Commonplace Book* from Wilson's pamphlet;[58] the passage quoted being that which asserts the welfare of a people to be of greater importance than legislative omnipotence; but Jefferson makes no reference to certain other passages which closely parallel a portion of the *Declaration of Independence*. The conclusion drawn from this by the editor of

[58] Art. 832; cf. Introduction, pp. 39 ff.

the *Commonplace Book* is that Jefferson's abstract was not made until after the *Declaration* was written. There is, however, a more plausible explanation of the omission. Jefferson's own *Summary View of the Rights of British America*[59] appeared in 1774, the same year as Wilson's pamphlet; and the point of Jefferson's argument is the same: submission to a common executive head is the only link between the colonies and the mother country, and the king is the only mediator between "the several states of the British empire." He possesses, by virtue of his office, the administrative power of the laws of every state in the imperial dominions, but these laws are made by the individual state for its own governance, and cannot be made for it by any other member of the empire. Jefferson also argues from precedent, as had Wilson, although he chooses to go back to the Saxon settlements in Britain rather than to the decisions of the King's Bench. The only point in Wilson's argument which Jefferson neglects is precisely the argument that sovereignty must be subject to the control of a more fundamental principle, the happiness of the society; and it is this argument he notes in the *Commonplace Book*. Neither Jefferson nor Wilson was ready, in 1774, to assert the complete independence of the American states, and the passages in the latter which would support complete separation were not written with that in view, any more than were similar phrases in Jefferson's pamphlet. It is thus possible to assume that the Virginian read Wilson's *Considerations* soon after its publication, while the subject was still uppermost in his own mind, and made note only of the phase of the argument which he had himself neglected.

It was only after the British king and ministry had turned a deaf ear to the constitutional argument that the more radical appeal to natural rights assumed a position of great importance in America, bringing with it the corollary, independence. And perhaps the most powerful single influence in convincing the colonists of the necessity of separation was the publication in

[59] *The Writings of Thomas Jefferson* (ed. by P. L. Ford. 10 vols. New York, 1892-1899), I, 429 ff.

January, 1776, of Thomas Paine's *Common Sense*. Although Jefferson probably arrived at the same conclusions independently, he expresses complete endorsement of Paine's views,[60] and seems to have valued them as highly as those of any of his contemporaries. The only other American source for any of Jefferson's political ideas is the *Federalist*, which he called the "best commentary on the principles of government, which ever was written";[61] and it was admittedly this volume which swung him from opposition to support of the constitution. John Adams's *Defense of the Constitutions of the United States*, he read in Paris, and endorsed with reservations, objecting to Adams's characterization of the confederation congress as a diplomatic rather than a legislative body. That the work might appear in the best light in Europe, Jefferson supervised its translation into French.[62]

v

The final source of Jefferson's political faith is to be found in legal history. As a lawyer, he conceived the state primarily from the juristic point of view, involving the surrender of certain rights, in return for security and the preservation of other rights. Now the fundamental assumption on which any legal state must rest is precisely the assumption that men are in some sense equal. The notion was perfectly familiar to Jefferson from his classical reading; he had probably met with it in the Stoic literature, he must have found it in Cicero, and by the time he studied Roman law it had become a commonplace. He presumably rediscovered it in reading Lord Kames, and was struck by it in the code of Alfred. And it was there that the principle most deeply impressed him. For Jefferson was a practitioner and student of the law at the time he and his compatriots were faced with the problem of justifying a separation from England. Their arguments from Locke and the doctrine

[60] To Monroe, July 10, 1791, *Writings*, VIII, 207; to Paine, Mar. 18, 1801, *ibid.*, X, 223; cf. Channing, *op. cit.*, III, 189-90.

[61] To Madison, Nov. 18, 1788, *Writings*, VII, 183; cf. to Norvell, June 11, 1807, *ibid.*, XI, 223.

[62] To Adams, Feb. 23, 1787, *ibid.*, VI, 97-98.

of natural rights were probably better known to the people generally, but the leaders of the Revolution, as we have seen, gave equal weight to the argument from legal precedent.

Virginia was under the common law, having no code of her own; and the common law Jefferson conceived to be the system introduced by the ancient Saxons into England—*lex non scripta*—and taken from them by their Norman conquerors. English history from the time of the Conquest reveals a struggle on the part of the people to regain their Saxon liberty, with Magna Charta the first popular victory.[63] The Saxon code, then, Jefferson reasons, is the true law of Virginia; and he seeks a restoration of this birthright, of which the people have been deprived by a long train of abuses. He argues, also, that the emigration to America, being an emigration of free agents, left England with no authority over them, and they were consequently free to resume their natural rights of conquest and settlement. In his draft of instructions to the delegates to the Continental Congress (published as the *Summary View of the Rights of British America*), Jefferson compared the position of the American colonies to that of Scotland before the union, and to that of Hanover, "having the same executive chief but no other necessary political connection." The emigration, he contended, gave England no more rights over the colonies than had the mother countries of the Saxons and Danes over England.[64]

Jefferson's historical studies carried him even further than this. He found in Pelloutier's *Histoire des Celtes* and *Histoire des Galates* confirmation of the principle of popular sovereignty, the doctrine of natural rights, and of the right of a colony to self-government;[65] and Stanyan's *Grecian History down to the death of Philip of Macedon* gave him still further precedent for the independence of colonies from the cities that planted them.[66] To these he adds examples from Plutarch, and from

[63] To Dr. Thomas Cooper, Feb. 10, 1814, *ibid.*, XIV, 90 ff.; *Commonplace Book*, Art. 873; cf. *Blackstone's Commentaries*, (4 vols. Philadelphia, 1897), IV, chap. 33.

[64] Autobiography, *Writings*, I, 11; Appendix C, 184 ff.

[65] *Commonplace Book*, arts. 708, 713, 715; Introduction, pp. 21 ff.

[66] *Ibid.*, arts. 717-31; Introduction, pp. 22 ff.

Sir Walter Raleigh's *History of the World;*[67] and an account of the introduction and practices of the feudal system, taken from various sources.[68]

Of still greater significance for Jefferson's thinking is a detailed comparative study of constitutions, after the manner of Aristotle's undertaking. The *Commonplace Book* reveals careful analyses of the Union of Utrecht, and the constitutions of Switzerland, Denmark, Sweden, and Poland, together with an account of the Anglo-Saxon and early English practice of electing kings. To this Jefferson adds a list of English kings from the year 640 to his own day, noting the manner in which each came to the throne. The conclusion from this list, which reveals that the direct line of descent had been more often ignored than otherwise, is inevitable: the people of England have reserved to them a right to choose their king. This is, as Professor Chinard points out, hardly the work of a theorist, weaving a fabric of government from untried schemes. It is rather the approach of a capable lawyer and careful scholar, who offers no principle for the utility of which he has not discovered adequate evidence.[69]

Among legal writers by whom Jefferson was influenced in a greater or less degree in his theory of natural rights and his choice of a constitutional system, Lord Kames, Dalrymple, and Montesquieu have already been mentioned in other connections. Blackstone he read, but after his admission to the bar, and apparently with an uniform disapproval. His only references to the *Commentaries* brand the work as superficial and biassed,[70] and there is no reason to believe that it was, in however slight a degree, a determining factor in his intellectual development. Bracton, Coke, and Matthew Bacon, on the other hand, Jefferson praises highly,[71] and it was probably largely from them that he drew the knowledge of English law which colored to a

[67] *Ibid.*, arts. 724, 725.
[68] *Ibid.*, arts. 733 ff., 737 ff.
[69] *Ibid.*, arts. 729-57; Introduction, pp. 24 ff.
[70] To Judge Tyler, June 17, 1812, *Writings*, XIII, 166-67; to Spafford, Mar. 17, 1814, *ibid.*, XIV, 120.
[71] To Cooper, Jan. 16, 1814, *ibid.*, pp. 54 ff.

considerable extent much of his later political thought. Beccaria, from whom he copied twenty-six articles in the *Commonplace Book*,[72] seems to have been largely responsible for the ideas in his *Bill for Proportioning Crimes and Punishments*, as the footnotes to that document testify;[73] and the Italian writer may also have exerted some influence on Jefferson's ethical beliefs. And finally, he was thoroughly acquainted with Grotius and Pufendorf, both of whom had influenced Locke's conception of natural rights, with Wolff, and with Vattel, whose work on international law was the standard text after the middle of the eighteenth century. These jurists were of signal importance for Jefferson's own handling of international questions, as we shall see in a later chapter.

We learn also from Jefferson's *Autobiography*[74] that among the men who framed the American government he was not alone in being fortified with carefully digested historical knowledge of federative and legal systems. In the light of this material, the American experiment ceases to be experimental. It was reared on the broad foundation of centuries of political theorizing and political experience, by men who were peculiarly fitted by training and by circumstances to adapt to their purposes such principles as time and use had sanctioned. If we may regard the development of political ideas in the western world, from the earliest times to the present, as forming in some sense a progressive whole, Jefferson belongs as surely to that tradition as any of the continental thinkers. The roots of his doctrine go back to the golden age of Greece, and its branches reach out to touch the multiplying problems of the twentieth century.

[72] Arts. 806-32. [73] *Writings*, I, 218 ff.

[74] *Ibid.*, I, 50-51; cf. Channing, *op. cit.*, III, 477, 496 ff.

BOOK II

THE JEFFERSONIAN STATE

We hold these truths to be self-evident, that all men are created equal, that they are endowed by their Creator with certain unalienable Rights, that among these are Life, Liberty, and the Pursuit of Happiness.

—THOMAS JEFFERSON

CHAPTER IV

THE PURSUIT OF HAPPINESS

I

JEFFERSON SHARED with eighteenth-century thinkers generally a conviction that the laws and institutions of the state must conform ultimately to certain moral principles. But although implicit in all his political thinking, the ethical basis of the social order was, in the period of his early writings, inchoate and undefined, and was accepted more or less uncritically. It was only after the strenuous years were over, when he was free to reflect and clarify his views at leisure, that he set down the theoretical foundation on which his ethical beliefs rested; and it is from this starting point that an attempt will be made to reconstruct his most mature position.

If Jefferson regarded Newton, Bacon, and Locke as the three greatest men who ever lived[1] it was because he shared with them a certain empirical quality of mind, which would suffer his faith to go no further than his facts. Abstract speculation was not in his nature; and the best statement of his metaphysical views begins with the simple proposition: "I feel, therefore I exist." "I feel bodies which are not myself: there are other existences then. I call them *matter*. I feel them changing place. This gives me *motion*. Where there is an absence of matter, I call it *void*, or *nothing*, or *immaterial space*. On the basis of sensation, of matter and motion, we may erect the fabric of all the certainties we can have or need. I conceive *thought* to be an action of a particular organization of matter, formed for that purpose by its Creator, as well as that *attraction* is an action of matter, or *magnetism* of loadstone. When he

---

[1] To Rush, Jan. 16, 1811, *Writings*, XIII, 4; cf. to G. F. Hopkins, Sept. 5, 1822, *ibid.*, XV, 394.

who denies the Creator the power of endowing matter with the mode of action called *thinking,* shall show how He could endow the sun with the mode of action called *attraction,* which reins the planets in the track of their orbits, or how an absence of matter can have a will, and by that will put matter into motion, then the Materialist may be lawfully required to explain the process by which matter exercises the faculty of thinking. When once we quit the basis of sensation, all is in the wind. To talk of *immaterial* existences, is to talk of *nothings.* To say that the human soul, angels, God, are immaterial, is to say they are *nothings,* or that there is no God, no angels, no soul. I cannot reason otherwise; but I believe I am supported in my creed of materialism by the Lockes, the Tracys and the Stewarts."[2] Dugald Stewart and Destutt de Tracy he had called, a few months earlier, the two ablest metaphysicians living, "by which I mean investigators of the thinking faculty of man."[3]

The doctrine is naïve enough; but it is a doctrine calculated to satisfy a mind primarily interested in the practical concerns of everyday life. The grouping of Locke, de Tracy, and Stewart together under the general head of materialism is certainly not the judgment of a man more than superficially familiar with their work; and it is improbable that Jefferson was actually influenced to any extent in its formulation by the writers whose names he couples with his creed. His admiration for Locke's political essays might easily lead him to project his agreement with the English thinker over into the more subtle and less familiar field of metaphysics; and his respect for de Tracy and Stewart was inspired more by personal friendship than by any detailed study of their writings. While he heartily endorsed de Tracy's political and economic treatises, the French Ideologist's final volume on moral philosophy did not appear until a year before Jefferson's death;[4] and he nowhere save for passing reference discusses any work of Stewart's, although he had

[2] To Adams, Aug. 15, 1820, *ibid.,* XV, 243-44. Cf. Dugald Stewart, *Elements of the Philosophy of the Human Mind* (3 vols. London, 1792), I. l. iv.

[3] To Adams, Mar. 14, 1820, *Writings,* XV, 240.

[4] Destutt de Tracy, *Éléments d'Idéologie* (4 vols., Paris, 1818; 5 vols., 1824-1825).

received an inscribed copy of *The Philosophy of the Human Mind*.

A closer parallel can be drawn with the Epicurean doctrine, a syllabus of which, based on Gassendi, Jefferson had sent to William Short less than a year before writing the passage quoted. The Epicurean basis of knowledge is sensation, which alone is true, and beyond which we cannot go. We can know with certainty, therefore, only that which the senses tell us; and where they furnish no evidence, we can only accept an hypothesis that does not contradict them. This Jefferson would call common sense.

Now on the basis of sensation, we can know only matter, which must accordingly be the only reality, together with motion, its property. And from these follows the assumption of empty, or immaterial space, in order that matter may have somewhere to move. So far Jefferson is in agreement with Epicurean doctrine, which he follows also in denying immateriality to the soul. But of the ultimate dissolution of the soul with the death of the body, he is not so sure as Lucretius; and when we come to the organization of society, and the social compact, the divergence is sharp. Here Jefferson is more original, and whatever parallel may be drawn is with English rather than with classic thought. Neither does he follow precisely the individualism of the Epicureans, although he was always the staunch champion of the individual man; for Jefferson, like Aristotle, sees man as primarily a social animal, and would probably have agreed that, in the Aristotelian sense, the state is prior to the individual, "since the whole is of necessity prior to the part." To consider man as divorced from society is to consider him as something other than human. The final, and perhaps the most fundamental, difference between Jefferson and the school of Epicurus is that the latter tends to be pessimistic, while the former shares to the full the romantic optimism of the eighteenth century. Lucretius finds nature, although governed by law, a chance and purposeless creation; Jefferson never doubts the ultimate reasonableness of the world order.

Translating metaphysical sensationalism into ethical terms, the basis for conduct appears to be the immediate perceptions of pleasure and pain. The one we seek instinctively, the other we avoid; in the broader sense, the one is happiness, the other misery. Thus the seed of morality is innate, is on the instinctive level; and its cardinal principle is the pursuit of happiness. This principle, however, must not be taken without qualification. The materialistic doctrine which makes matter and motion the only realities is precisely the premise of Hobbes; and if Jefferson had carried it out logically, there would have been no room for natural rights. He did not, however, carry the materialistic reasoning over into his psychology, where the moral nature of man is admitted as a reality quite as fundamental as matter or motion. In the order of nature, Jefferson finds individual happiness inseparable from virtue. Even wisdom cannot bring happiness unless the wise man is also virtuous; and the social test of virtue is utility to man.[5] Call it enlightened self-interest if you will, but the emphasis must be decidedly on the qualifying adjective: an enlightenment which recognizes as prior to individual welfare, the welfare of the group, and which holds individual happiness impossible on any other basis.

Jefferson arrives at this conclusion through a process of elimination. The foundation of morality cannot be truth, for that is elusive; it cannot be the love of God, for an atheist may have morality; it cannot be the desire for the beautiful, for many men are deprived of any aesthetic sense. If self-interest is more convincing, it is because it is interpreted as a social rather than an egoistic maxim. Helvetius had declared the humane man to be "he to whom the sight of misfortune is insupportable, and who to rescue himself from this spectacle, is forced to succor the unfortunate object." With this, Jefferson agrees, but adds that "it is one step short of the ultimate question. These good acts give us pleasure, but how happens it that they give us pleasure? Because nature hath implanted in our breasts a love of

---

[5] To Correa de Serra, Apr. 19, 1814, *Writings*, XIX, 210; to Amos J. Cook, Jan. 21, 1816, *ibid.*, XIV, 405; to Thomas Law, June 13, 1814, *ibid.*, p. 141.

others, a sense of duty to them, a moral instinct, in short, which prompts us irresistibly to feel and succor their distresses. . . . The Creator would indeed have been a bungling artist, had he intended man for a social animal, without planting in him social dispositions. It is true they are not planted in every man, because there is no rule without exceptions; but it is false reasoning which converts exceptions into the general rule."[6]

Jefferson was not a philosopher in any rigorous sense; he was rather a political theorist, seeking a principle of life which would justify a democratic state. And he saw no inconsistency in combining with the hedonistic belief in the pursuit of happiness the intuitionist dogma of an innate moral sense. The manner in which this intuitive knowledge of right and wrong makes itself manifest in man is more fully described in another passage: "This sense is as much a part of his nature as the sense of hearing, seeing, feeling. It is the true foundation of morality. . . . It is given to all human beings in a stronger or weaker degree, as force of members is given them in a greater or less degree. It may be strengthened by exercise, as may any particular limb of the body. This sense is submitted, indeed, in some degree, to the guidance of reason; but it is a small stock which is required for this: even a less one than what we call common sense. State a moral case to a ploughman and a professor. The former will decide it as well, and often better than the latter, because he has not been led astray by artificial rules."[7] And again, he speaks of the moral sense as being so much a part of our constitution that "no errors of reasoning or of speculation might lead us astray in practice." The parallel with the Scottish Common Sense philosophy is too striking to be overlooked. Reid had declared, in language which Jefferson has virtually paraphrased, that the "learned and the unlearned, the philosopher and the day laborer, are upon a level, and will pass the same judgment, when they are not misled by some bias, or taught to renounce their understanding from some mistaken

[6] To Law, June 13, 1814, *ibid.*, pp. 138 ff.
[7] To Peter Carr, Aug. 10, 1787, *ibid.*, VI, 257-58; cf. to Law, June 13, 1814, *ibid.*, XIV, 139.

religious principle";[8] and it is impossible not to believe that Jefferson was greatly influenced, if not by Reid himself, at least by members of the school. This conclusion is considerably strengthened by the fact that the passage restating Reid's argument was written from Paris during the period of his intimacy with Dugald Stewart.

Now if we have a moral sense to enable us to distinguish right from wrong, the virtuous from the vicious, it may legitimately be asked why right and wrong are not always so marked as to be distinguishable; for we see in fact that time and place often reverse moral judgments, and the same act deemed virtuous in one country may be vicious in another. Jefferson answers that "nature has constituted *utility* to man, the standard and test of virtue. Men living in different countries, under different circumstances, differert habits and regimens, may have different utilities; the same act, therefore, may be useful, and consequently virtuous in one country, which is injurious and vicious in another differently circumstanced."[9] The hedonistic and intuitional principles are thus reconciled; for the greatest happiness of the individual is to be achieved only by following as sincerely as he may the dictates of his own conscience, "as the only sure clue, which will eternally guide a man clear of all doubts and inconsistencies." The only appeal is the appeal to reason. "Your own reason," writes Jefferson to his nephew, "is the only oracle given you by heaven, and you are answerable, not for the rightness, but uprightness of the decision."[10]

II

If the basis of right conduct is innate, so also is the key to social organization. For on the assumption that man is born for society, he must also have been born with such innate equipment as will enable him to live peaceably with his fellows. The moral sense is accordingly understood by Jefferson to compre-

---

[8] *The Works of Thomas Reid* (2 vols. Edinburgh, 1863), I, 438.
[9] To Law, June 13, 1814, *Writings*, XIV, 143; cf. to Adams, Oct. 14, 1816, *ibid.*, XV, 76-77.
[10] To Peter Carr, Aug. 16, 1787, *ibid.*, VI, 261.

hend a sense of justice. "Assuming the fact, that the earth has been created in time, and consequently the dogma of final causes, we yield, of course, to this short syllogism. Man was created for social intercourse; but social intercourse cannot be maintained without a sense of justice; then man must have been created with a sense of justice."[11] The dictum of Hobbes, who follows Epicurus, that justice is based on convention only, Jefferson regards as "humiliation to human nature."

So man is pictured as a gregarious animal, endowed by nature with a moral sense which enables him to distinguish right from wrong, and with a sense of justice to keep him from encroaching on his fellows. His ethical end is happiness, which can be achieved only in society; and the end of society itself is to promote the individual happiness of its members. But society cannot be effectively organized until the sphere of the individual has been defined. For this purpose, Jefferson adopts the doctrine of natural rights, laid down originally by the Stoics, and reaffirmed in various forms throughout the seventeenth and eighteenth centuries. His position is nowhere more explicitly stated than in the second paragraph of the *Declaration of Independence:* "We hold these truths to be self-evident, that all men are created equal, that they are endowed by their Creator with certain unalienable Rights, that among these are Life, Liberty, and the Pursuit of Happiness. That to secure these Rights, governments are instituted among Men, deriving their just powers from the consent of the governed. That whenever any form of Government becomes destructive of these ends, it is the Right of the People to alter or abolish it, and to institute a new Government, laying its foundations on such principles, and organizing its powers in such form, as to them shall seem most likely to effect their Safety and Happiness."

Both Hobbes and Locke had held that men in a presocial state were free and equal, and the Roman law had recognized that the freedom of the individual was limited only by the

---

[11] To Gilmer, June 7, 1816, *ibid.*, XV, 25; cf. to Adams, Oct. 14, 1816, *ibid.*, pp. 76-77.

rights of others; but the happiness principle is less easy to trace. Since there is no reference to Epicurus in either of the *Commonplace Books,* and no mention of him in the letters until the period of Jefferson's old age, it is probable that he was not well acquainted with the Epicurean doctrine at the time the *Declaration* was written. It was a common assumption of Greek political thought generally that happiness was a desirable end; the principle appears in Locke, and is likewise to be found in Hutcheson and Priestley, although the latter two were hardly well enough known to Jefferson at this date to have influenced him. The greatest happiness of the greatest number is Beccaria's phrase, plagiarized by Bentham;[12] and the pursuit of happiness might well be the turn given it by one with as fine a feeling for language as had Jefferson. The notion of happiness as the end of political organization is also included in Burlamaqui's definition of the state,[13] and it is taken for granted by Bolingbroke.[14] Since Jefferson assumes the principle without question or reference, it is probable that he had met with it in most, or all, of these possible sources. The notion was generally accepted by Americans of the revolutionary period, and there is no record of any question raised in regard to it in the convention which voted the *Declaration.* It appears also in Wilson's *Considerations,* and in the Virginia *Declaration of Rights,* which preceded the national declaration by a month.

The happiness principle is undoubtedly the most significant feature of Jefferson's theory of rights, for it raises government above the mere negative function of securing the individual against the encroachments of others. By recognizing a right to the pursuit of happiness, the state is committed to aid its citizens in the constructive task of obtaining their desires, whatever they

---

[12] Beccaria, *Essay on Crimes and Punishments* (English translation, Dublin, 1767), Introduction. See T. E. Holland, "Jeremy Bentham," in *Encyclopedia Britannica* (14th ed., 1929), III, 416-18; Bernard Bosanquet, *Philosophical Theory of the State* (London and New York, 1899), p. 56. Cf. *Commonplace Book,* arts. 806-32.

[13] *Principles of Natural and Politic Law* (English translation by Nugent, 2 vols. London, 1763), II, part I, chap. 3, ix; see also chap. 5, ii, and I, part I, chap. 5, especially iv-ix.

[14] *E.g.,* see *Political Tracts* (London, 1748), pp. 284 ff.

may be. It should also be noted that this principle is universal, and therein is distinct from the hedonistic maxim of Bentham. The state is to secure, not merely the greatest happiness of the greatest number, but so far as possible the greatest happiness of all its citizens, whatever their condition. It may well mean, therefore, that many will be restrained from achieving the maximum of happiness, that others less fortunate may obtain more than the minimum. No one will get all he wants, perhaps, but so far as the power of the state can go, everyone will get something.

In a sense all the natural rights are subsumed by Jefferson under this one principle, because the right to pursue happiness presupposes the guarantee of life and liberty. But it is not to be assumed that the rights named in the *Declaration* exhaust the list, except in so far as the last named is inclusive. These form the starting point of Jefferson's political creed because they are the rights it was necessary to assert in order to establish the argument for separation from England; but he announces others as occasion arises, such as the right to settle unoccupied territory, the right of expatriation, and the right to a free use of the ocean. In general, the appeal to natural rights is identical with the appeal of the Scottish philosophers to the common sense and reason of mankind.

How far the rights affirmed by Jefferson and the other American colonists, determined to free themselves from British rule, are derived from the English common law is a matter of conjecture. Certainly those who wrote and spoke most eloquently in their favor were lawyers, well versed in the common law system, although Jefferson, writing years after the event to Judge Tyler, derides the notion that Americans brought with them from England the common-law rights. "This narrow notion was a favorite in the first moment of rallying to our rights against Great Britain. But it was that of men who felt their rights before they had thought of their explanation. The truth is, that we brought with us the *rights of men;* of expatriated men."[15] It remained for later scholarship to suggest that the common-law rights of Englishmen became the natural rights of man.[16] And the fact remains that the rights to life, liberty, property, were precisely the rights enjoyed by Englishmen under the common law.

III

Inalienable natural rights, however, are not enough on which to found a stable society. If Jefferson's insistence on a bill of rights as a necessary part of the constitution implies the possession of certain fundamental rights which the state has no power to transgress, the necessity for entering into a compact at all implies rights of a different nature, contractually based, and carrying with them correlative duties. The distinction might be called one between individual and social rights, or as Jefferson puts it, between natural and civil rights. Man can exercise no rights in opposition to his social duties,[17] and he can retain only those rights which he has power to exercise fully. This notion is embodied in a highly interesting document discovered by Professor Chinard among the Jefferson papers in the Library of Congress, which comprises Jefferson's reflections on his return from the debates on the Articles of Confederation:

"Suppose 20 persons, strangers to each other, to meet in a country not before inhabited. Each would be a sovereign in his own natural right. His will would be his Law,—but his power, in many cases, inadequate to his right, and the consequence would be that each might be exposed, not only to each other but to the other nineteen.

"It would then occur to them that their condition would be much improved, if a way could be devised to exchange that quantity of danger into so much protection, so that each individual should possess the strength of the whole number. As all their rights, in the first case are natural rights, and the exercise of those rights supported only by their own natural individual

---

[15] To Judge Tyler, June 17, 1812, *Writings*, XIII, 165.
[16] Roscoe Pound, *The Spirit of the Common Law* (Boston, 1921), p. 90.
[17] Replies, etc., Jan. 1, 1802, *Writings*, XVI, 282.

power, they would begin by distinguishing between those rights they could individually exercise fully and perfectly and those they could not.

"Of the first kind are the rights of thinking, speaking, forming and giving opinions, and perhaps all those which can be fully exercised by the individual without the aid of exterior assistance—or in other words, rights of personal competency— Of the second kind are those of personal protection of acquiring and possessing property, in the exercise of which the individual natural power is less than the natural right.

"Having drawn this line they agree to retain individually the first Class of Rights or those of personal Competency; and to detach from their personal possession the second Class, or those of defective power and to accept in lieu thereof a right to the whole power produced by the condensation of all the parts. These I conceive to be civil rights or rights of Compact, and are distinguishable from Natural rights, because in the one we act wholly in our own person, and in the other we agree not to do so, but act under the guarantee of society.

"It therefore follows that the more of those imperfect rights, or rights of imperfect power we give up and thus exchange the more security we possess, and as the word liberty is often mistakenly put for security Mr. Wilson has confused his Argument by confounding his terms.

"But it does not follow that the more natural rights of *every kind* we resign the more security we possess,—because if we resign those of the first class we may suffer by the exchange, for where the right and the power are equal with each other in the individual naturally they ought to rest there."[18]

Only one class of rights is ever surrendered on entering into society—those rights which would be useless without power to back them up. The natural rights in the strict sense are never so surrendered. In this division, however, Jefferson cannot be given credit for any great amount of originality. Shorn of its illustrative material and reduced to abstractions, the distinction

[18] Cf. *Thomas Jefferson*, pp. 80-81.

is strikingly close to that made by Wolff between natural or innate, and acquired or contractual rights, and it was most probably from this source that Jefferson derived it. Wolff's *Droit de la Nature* in a Latin and French edition of 1772 is one of the volumes in Jefferson's collection.[19] Blackstone was also influenced by Wolff in his theory of absolute rights; and a similar distinction is made by Burlamaqui.[20]

Robinson Crusoe on his island must have enjoyed to the full his rights to liberty and property, although he was, Jefferson would have insisted, the most miserable of men. But when the number of castaways is increased to twenty, the problem becomes one of quite a different nature. Each of the twenty may think as he pleases, and may speak his mind; but no one of them could hold property without first bargaining with the others that it should be respected. It follows that property is not, as Locke had held, a natural right, but is a right of compact. The word "property" does not occur in the preamble to the *Declaration of Independence;* and when Lafayette submitted to Jefferson his *Déclaration des droits de l'homme,* the latter put in brackets the words *droit à la propriété.*[21] This view of property is an old one, and in Jefferson's case probably goes back to Grotius, who had argued that agreement is the original source of title.[22] The theory of property will be more fully discussed in a later chapter.

The society, when it has been brought under some form of organization, possesses as a unit rights similar to those previously claimed by the individuals composing it. First among these is the right to self-government. "Every man, and every body of men on earth, possesses the right of self-government. They receive it with their being from the hand of nature. Individuals exercise it by their single will; collections of men by that of their majority; for the law of the *majority* is the natural law

[19] Cf. Christian Wolff, *Institutions du Droit de la Nature et des Gens* (6 vols. Leide, 1772), I, chap. 1.
[20] Burlamaqui, *op. cit.,* especially II, i, 3.
[21] Chinard, *Thomas Jefferson,* p. 84.
[22] *De Jure Belli ac Pacis Libri Tres* (3 vols. Cambridge, 1853), II, 2, 2, 5.

of every society of men."[23] The society can, moreover, "fix the fundamental principles of its association," and "say to all individuals, that, if they contemplate pursuits beyond the limits of these principles, and involving dangers which the society chooses to avoid, they must go somewhere else for their exercise."[24] When a government is formed, these fundamental principles will be embodied in the constitution.

What distinction, if any, Jefferson made between the social compact whereby, as we have seen, men yield certain rights of imperfect power in return for greater security, and the governmental compact, or constitution of the state, is not clear. From what has already been said, it would seem safe to assume a distinction. But he writes in the *Notes on Virginia* that "necessities which dissolve a government, do not convey its authority to an oligarchy or a monarchy. They throw back, into the hands of the people, the powers they had delegated, and leave them as individuals to shift for themselves."[25] If the condition of these individuals shifting for themselves is comparable to that of the twenty men in an uninhabited country of a previous illustration, then the social compact and the governmental compact would be identical. It is, however, difficult to accept such a conclusion. Jefferson had repeatedly held that a people may "govern itself internally under what forms it pleases, and . . . change these forms at its own will,"[26] which certainly implies that the form of the government is distinct from the organization of the society itself; and that the form may be changed without dissolving the society, although some of its essential machinery may, for a time, be destroyed.

Whenever grave emergency sweeps away a government, some form of temporary organization remains in effect until a new order can be instituted. There is in fact no example within the scope of history of men without some form of government,

[23] Official Papers, *Writings*, III, 60; cf. to Adams, Jan. 21, 1812, *ibid.*, XIII, 123.
[24] To Crawford, June 20, 1816, *ibid.*, XV, 28.
[25] *Ibid.*, II, 175.
[26] To Pinckney, Dec. 30, 1792, *ibid.*, IX, 7-8; cf. to Morris, Mar. 12, 1793, *ibid.*, pp. 36-37; Anas, *ibid.*, I, 330.

and such a situation is for Jefferson inconceivable. While he pictures the presocial state as lacking in many points desirable for human welfare, most important of which is security, he nowhere gives any hint that he regards the state of nature as presenting anything like the anarchy of Hobbes's conception, nor yet the idyllic virtues of Rousseau's. In attempting to reconstruct the life of uncivilized man, Jefferson is influenced, not by any imaginative theorist, but by his own observations of the American Indians, from which he draws a fairly consistent picture of the evolution of society.

Locke speaks of a golden age, which was the natural state of primitive man, but Jefferson's golden age is in the future. For him, the state of nature is the state of the American Indian; and it is from his empirical knowledge of Indian societies that he deduces his conclusion in regard to the earliest form of the state. "There is an error into which most of the speculators on government have fallen, and which the well known state of society of our Indians ought, before now, to have corrected. In their hypothesis of the origin of government, they suppose it to have commenced in the patriarchal or monarchical form. Our Indians are evidently in that state of nature which has passed the association of a single family; and not yet submitted to the authority of positive laws, or of any acknowledged magistrate. Every man, with them, is perfectly free to follow his own inclinations. But if, in doing this, he violates the rights of another, if the case be slight, he is punished by the disesteem of his society, or, as we say, by public opinion; if serious, he is tomahawked as a dangerous enemy. Their leaders conduct them by the influence of their character only; and they follow, or not, as they please, him of whose character for wisdom or war they have the highest opinion. Hence the origin of the parties among them adhering to different leaders, and governed by their advice, not by their command. The Cherokees, the only tribe I know to be contemplating the establishment of regular laws, magistrates, and government, propose a government of representatives, elected from every town. But of all things, they think least of subjecting themselves to the will of one man. This, the only instance of actual fact within our knowledge, will be then a beginning by republican, and not by patriarchal or monarchical government, as speculative writers have generally conjectured."[27]

While he thinks the position of the Indians ought to be improved, Jefferson regards them with sympathy and understanding. It is rather for civilized man, who fails to follow rational precepts, that he reserves his scorn; and it is of civilized man he is thinking when he writes to Madison: "In truth I do not recollect in all the animal kingdom a single species but man which is eternally and systematically engaged in the destruction of its own species. What is called civilization seems to have no other effect on him than to teach him to pursue the principle of *bellum omnium in omnia* on a larger scale, and in place of the little contests of tribe against tribe, to engage all the quarters of the earth in the same work of destruction. When we add to this that as to the other species of animals, the lions and tigers are mere lambs compared with man as a destroyer, we must conclude that it is in man alone that nature has been able to find a sufficient barrier against the too great multiplication of other animals and of man himself, an equilibriating power against the fecundity of generation. My situation points my views chiefly to his wars in the physical world: yours perhaps exhibit him as equally warring in the moral one. We both, I believe, join in wishing to see him softened."[28]

It is rare indeed that Jefferson so far loses his calm faith in man as to give way to such an outburst as this; and even here he does not rise to the passionate crescendo of Rousseau. The mood is no doubt a passing one, prompted, perhaps, by the bitterness of his first campaign for the presidency. A later passage is colder, and more explanatory: The "*bellum omnium in omnia*, which some philosophers observing to be so general in the world, have mistaken for the natural, instead of the abusive

[27] To Gilmer, June 7, 1816, *ibid.*, XV, 25-26.
[28] To Madison, Jan. 1, 1797, *ibid.*, IX, 359-60.

state of man," only begins when man has been reduced by bad government—public debt and heavy taxation—to the most abject level of misery.[29] This is probably the explanation of the reference in his first inaugural address to the "agonizing spasms of infuriated man, seeking through blood and slaughter his long-lost liberty";[30] it is not the liberty of a presocial state that has been lost, but the rational liberty of a legal order, destroyed by bad government.

From a comparison of Indian tribes Jefferson draws a condensed picture of countless centuries of social progress. "Let a philosophic observer commence a journey from the savages of the Rocky Mountains, eastwardly towards our seacoast. These he would observe in the earliest stage of association living under no law but that of nature, subsisting and covering themselves with the flesh and skins of wild beasts. He would next find those on our frontiers in the pastoral state, raising domestic animals to supply the defects of hunting. Then succeed to our own semibarbarous citizens, the pioneers of the advance of civilization, and so in his progress he would meet the gradual shades of improving man until he would reach his, as yet, most improved state in our seaport towns. This, in fact, is equivalent to a survey, in time, of the progress of man from the infancy of creation to the present day."[31]

The precise point in this ascending scale of civilization at which the social compact arises is not clear. Nor need it be so; for there is no hint in Jefferson that he regards the compact as anything more than a legal fiction, ultimately to be given concrete embodiment in the constitution of the state. He conceives it with the rigor of a lawyer, and adds a bill of rights as a safeguarding clause. Like Hobbes, he is not seeking an historical origin, but a rational justification of government. The compact is implicit in his description of the basis of social organization, in which he declares that society is "one of the natural wants with which man has been created; that he has been endowed

---

[29] To Kercheval, July 12, 1816, *ibid.*, XV, 40.
[30] *Ibid.*, III, 319.
[31] To William Ludlow, Sept. 16, 1824, *ibid.*, XVI, 74-75.

with faculties and qualities to effect its satisfaction by concurrence of others having the same want; that when, by the exercise
of these faculties, he has procured a state of society, it is one of
his acquisitions which he has a right to control, jointly, indeed
with all those who have concurred in the procurement, whom
he cannot exclude from its use or direction more than they
him."[32] It is a *pactum foederis* rather than the *pactum subjec-
tionis* of Hobbes.

IV

Since the form of the government is rightfully for the
people to select, there will necessarily be various types of organization in actual use. In his classification of these, Jefferson
combines his historical knowledge, his observations of Indian
tribes, a keen analysis of existing European monarchies, and an
idealized vision of the republic he helped so materially to create.
Other political writers had classified societies according to various categories, from the days of Plato and Aristotle down to
Jefferson's own times, and he was undoubtedly familiar with
many of the earlier lists; but the vast accumulation of empirical
data at his command leads him to a startlingly different result.
He cuts clear across the old line of division into democracy and
aristocracy with a new principle of classification. "Societies exist
under three forms, sufficiently distinguishable. 1. Without
government, as among our Indians. 2. Under governments,
wherein the will of everyone has a just influence; as is the case
in England, in a slight degree, and in our States, in a great one.
3. Under governments of force; as is the case in all other
monarchies, and in most of the other republics. To have an
idea of the curse of existence under these last, they must be
seen. It is a government of wolves over sheep. It is a problem,
not clear in my mind, that the first condition is not the best.
But I believe it to be inconsistent with any great degree of
population. The second state has a great deal of good in it.
The mass of mankind under that enjoys a precious degree of
liberty and happiness. It has its evils, too; the principal of

[32] To Dupont de Nemours, Apr. 24, 1816, *ibid.*, XIV, 487.

which is the turbulence to which it is subject. But weigh this against the oppressions of monarchy, and it becomes nothing. *Malo periculosam libertatem quam quietam servitutem.* Even this evil is productive of good. It prevents the degeneracy of government, and nourishes a general attention to the public affairs."[33] This classification makes the preservation of order secondary to the promotion of individual self-expression and self-realization.

The only legitimate end of government is "to secure the greatest degree of happiness possible to the general mass of those associated under it."[34] Government, then, exists for men, and to "inform the minds of the people, and to follow their will, is the chief duty of those placed at their head."[35] The state is a human institution, built to serve an ethical end; but the end is broader than the institution. The "freedom and happiness of man" are not only the objects of political organization; they are the ends of all science, of all human endeavor.[36]

Since men live under widely differing conditions, and have interests as varied as their characters, it follows that the same institutions will not always serve them in the same way. Hence, each association of men has, as we have seen, the right to fix for itself the fundamental tenets of its organization; and the "excellence of every government is its adaptation to the state of those to be governed by it."[37] The principle that the best government is that best suited to the temper and inclination of the people concerned is hardly new: it is in Montesquieu, and it had been affirmed in America at a still earlier date by John Wise, in his *Vindication*.[38] It is also in Aristotle, but in holding that government should conform to the habits of the people, Jefferson does not mean precisely what Aristotle means when he names the types of people which will produce different types of state. For Jefferson, there is an ideal form of government—the

[33] To Madison, Jan. 30, 1787, *ibid.*, VI, 65.
[34] To F. A. Van der Kemp, Mar. 22, 1812, *ibid.*, XIII, 135.
[35] To Dumas, Oct. 14, 1787, *ibid.*, VI, 342.
[36] To Kosciusko, Feb. 26, 1810, *ibid.*, XII, 369-70.
[37] To Dupont de Nemours, Apr. 24, 1816, *ibid.*, XIV, 487.
[38] See Riley, *American Philosophy*, p. 30.

republican—which is ideally best. And however its principles may be modified to meet the needs of different peoples under different circumstances, they are not to be altered in essentials. The representative principle is, he believes, sufficiently elastic to respond to whatever demands may be made upon it. Life, liberty and the pursuit of happiness are universal and inalienable rights; it is only the means of procuring them which vary, and these only in detail.

Within every society, the members will divide roughly into two groups, because men "by their constitutions are naturally divided into two parties: 1. Those who fear and distrust the people, and wish to draw all powers from them into the hands of the higher classes. 2. Those who identify themselves with the people, have confidence in them, cherish and consider them as the most honest and safe, although not the most wise depository of the public interests."[39] It is a significant principle that public interests are better preserved by honesty than by wisdom, and one which must be admitted by any consistent advocate of democracy. Thirty years earlier, Jefferson had voiced his distrust of placing power in the hands of the higher classes. "I do not believe with the Rochefoucaults and Montaignes, that fourteen out of fifteen men are rogues: I believe a great abatement from that proportion may be made in favor of general honesty. But I have always found that rogues would be uppermost, and I do not know that the proportion is too strong for the higher orders, and for those who, rising above the swinish multitude, always contrive to nestle themselves into the places of power and profit."[40] The honesty and inertia of the lower classes are necessary to counterbalance the ambition and unscrupulousness of the more favorably situated.

Jefferson views the conflict between aristocrat and democrat with larger vision four years after his own retirement from the public stage, when he writes to Adams that men "have differed in opinion, and been divided into parties by these opinions, from

[39] To Henry Lee, Aug. 10, 1824, *Writings*, XVI, 73-74; cf. to Short, Jan. 8, 1825, *ibid.*, p. 96.
[40] To Mann Page, Aug. 30, 1795, *ibid.*, IX, 306-7.

the first origin of societies, and in all governments where they have been permitted freely to think and to speak. The same political parties which now agitate the United States, have existed through all time. Whether the power of the people or that of the *aristoi* should prevail, were questions which kept the states of Greece and Rome in eternal convulsions, as they now schismatize every people whose minds and mouths are not shut up by the gag of a despot. And in fact, the terms of whig and tory belong to natural as well as to civil history. They denote the temper and constitution of mind of different individuals."[41] He takes care, however, to qualify his position by defining his terms. He distinguishes sharply between a pseudo-aristocracy of wealth and family, and a natural aristocracy of talents and virtue. The former he seeks to annihilate, and refers to his early Virginia laws abolishing entails and primogeniture, as being for this purpose.[42] Talents and virtue, on the other hand, are to be encouraged by all legitimate means, principal among which is education. It is to the talented and the virtuous that the government is to be committed, a doctrine suggesting the Greek ideal of the wise man. The criticism of Adams, that talents and virtue will, in the end, breed wealth and family, he seems to have ignored.

Jefferson never wearies of reiterating that the natural equality of man is the basis of free government. It involves the denial of every preëminence but that annexed to legal office, and most specifically of all, preëminence by birth. He is therefore outspoken against anything resembling hereditary aristocracy or hereditary office. This is the basis of his objection to the Cincinnati, an organization of officers of the revolutionary army which flourished for a brief time after the war; adding the further point that such an order would tend to keep up a distinction between the civil and the military "which it is for the happiness of both to obliterate."[43]

[41] To Adams, June 27, 1813, *ibid.*, XIII, 279-80.
[42] To Adams, Oct. 28, 1813, *ibid.*, pp. 394 ff., especially p. 399.
[43] To Washington, Apr. 16, 1784, *ibid.*, IV, 215 ff.; Nov. 14, 1786, *ibid.*, VI, 3-4; cf. Observations on Article États Unis, etc., *ibid.*, XVII, 81 ff.

V

Democracy is a faith rather than a philosophy. Its tremendous appeal to the great mass of mankind is akin to a religious appeal; and however inadequate its logic, however cumbersome its processes, it is still able to inspire a passionate loyalty in the most humble of men, if he can but be made to believe that his will is equal in weight to that of his more fortunate neighbor. The government rests upon the will of the whole society, where each individual counts as one; and that government is best which most adequately and faithfully expresses that will. For Jefferson, therefore, the ideal form is a republic, which he defines as a "government by its citizens in mass, acting directly and personally, according to rules established by the majority; and . . . every other government is more or less republican, in proportion as it has in its composition more or less of this ingredient of the direct action of the citizens. Such a government is evidently restrained to very narrow limits of space and population. I doubt if it would be practicable beyond the extent of a New England township. The first shade from this pure element, which, like that of pure vital air, cannot sustain life of itself, would be where the powers of the government, being divided, should be exercised each by representatives chosen either *pro hac vice,* or for such short terms as should render secure the duty of expressing the will of their constituents. This I should consider the nearest approach to a pure republic, which is practicable on a large scale of country or population."[44]

The pure republic, or ideal form, differs from the Greek democracy in that its citizens apparently are to choose their magistrates by vote, rather than by lot as was the Athenian custom. In general, Jefferson limits the use of the term republic to the familiar representative type. "A government is republican in proportion as every member composing it has his equal voice in the direction of its concerns, (not indeed in person, which would be impracticable beyond the limits of a city, or

[44] To John Taylor, May 28, 1816, *ibid.,* XV, 19.

small township), but by representatives chosen by himself, and responsible to him at short periods."[45]

A government based on such principles as these presupposes a supreme faith in the honesty and good sense of the great mass of mankind—an assumption which Jefferson fully realizes and freely accepts. "I cannot," he says, "act as if all men were unfaithful because some are so; nor believe all will betray me, because some do. I had rather be the victim of occasional infidelities, than relinquish my general confidence in the honesty of man."[46] And to Dupont de Nemours he writes: "we both consider the people as our children, and love them with parental affection. But you love them as infants whom you are afraid to trust without nurses; and I as adults whom I freely leave to self-government."[47] It is only a logical consequence for Jefferson to believe "that the mass of the citizens is the safest depository of their own rights and especially, that the evils flowing from the duperies of the people, are less injurious than those from the egoism of their agents."[48]

As we have seen, every society will be divided in opinion, and since there is an equality between the members, an acquiescence in the will of the majority is a necessary corollary. "The first principle of republicanism is that the *lex majoris partis* is the fundamental law of every society of individuals of equal rights; to consider the will of the society enounced by the majority of a single vote, as sacred as if unanimous, is the first of all lessons in importance, yet the last which is thoroughly learnt. This law once disregarded, no other remains but that of force, which ends necessarily in military despotism."[49] Where individuals are equal, the *lex majoris partis* has become a law of the numerical majority, rather than the law of the better part, which was its significance in mediaeval theory. It is strong medicine; and

[45] To Kercheval, July 12, 1816, *ibid.*, p. 33.
[46] To Thomas Leiper, Jan. 1, 1814, *ibid.*, XIV, 43.
[47] To Dupont de Nemours, Apr. 24, 1816, *ibid.*, pp. 489-90.
[48] To Taylor, May 28, 1816, *ibid.*, XV, 23.
[49] To Baron Alexander von Humboldt, June 13, 1817, *ibid.*, p. 127; cf. First Inaugural Address, *ibid.*, III, 321-22.

the republic above all other governments must make a place, and an honored place, for the dissenter. The majority may be wrong. So Jefferson adds the qualification "that though the will of the majority is in all cases to prevail, that will, to be rightful, must be reasonable; that the minority possess their equal rights, which equal laws must protect, and to violate which would be oppression."[50]

The American war for independence had demonstrated to Jefferson's entire satisfaction the "happy truth that man is capable of self-government, and only rendered otherwise by the moral degredation designedly superinduced on him by the wicked acts of his tyrants." Every man cannot, of course, govern himself in all things, but he ought to exercise in person every function his qualifications will permit him to exercise, "consistently with the order and security of society."[51] To hold public office, from the least to the greatest, is both a privilege and a duty. Like the Athenians of old, and like Cicero in the Roman world, Jefferson regards the good magistrate as one who has been a good citizen. Every man should look forward to a possible period of public service, and every officeholder should bear it always in mind that in a short time he will once more be in private life. Public office is not for personal aggrandizement or personal glorification. "An honest man can feel no pleasure in the exercise of power over his fellow citizens." And Jefferson has superb faith that men will always be found to meet whatever crisis may arise.[52]

For all his idealistic belief in the capacity and honesty of men, however, Jefferson is well aware of the innumerable petty dissensions which render precarious the course of popular assemblies. For example, during his term as vice-president the dominance of policies by the New England states had become so galling to the South that the suggestion was made to form a

---

[50] First Inaugural Address, *ibid.*, p. 318.

[51] To Dr. Walter Jones, Jan. 2, 1814, *ibid.*, XIV, 46 ff.; cf. to Barre de Marbois, June 14, 1817, *ibid.*, XV, 130.

[52] To Duane, Apr. 4, 1813, *ibid.*, XIII, 231; cf. to Melish, Jan. 13, 1813, *ibid.*, p. 211.

separate union of North Carolina and Virginia. Jefferson refused to countenance the idea, slyly remarking that "an association of men who will not quarrel with one another is a thing which never yet existed, from the greatest confederacy of nations down to a town meeting or a vestry; seeing that we must have somebody to quarrel with, I had rather keep our New England associates for that purpose, than to see our bickerings transferred to others."[53] Yet after sharing for more than forty years in the burdens of his country's government, during which time he was exposed to the full to all its weaknesses and shortcomings, he is still firmly convinced that a republic, typified by the United States, is the best form of political order. "A government regulating itself by what is wise and just for the many, uninfluenced by the local and selfish views of the few who direct their affairs, has not been seen, perhaps, on earth. Or if it existed, for a moment, at the birth of ours, it would not be easy to fix the term of its continuance. Still, I believe it does exist here in a greater degree than anywhere else."[54]

No sane man could follow, even for a few months, the actual workings of any government the world has yet seen, and have any lingering doubts as to its fallibility. Governments are human institutions, existing at the instigation of men, and supposedly for the benefit of men. They will have their share of friction and of cross-purposes; and they will fail, now and again, to serve their avowed end. When they stray, they must be brought back to their rightful path. Jefferson's own state was conceived in revolution and carried through with arms. He cannot deny to the people a right of protest, even of violent protest, if they sincerely think it warranted. "I hold it," he writes, after news of Shay's rebellion had reached him in Paris, "that a little rebellion, now and then, is a good thing, and as necessary in the political world as storms in the physical."[55] And in another passage: "If the happiness of the mass of the

[53] To Taylor, June 1, 1798, *ibid.*, X, 46.
[54] To Crawford, June 20, 1816, *ibid.*, XV, 31.
[55] To Madison, Jan. 30, 1787, *ibid.*, VI, 65; cf. to Styles, Dec. 24, 1786, *ibid.*, p. 25.

people can be secured at the expense of a little tempest now and then, or even of a little blood, it will be a precious purchase. . . . Let common sense and common honesty have fair play, and they will soon set things to rights."

Without harmony and affection in social intercourse, "liberty and even life itself are but dreary things";[56] yet Jefferson rests his faith in a certainty that common sense and common honesty will make such harmony possible. A spirit of mutual accommodation will go a long way; and he believes much would be gained by reducing the relations between governor and governed, between diplomat and diplomat, to the footing of "friendly intercourse between individuals."[57] Where men are ruled by native good sense and integrity, the rôle of political authority is reduced to a minimum. In the first inaugural address, Jefferson describes the wise and frugal government as one which "shall restrain men from injuring one another, which shall leave them otherwise free to regulate their own pursuits of industry and improvement, and shall not take from the mouth of labor the bread it has earned."[58]

[56] First Inaugural Address, *ibid.*, III, 318.
[57] To Monroe, June 17, 1785, *ibid.*, V, 11-12.
[58] *Ibid.*, III, 320-21.

CHAPTER V

THE BURDEN OF AUTHORITY

I

THE CONSTITUTION of the state determines its form, the distribution of its powers, the mechanics of its operation. It is an accommodation of the various interests represented in the state,[1] and is effective to the extent that these interests are harmonized with one another, and brought under a common rule of law. It is the legal instrument by which the state is made actual. But the framers of the constitution must steer a delicate course between Scylla and Charybdis. If the document lacks energy, the government will be inefficient, and terminate in anarchy; if too energetic, it will be oppressive.[2] The historical cycle of governments is one of oppression, rebellion, reformation in continuous recurrence; and the problem is to provide for progressive reformation, without waiting for oppression to force rebellion.[3] Jefferson expresses the belief that the world has much to learn from the American example of "changing a constitution, by assembling the wise men of the State, instead of assembling armies."[4]

His definition of the constitution, and in fact his whole discussion of that document is colored by the economic interpretation of history. But it is an attitude which does not enter his writings to any noticeable degree until after he had read the *Federalist,* and it seems safe to assume that he borrowed it from his young friend, James Madison. In particular, his reference to the constitution as an "accomodation of interests" recalls

---

[1] To Col. Humphreys, Mar. 28, 1789, *Writings*, VII, 322.
[2] To Madison, Dec. 20, 1787, *ibid.*, VI, 391; cf. to George Mason, June 13, 1790, *ibid.*, VIII, 35.
[3] To Kercheval, July 12, 1816, *ibid.*, XV, 43.
[4] To Humphreys, Mar. 28, 1789, *ibid.*, VII, 322.

Madison's number ten of the *Federalist*, a paper which Jefferson could not have seen much before writing the passage summarized above. It is equally safe to assume, however, that he would not have been influenced by Madison's doctrine, if he had not already been inclining in the direction of the economic theory it involved.

Since he had no hand in framing the American constitution, the views here ascribed to Jefferson are drawn mainly from his comments on the work of the convention of 1787, and from his observations on the practical operation of the instrument in the light of his later experience in administering it. Some of his constitutional theories, also, date from the debates on the Articles of Confederation, while others are recorded in the *Notes on Virginia*. Although he came to regard the Constitution of the United States as a model document, many of its provisions were new to him at the time; and he was quite unprepared to accept it at first blush. His initial reaction was one of surprize, not unmixed with disapproval. "How do you like our new constitution?" he writes to Adams. "I confess there are things in it which stagger all my dispositions to subscribe to what such an Assembly has proposed."[5] Gradually, however, he was won over, partly by reflection, partly by the arguments of Madison; and by the date of its actual ratification in 1789, he had fully endorsed it, with the single exception of its omission of a bill of rights. His letters from Paris, and his personal influence after his return, were powerful factors in securing the adoption of the first ten amendments.

Yet this very constitution, "unquestionably the wisest ever yet presented to men,"[6] he regards as far from final. It was born from the womb of rebellion, and carried to fruition by men who had scarce a decade before been under arms. At eighty, Jefferson looks back over the stormy road to free government, reflects upon the outcome of the French and Mexican revolutions, and writes to Adams: "The generation which commences

[5] To Adams, Nov. 13, 1787, *ibid.*, VI, 370.
[6] To Humphreys, Mar. 28, 1789, *ibid.*, VII, 322.

a revolution rarely completes it. Habituated from their infancy to passive submission of body and mind to their kings and priests, they are not qualified when called on to think and provide for themselves; and their inexperience, their ignorance and bigotry make them instruments often, in the hands of the Bonapartes and Iturbides, to defeat their own rights and purposes."[7]

A written constitution Jefferson regards as superior to an implicit one, for "though written constitutions may be violated in moments of passion or delusion, yet they furnish a text to which those who are watchful may again rally and recall the people; and they fix too for the people the principles of their political creed."[8] A written constitution, further, is to be taken at its face value; and where it does not function smoothly, it is to be changed. Interpretation and construction only render it worthless. "Our peculiar security is in the possession of a written Constitution. Let us not make it a blank paper by construction." Where it has been found imperfect, "let us go on then perfecting it, by adding, by way of amendment . . . those powers which time and trial show are still wanting."[9]

These are the cautious observations of the lawyer on a legal document, and of the president in office on the basic law of the land. The younger man had been more impetuous, and more concerned with the question of securing individual liberty, arguing in the *Notes on Virginia* that a constitution, like any other legislative enactment, should be alterable by the legislature. The Virginia constitution at this date was a part of statute law, and could actually be amended by legislative act; but Jefferson probably did not mean to imply that the instrument should be comparable to a common statute. The popular notion, when the colonial charter came to be replaced by the constitution, was that it should be framed by a specially chosen convention, and ratified by the people. It was necessarily superior to the legislature, for by its phrases it called the legislature into being, and

[7] To Adams, Sept. 4, 1823, *ibid.*, XV, 464.
[8] To Priestley, June 19, 1802, *ibid.*, X, 325.
[9] To Wilson C. Nicholas, Sept. 7, 1803, *ibid.*, X, 419.

by its ratification delegated to the government those functions which the people could not conveniently exercise for themselves. A few pages further along, Jefferson voices the familiar conception. When the constitution is found inadequate, the remedy is a convention to amend its defects, "to bind up the several branches of government by certain laws, which, when they transgress, their acts shall become nullities; to render unnecessary an appeal to the people, or in other words a rebellion, on every infraction of their rights, on the peril that their acquiescence shall be construed into an intention to surrender those rights."[10]

The older Jefferson, the cares of public office not altogether unwillingly laid aside, lets his mind range more freely over broader aspects of the constitutional problem. "The idea that institutions established for the use of the nation cannot be touched nor modified, even to make them answer their end, because of rights gratuitously supposed in those employed to manage them in trust for the public, may perhaps be a salutary provision against the abuses of a monarch, but is most absurd against the nation itself."[11] He sees clearly the danger of a static constitution, and offers a constructive suggestion. "Let us provide in our Constitution for its revision at stated periods. What these periods should be, nature herself indicates. By the European tables of mortality, of the adults living at any one moment of time, a majority will be dead in about nineteen years. At the end of that period then, a new majority is come into place; or, in other words, a new generation. Each generation is as independent of the preceding, as that was of all which had gone before. It has then, like them, a right to choose for itself the form of government it believes most promotive of its own happiness; consequently, to accomodate to the circumstances in which it finds itself, that received from its predecessors; and it is for the peace and good of mankind, that a solemn opportunity

---

[10] Notes on Virginia, *ibid.*, II, 165 ff., 178; cf. Dunning, *A History of Political Theories* (3 vols. New York, 1902-1920), III, 98; Channing, *History of the United States*, IV, 157.

[11] To Gov. Plumer, July 21, 1816, *Writings*, XV, 46.

of doing this every nineteen or twenty years, should be provided by the Constitution; so that it may be handed on, with periodical repairs, from generation to generation, to the end of time, if anything human can so long endure."[12]

He has passed his three-score years and ten, and it is his privilege to look back, and point out in mellow phrases the fallibility of man; it is his genius to look forward down the ever widening vista of the years, and plead for laws and institutions that will expand to meet new problems, that will grow with the ceaseless growing of the human mind. "Some men look at constitutions with sanctimonious reverence, and deem them like the ark of the covenant, too sacred to be touched. They ascribe to the men of the preceding age a wisdom more than human, and suppose what they did to be beyond amendment. I knew that age well; I belonged to it, and labored with it. It deserved well of its country. It was very like the present, but without the experience of the present; and forty years of experience in government is worth a century of book-reading; and this they would say themselves, were they to rise from the dead. I am certainly not an advocate for frequent and untried changes in laws and constitutions. I think moderate imperfections had better be born with; because, when once known, we accommodate ourselves to them, and find practical means of correcting their ill effects. But I know also, that laws and institutions must go hand in hand with the progress of the human mind. As that becomes more developed, more enlightened, as new discoveries are made, new truths disclosed, and manners and opinions change with the change of circumstances, institutions must advance also, and keep pace with the times. We might as well require a man to wear still the coat which fitted him when a boy, as civilized society to remain ever under the regimen of their barbarous ancestors."[13]

II

Since government exists only to further the happiness of its citizens, the will of those citizens will be its sanction, and the voice of the majority will be law. The citizenry, taken col-

[12] To Kercheval, July 12, 1816, *ibid.*, p. 42.   [13] *Ibid.*, pp. 40-41.

lectively, Jefferson calls the nation. "I consider the source of authority with us to be the Nation. Their will, declared through its proper organ, is valid, till revoked by their will," again declared through its proper organ.[14] If there exists in Jefferson's state any body whose authority is ultimate and final, in which, in the sense of Hobbes and Blackstone, the sovereignty resides, it is the body of the people themselves; and this authority they cannot alienate. Whatever organization they may set up for its exercise is always responsible to and dissoluble by the people. Thus the element of continuity in the state is the will of the nation, or the people as a whole, expressed through legally constituted channels. The strength of the government, therefore, lies in the willingness of the people to coöperate with it, and "the government which can wield the arm of the people must be the strongest possible."[15]

The popular will, however, is too unwieldy for practical purposes, and in the interest of good government the people must delegate their sovereignty to a small body. This they do by means of the constitution; but there is no thought in Jefferson's mind of vesting this popular sovereignty in any *one* group. It must be distributed among several, for its more jealous preservation, and behind these designated repositories of power looms the shadow of the fundamental law. "The whole body of the nation is the sovereign legislative, judiciary and executive power for itself. The inconvenience of meeting to exercise these powers in person, and their inaptitude to exercise them, induce them to appoint special organs to declare their legislative will, to judge and to execute it. It is the will of the nation which makes the law obligatory; it is their will which creates or annihilates the organ which is to declare and announce it. They may do it by a single person, as an Emperor of Russia (constituting his declarations evidence of their will), or by a few persons, as the aristocracy of Venice, or by a complication of councils, as in our former regal government, or our present republican one. The law being law because it is the will of the

[14] To Washington, Feb. 4, 1792, *ibid.*, VIII, 301.
[15] To Isaac Weaver, Jr., June 7, 1807, *ibid.*, XI, 221.

nation, is not changed by their changing the organ through which they choose to announce their future will; no more than the acts I have done by one attorney lose their obligation by my changing or discontinuing that attorney."[16]

The constitution is the instrument whereby these powers are delegated, and which prescribes their use. But the sovereign people, even though they have delegated the exercise of their sovereignty to others, must retain in their own hands some means of control over their agents, lest their power be usurped. "The natural progress of things is for liberty to yield and government to gain ground."[17] Jefferson takes the fact of the adoption of the federal constitution in America as proof that an informed people can be trusted with their own government: that when things go wrong, they can and will be set right.[18]

Now the best way to set things right is to keep them from going wrong. "The time to guard against corruption and tyranny is before they shall have gotten hold of us. It is better to keep the wolf out of the fold, than to trust to drawing his teeth and claws after he shall have entered."[19] Hence Jefferson believes it unwise to have public functionaries far removed from the control of the society. For "human character . . . requires in general constant and immediate control, to prevent its being biased from right by the seductions of self-love."[20] In another passage, he states the case even more emphatically: "unless the mass retains sufficient control over those intrusted with the powers of their government, these will be perverted to their own oppression, and to the perpetuation of wealth and power in the individuals and their families selected for the trust." Whether the American constitution has hit upon the degree of control necessary, he regards, after more than twenty years of its operation, as being still under experiment.[21]

[16] To Edmund Randolph, Aug. 18, 1799, ibid., X, 126-27.
[17] To Carrington, May 27, 1788, ibid., VII, 37.
[18] To Dr. Price, Jan. 8, 1789, ibid., p. 253.
[19] Notes on Virginia, ibid., II, 165.
[20] To Dupont de Nemours, Apr. 24, 1816, ibid., XIV, 489.
[21] To Van der Kemp, Mar. 22, 1812, ibid., XIII, 136.

But however he may wish to see the constitution of the United States improved, Jefferson never fails to find consolation for its shortcomings by comparing it with those of other nations. England, for example, "presents a singular phenomenon of an honest people whose constitution, from its nature, must render their government forever dishonest."[22] And another typical comment occurs in one of his letters from Europe—this while the states were still floundering under the Articles of Confederation. "I am sensible that there are defects in our federal government, yet they are so much lighter than those of monarchies, that I view them with much indulgence. I rely, too, on the good sense of the people for remedy, whereas the evils of monarchical government are beyond remedy. If any of our countrymen wish for a King, give them Aesop's fable of the frogs who asked a King; if this does not cure them, send them to Europe."[23]

III

The feature of the constitution which Jefferson believed to be its greatest strength is the feature which, in American experience at least, has proved to be the primary source of friction: the system of checks and balances among the several departments of the government. In theory, he follows the principle that the powers of government "should be so divided and balanced among several bodies of magistracy, as that no one could transcend their legal limits, without being effectually checked and restrained by the others."[24] In practice, the powers are so distributed that it is difficult for any one branch to act at all without being effectually thwarted by one of the others. Such is the effect of a divided sovereignty, made only a little less awkward by the rapid growth of the party system under Jefferson's own skillful guidance. As we shall see in a later chapter, he is himself forced to introduce a modification of the balance to allow for quick action in emergencies.

[22] To James Ronaldson, Dec. 13, 1810, *ibid.*, XII, 435.
[23] To Dr. David Ramsay, Aug. 4, 1787, *ibid.*, VI, 226; cf. to Joseph Jones, Aug. 14, 1787, *ibid.*, p. 274.
[24] Notes on Virginia, *ibid.*, II, 163.

Jefferson's real fear was of a government that should arrogate to itself unlimited powers. In the Alien and Sedition laws of 1798, with the arbitrary deportations and despotic imprisonments that followed, he saw an attempt on the part of the Federalist majority to assume such power; and to avoid submission to it, he was willing that the union itself should be dissolved.[25] Better the government should move slowly and indecisively, or not at all, than move quickly and with decision in the wrong direction. The system of checks and balances, by erecting such barriers between the various departments that no one could encroach upon the functions of the others, was designed to prevent this very thing; and a few years later the Supreme Court would certainly have had a word to say in regard to the passage of such doubtful measures.

In this system of checks and balances, arising out of the separation of powers, Jefferson is presumably following Montesquieu, and Locke, from whom the French writer borrowed, although his sources may include still older theorists. The doctrine is in fact simply a development of the mixed constitution of Aristotle, which is expanded in Polybius, the purpose being so to balance the various interests against each other that a constant equilibrium will be maintained. With Jefferson it is of fundamental importance. "The first principle of a good government, is certainly, a distribution of its powers into executive, judiciary and legislative, and a subdivision of the latter into two or three branches. It is a good step gained, when it is proved that the English constitution, acknowledged to be better than all which have preceded it, is only better in proportion as it has approached nearer to this distribution of powers."[26] If the distribution is not adequate, and one branch possesses more than its share of power, only a despotism can result—a despotism no better for the fact that it may have been elected, or may be exercised by a plurality of hands. For "mankind soon learn to

---

[25] See drafts of Kentucky and Virginia Resolutions, *ibid.*, XVII, 379 ff., 442 ff.

[26] To Adams, Sept. 28, 1787, *ibid.*, VI, 321; cf. Montesquieu, *The Spirit of Laws* (2 vols. New York, 1900), I, Bk. XI, chap. 6. Aristotle, *Politics*, ii, 6, 17; Polybius, *Histories*, Bk. VI.

make interested uses of every right and power which they possess, or may assume. The public money and public liberty, intended to have been deposited with three branches of magistracy, but found inadvertently to be in the hands of one only, will soon be discovered to be sources of wealth and dominion to those who hold them; distinguished, too, by this tempting circumstance, that they are the instrument as well as the object of acquisition. With money we will get men, said Caesar, and with men we will get money."[27]

Since Jefferson never fully develops his views on the contitution in any single passage, it is difficult to determine with certainty what attitude he took toward certain constitutional problems. He seems to have held that each of the three branches of the government should have final authority to interpret the document in so far as it relates to them. "In general, that branch which is to act ultimately, and without appeal, on any law, is the rightful expositor of the validity of the law, uncontrolled by the opinions of the other coördinate authorities."[28] This passage might, however, be construed as a defense of an executive interpretation, for it is the executive who acts on the law: the legislative makes it, and the judiciary applies it to the specific case. Jefferson had earlier been impressed, however, by the principle laid down in a proposed Spanish constitution that "when the three coördinate branches differ in their construction of the constitution, the opinion of two branches shall overrule the third," and made the comment that "our constitution has not sufficiently solved this difficulty."[29] Marshall had, in fact, effectually solved the difficulty by the time Jefferson's statement was made; but despite the fact that he himself argues, as we shall see, for a judicial rather than a presidential veto, he was not prepared to grant to the Supreme Court the power of passing upon legislation, regarding it rather as an usurpation of power.

Another constitutional provision which Jefferson held to be

[27] Notes on Virginia, *ibid.*, II, 163-64.
[28] To W. H. Torrance, June 11, 1815, *ibid.*, XIV, 304.
[29] To Don Valentine de Foronda, Oct. 4, 1809, *ibid.*, XII, 318-19.

essential is that of necessary rotation in office, a principle which he sought to have included by the American framers;[30] and he contends that offices should be held for short terms only. Presumably his inspiration for this insistence came from Athenian practice; and more specifically from Thucydides, for whom, as has been pointed out, he had high respect. The theory of rotation is best developed, to be sure, in Harrington's *Oceana*, and the principle as it is laid down in Jefferson's draft of the Virginia constitution of 1776 strongly suggests this source;[31] although Jefferson nowhere makes any reference to the English writer which could be used to establish any direct influence. He may, of course, have imbibed something of Harrington's doctrine from Adams or Madison, but his most direct source for the principle of rotation was undoubtedly Greek, as was Harrington's own. It rests on the assumption that government is everybody's business; and it reflects to considerable degree the boast the historian puts into the mouth of Pericles, that the peculiar pride of the Athenian was his ability to carry on simultaneously his own affairs and the affairs of the state, and to do both better than anybody else.[32] Athens paid heavily for her pride, and the United States might have learned from her example. For such an assumption necessarily precludes the possibility of a governing class, trained to the task of administration and lawmaking. Government is never a career, and is rarely more than an interlude in the life of a man; and the tenure of office is so problematical that the most capable look elsewhere for security. Jefferson feels himself driven to this extreme to escape monarchy. Professor Laski raises an interesting, if speculative, point when he suggests that the course of American government might have been towards the neo-parliamentary form if Jefferson and Madison had taken a different view of Hamilton.[33]

<hr />

[30] To Madison, *ibid.*, VI, 389-90.
[31] See *Writings* (Ford Edition), II, 16.
[32] Peloponnesian War, *Writings*, II, 35 ff.
[33] H. S. Laski, *The Dangers of Obedience and Other Essays* (New York, 1931), pp. 40-41.

IV

If Jefferson had been slow to approve the constitution, it was because he feared its centralization of power would rob the common man of his liberty. Hamilton disapproved of it till the day of his death because it did not do that very thing. The controversy between these two men, who battled for power during the formative years of the American government, is the age-old controversy between authority and liberty, between Hobbes and Locke. For Hamilton, under the influence of the two political theorists most distasteful to Jefferson, Hobbes and Hume, was frankly the champion of the leviathan state.[34] He combined with a deep distrust of democracy a sincere belief that no government could endure which did not identify its interests with the interests of property and wealth. Starting from the premise of Hobbes that the sovereign must be absolute, he discards the republican form because it "does not admit of vigorous execution." The chief support of the state should be an aristocratic class, committed by ties of property and privilege to maintaining the existing order; and the monarch "ought to be hereditary, and to have so much power that it would not be his interest to risk much to gain more."[35]

It is not, therefore, surprising that Hamilton should have been one of the earliest and most insistent critics of the Articles of Confederation. Weakness and decentralization were to him intolerable; and his efforts were perhaps the most important single influence in persuading the Congress to summon a convention for amending the fundamental law. For the first month of the protracted session, Hamilton watched in silence the efforts of his colleagues; but an impasse having been reached between those who sought a central power and those who wished to maintain the sovereignty of the states, he took the floor on the eighteenth of June, 1787, to present his own plan for a new

[34] See Parrington, *The Colonial Mind*, pp. 296 ff.

[35] Claude G. Bowers, *Jefferson and Hamilton* (Boston and New York, 1925), pp. 29 ff.

constitution, modified somewhat out of deference to the known opinions of his collaborators.[36]

In Hamilton's view, there are five supporting pillars in the governmental structure: an active and constant interest on the part of the people in maintaining the edifice; the love of power natural to man; the habitual attachment of the people; force, which may take the form either of legal or of military coercion; and influence, or patronage. Built upon these supports, Hamilton's plan included a president and senate chosen for life from the propertied class, by electors having themselves a substantial property qualification; state governors appointed by the president to serve a life term, and having an absolute veto over acts of the state legislatures; and a representative house, or assembly, whose members were to be elected by the people for a term of three years. The president was to have power, not only to veto acts of the legislature, but to convene, adjourn or prorogue that body at will, and to enforce existing laws or not, as he chose. Although treaties and lesser appointments were to be subject to the advice and consent of the senate, the heads of the all-important departments of finance, war and foreign affairs were to be named by the executive alone. Revenue bills, while they were to originate in the assembly, were subject to alteration and amendment by the senate. A supreme court was also to be established, having appellate jurisdiction from the state courts; and the state courts were to be the tools of the national legislature, which might create or abolish them at its pleasure.

Having offered his plan, Hamilton left the convention, knowing well enough that it would not be considered by men committed, if not to out and out democracy, at least to a government which a substantial proportion of the people could look upon as their own. And when the compromise had been effected

<hr>

[36] See *The Works of Alexander Hamilton* (ed. by H. C. Lodge. 9 vols. New York and London, 1885-1886), I, 353-60, for the brief from which he spoke, together with the comprehensive reports of it by Madison, pp. 363-75, and by Yates, pp. 375-84. See also Madison's Journal of the Convention in the supplement to Elliot's *Debates* (5 vols. Philadelphia, 1907), V, 198-206; Appendix V, 584-90.

and the constitution as we know it drawn up, he supported the "frail and worthless fabric" in the *Federalist* with logic and vigor, on the principle that half a loaf was better than no bread. "No man's ideas are more remote from the plan than my own are known to be; but is it possible to deliberate between anarchy and convulsion on one side, and the chance of good to be expected from the plan on the other?"[37]

Jefferson was entirely justified in charging that Hamilton held the English constitution to be perfect as it stood; that a correction of its abuses would only render it impotent.[38] For Hamilton was following a theory of the state which held force to be the basis of government, and coercion a necessary instrument of control. In doing this, he was perfectly sincere—Jefferson himself had called him "disinterested, honest and honorable in all private transactions"—and he was disconcertingly logical. On the assumption that the purpose of government is the maintenance of order, it follows that the best government is that which is best administered;[39] and, in theory at least, the most efficient state is the absolute monarchy. Jefferson arrives at a contradictory conclusion because he starts from a contradictory premise: the end of the state is not the preservation of order, but the furtherance of individual happiness and well-being. Following Locke, therefore, he rests the sovereignty, not with the executive head of the estate, nor with its legislative body, but with the people themselves. Hamilton's ideal was stability, Jefferson's was liberty; the one built on property and wealth, the other on equality and freedom. Both views were legitimate; but in the immediate conflict between the two, the democratic ideal won out because Jefferson had judged more soundly of the temper of the men with whom both had to deal. Yet after more than a century, the issue between them is not finally settled, and both theories still play an active rôle in our national life.

[37] Quotations from Bowers, *op. cit.*, p. 32.

[38] To Melish, Jan. 13, 1813, *Writings*, XIII, 209; to Dr. Jones, Jan. 2, 1814, *ibid.*, XIV, 51; cf. Madison's Journal, *loc. cit.*, p. 202.

[39] Cf. John Sharpe Williams, *Thomas Jefferson: His Permanent Influence on American Institutions* (New York, 1913), pp. 149-50.

V

Jefferson's vision of the state is colored by the conditions of life to which he was brought up; and by the contrast he found between the hardy, self-reliant simplicity of pioneer America and the wasteful luxury of Europe. The chief threat to the preservation of republican government is the corruption of men. Jefferson must have seen a prophecy in the lines of Goldsmith,

Ill fares the land, to hastening ills a prey,

Where wealth accumulates and men decay;

for free government is built upon the shoulders of men in whom the love of liberty is stronger than the love of gain. He had his own fears, too, for a future not quite so distant as he had hoped. The people, he writes to Madison, can be relied upon to set their own house in order as long as they remain virtuous; "and I think we shall be so, as long as agriculture is our principal object which will be the case while there remain vacant lands in any part of America. When we get piled upon one another in large cities, as in Europe, we shall become corrupt as in Europe, and go to eating one another as they do there." Great cities he views as "pestilential to the morals, the health and the liberties of man. True, they nourish some of the elegant arts, but the useful ones can thrive elsewhere, and less perfection in the others, with more health, virtue and freedom, would be my choice."[40] There is something of the Spartan in Jefferson's preference for a stalwart and hardy race, rather than a people softened and become degenerate through self-indulgence. During one of America's earlier financial crises, he writes: "I own it to be my opinion, that good will arise from the destruction of our credit. I see nothing else which can restrain our disposition to luxury, and to change those manners which alone can preserve republican government."[41]

The Greek democracies were necessarily small, as were the Italian republics later. But when the principle of direct control by the people in public assembly is discarded, the repre-

[40] To Rush, Sept. 23, 1800, *Writings*, X, 173; to Madison, Dec. 20, 1787, *ibid.*, VI, 392-93.
[41] To A. Stuart, Jan. 25, 1786, *ibid.*, V, 259.

sentative system seems capable of indefinite expansion. Certainly Jefferson regarded it in this light, holding that it was not only possible for a republic to be large, but necessary that it should be so. "I suspect that the doctrine, that small states alone are fitted to be republics, will be exploded by experience, with some other brilliant fallacies accredited by Montesquieu and other political writers. Perhaps it will be found, that to obtain a just republic (and it is to secure our just rights that we resort to government at all) it must be so extensive as that local egoisms may never reach its greater part; that on every particular question, a majority may be found in its councils free from particular interests, and giving, therefore, an uniform prevalence to the principles of justice. The smaller the societies, the more violent and more convulsive their schisms."[42]

Perhaps Jefferson the visionary saw in this principle the ultimate triumph of free government; certainly Jefferson the statesman saw in it a brilliant—Seillière would say imperialistic—future for his own country. As president, more than a year before the purchase of Louisiana, he wrote to Monroe that "however our present interests may restrain us within our own limits, it is impossible not to look forward to distant times, when our rapid multiplication will expand itself beyond those limits, and cover the whole northern, if not the southern continent, with a people speaking the same language, governed in similar forms, and by similar laws; nor can we contemplate with satisfaction either blot or mixture on that surface."[43] If this is a first, inchoate expression of the doctrine later enounced by President Monroe, and which has ever since been the storm center of American diplomacy, Jefferson laid down the principle still more emphatically in a letter to the president dated October 24, 1823 —some six weeks before it received official form in Monroe's message to Congress of December 2, the same year.[44]

[42] To D'Ivernois, Feb. 6, 1795, *ibid.*, IX, 299-300; cf. to Nathaniel Niles, Mar. 22, 1801, *ibid.*, X, 222-23; to Gov. Williams, Nov. 1, 1807, *ibid.*, XI, 390.

[43] To Monroe, Nov. 24, 1801, *ibid.*, X, 296; cf. to Stuart, Jan. 25, 1786, *ibid.*, V, 259.

[44] *Ibid.*, XV, 477 ff.; cf. H. S. Randall, *The Life of Thomas Jefferson* (3 vols. New York, 1858), III, 493.

We have seen the fabric of the state woven from the principles of equality, liberty, and happiness: a state wherein men are to be governed by representatives chosen by themselves. Let us see to whom the privilege of the vote is to be extended. Jefferson objects to a property qualification, because individuals not having property "are the greater number in every society of long standing."[45] And he deplores the fact that in his own Virginia, "one half of our brethren who fight and pay taxes, are excluded, like Helots, from the rights of representation, as if society were instituted for the soil, and not for the men inhabiting it; or one half of these could dispose of the rights and the will of the other half, without their consent."[46] But even in a pure democracy, in which all the citizens could meet together to transact their business, "there would yet be excluded from their deliberations, 1, infants, until arrived at years of discretion. 2. Women, who, to prevent depravation of morals and ambiguity of issue, could not mix promiscuously in the public meetings of men. 3. Slaves, from whom the unfortunate state of things with us takes away the rights of will and property."[47] Jefferson's reason for excluding women is curious for a man who had known Madame d'Houdetot and Madame de Staël, and the brilliant Dolly Madison. Presumably, however, his objection would be overcome with the substitution of the ballot box for the public meeting.

Slavery, of course, Jefferson could not justify on any ground. If he feels that, as a public servant, he cannot work ardently for abolition against the wishes of a majority of those he serves,[48] he is outspoken in his private capacity. "A man's moral sense must be unusually strong," he writes, "if slavery does not make him a thief. He who is permitted by law to have no property of his own can with difficulty conceive that property is founded in anything but force."[49] His draft of the Virginia constitution

[45] To Dupont de Nemours, Apr. 24, 1816, *Writings*, XIV, 489.
[46] To Taylor, May 28, 1816, *ibid.*, XV, 21.
[47] To Kercheval, Sept. 5, 1816, *ibid.*, pp. 71-72.
[48] To Warville, Feb. 12, 1788, *ibid.*, VI, 428.
[49] To Edward Bancroft, Jan. 26, 1788, *ibid.*, XIX, 41.

provides that no more slaves shall be imported, and in his revision of the laws of that state slavery is abolished altogether.[50] But he remained convinced that abolition, without adequate preparation for it, would precipitate a worse evil. In his *Notes on Virginia* he advanced a plan to which he still adhered in 1815. "The mind of the master is to be apprised by reflection, and strengthened by the energies of conscience, against the obstacles of self-interest to an acquiescence in the rights of others; that of the slave is to be prepared by instruction and habit for self-government, and for the honest pursuits of industry and social duty. Both of these courses of preparation require time, and the former must precede the latter."[51] He cannot understand how any man, on reflection, can fail to see that slavery is wrong; and he cannot believe that an admitted evil will be tolerated for long.

Nor can Jefferson's opposition to slavery be discredited by observing that he was himself a slaveholder. He could not have freed his own slaves, even had he wished to, because he was in debt during most of his life, and the law would not allow him to deprive his creditors of that security. Then, too, it was more humane to keep them than to let them go. There was no place in the southern system for a free negro; and in most of the northern states, they were forbidden to live at all.[52] The Ordinance of the Northwest Territory, from Jefferson's hand, prohibiting slavery in any of the states that might be made from it after 1800, is further testimony to his sincerity in the cause of abolition; and he had been shocked by the Missouri compromise. "A geographical line, coinciding with a marked principle, moral and political, once conceived and held up to the angry passions of men, will never be obliterated; and every new irritation will mark it deeper and deeper."[53]

[50] *Writings* (Ford Edition), II, 26, 201; cf. Channing, *op. cit.*, III, 557.

[51] To David Barrow, May 1, 1815, *Writings*, XIV, 296-97; cf. Notes on Virginia, *ibid.*, II, 191 ff.

[52] Williams, *op. cit.*, pp. 75 ff.

[53] To John Holmes, Apr. 22, 1820, *Writings*, XV, 249.

CHAPTER VI

THE SEPARATION OF POWERS

I

LET US EXAMINE in greater detail the three branches of the government, and the functions Jefferson was disposed to assign to them. First in importance, if any may be regarded as more essential than the others, is the legislative, whose duty it is to make the laws by which the state is governed. Holding as he does to a theory of natural rights, Jefferson argues that the legislative power must of necessity be circumscribed by these rights, and that in so far as they are defined, the office of the legislator is predetermined within a certain course. Thus, "their true office is to declare and enforce only our natural rights and duties, and to take none of them from us. No man has a natural right to commit aggression on the equal rights of another; and this is all from which the laws ought to restrain him; every man is under the natural duty of contributing to the necessities of the society; and this is all the laws should enforce on him; and, no man having a natural right to be the judge between himself and another, it is his natural duty to submit to the umpirage of an impartial third. When the laws have declared and enforced all this, they have fulfilled their function; and the idea is quite unfounded, that on entering into society we give up any natural right. The trial of every law by one of these texts, would lessen the labors of our legislators, and lighten equally our municipal codes."[1]

In structure, the legislature should be bicameral. Jefferson believes American experience has "proved the necessity of two Houses to prevent the tyranny of one," even if theoretical arguments be discounted; but he adds the personal conviction that

---

[1] To Gilmer, June 7, 1816, *Writings*, XV, 24.

"theory and practice are not at variance in this instance."[2] In an earlier passage, he explains that "the purpose of establishing different houses of legislation is to introduce the influence of different interests or different principles. Thus in Great Britain it is said their constitution relies on the house of commons for honesty and the lords for wisdom; which would be a rational reliance, if honesty were to be bought with money, and if wisdom were hereditary."[3] The interests he proposed, less than a year after independence had been declared, to incorporate in the respective houses, are the same as those later embodied in the American constitution. The one house is to represent geographical or sectional interests, the other the people directly.[4] There can be no question but that the principle had its origin in the existing organization of the American states, and the necessities of the time. Only by some such compromise could any sort of union be effected, the representation by states serving to protect the smaller units, and that by population the larger. But though the division grew in fact out of practical expediency, Jefferson finds it sound in principle.

For all his insistence that the common man is capable of governing himself, Jefferson is dubious as to the advisability of letting him choose his representatives directly. He thinks a house so chosen "will be very far inferior" to the Congress of the Confederation, members of which were selected by the state legislatures; and it was only with reluctance that he approved the direct vote in the case of the house whose business it was to protect the interests of the people. Members of the second chamber are to be chosen as were the members of the Continental Congress, by vote of the state assemblies; each state being allowed two Senators, who are to vote as individuals rather than by states. Members of the popular house are to be elected on the basis of population, apportioned according to a fixed ratio.[5] The voters should retain the right to instruct their repre-

[2] To Rochefoucault, Apr. 3, 1790, *ibid.*, VIII, 19; cf. to Lafayette, May 6, 1789, *ibid.*, VII, 334.   [3] Notes on Virginia, *ibid.*, II, 162.
[4] To Adams, May 17, 1777, *ibid.*, IV, 287.
[5] Official Papers, *ibid.*, III, 201 ff.

sentatives; and it is the duty of the latter to be guided by such instructions.[6] Both houses are to be governed by the law of the majority, which is founded in common law as well as common right. "It is the natural law of every assembly of men, whose numbers are not fixed by any other law." Hence the legislative assembly does not have a right to determine a quorum of its own body; for if a quorum may be fixed at forty, it may be fixed at four, or at one, and an oligarchy or monarchy result.[7]

The legislative houses are coördinate, and in general the approval of both is required to give any measure the force of law. Certain types of legislation, however, are to originate in a specific chamber. The popular House of Representatives should have power to institute inquiries and call for papers, although the executive may refuse these if the disclosure of their contents would in his opinion injure the public good.[8] But above all, the House has the power to originate tax measures, and it is for this reason solely that Jefferson is willing to approve its members being chosen by the people directly, to preserve inviolate "the fundamental principle, that the people are not to be taxed but by representatives chosen immediately by themselves."[9] In Jefferson's draft of the Virginia constitution, he went so far as to deny to the senate the power to amend money bills, although the approval of that house was required to give such measures the force of law.[10]

The problem of taxation was, in fact, largely responsible for the abandonment of the Articles of Confederation. "It is not unknown to you," Jefferson writes to l'Abbé Morellet in 1787, "that the part of our new machine of government which works the worst, is that which respects the raising of money; and it is that which has occasioned the late attempts to amend our confederation."[11] By the end of another year, with war clouds gath-

---

[6] To John Taylor, May 28, 1816, *ibid.*, XV, 18; cf. Taylor's *An Enquiry into the Principles and Tendency of Certain Public Measures* (Philadelphia, 1794), p. 6.

[7] Notes on Virginia, *Writings*, II, 172-73.

[8] Anas, *ibid.*, I, 303-4.

[9] To Madison, Dec. 20, 1787, *ibid.*, VI, 387.

[10] *Writings* (Ford Edition), II, 17.

[11] To Morellet, Oct. 24, 1787, *Writings*, VI, 347-48.

ering on more than one horizon, Jefferson had persuaded himself that adequate taxing powers alone can preserve a government. "Calculation has convinced me that circumstances may arise, and probably will arise, wherein all the resources of taxation will be necessary for the safety of the State. For though I am decidedly of the opinion we should take no part in European quarrels, but cultivate peace and commerce with all, yet who can avoid seeing the source of war, in the tyranny of those nations, who deprive us of the natural right of trading with our neighbors?"[12]

But although the taxing power is a vital one, it is also a dangerous one, which must be exercised with caution and circumscribed with constitutional checks. Hence Jefferson argues for strict interpretation of the Constitution, where it provides (Art. I, sec. 8) that "the Congress shall have power to lay and collect taxes, duties, imposts and excises, to pay the debts and provide for the general welfare of the United States." In opposing the proposal to establish a national bank, he contends that the members of Congress "are not to lay taxes *ad libitum for any purpose they please; but only to pay the debts or provide for the welfare of the Union.* In like manner, they are not *to do anything they please* to provide for the general welfare, but only to *lay taxes* for that purpose. To consider the latter phrase, not as describing the purpose of the first, but as giving a distinct and independent power to do any act they please, which might be for the good of the Union, would render all the preceding and subsequent enumerations of power completely useless. . . . It would reduce the whole instrument to a single phrase, that of instituting a Congress with power to do whatever would be for the good of the United States; and, as they would be the sole judges of the good or evil, it would also be a power to do whatever evil they please."[13]

To the upper house, or Senate, goes the treaty-making power,

[12] To Washington, Dec. 4, 1788, *ibid.*, VII, 223-24; cf. to Carmichael, Dec. 25, 1798, *ibid.*, VII, 248.

[13] Official Papers, *ibid.*, III, 148; cf. *ibid.*, pp. 212-13; Madison, *The Federalist* (New York, 1898), No. 41.

conjointly with the president; such at least is the theory of the American constitution. But Jefferson would have the principle qualified. He insists that "in giving to the President and Senate a power to make treaties, the Constitution meant only to authorize them to carry into effect, by way of treaty, any powers they might constitutionally exercise."[14] And there is also a further limitation urged by Jefferson as to the treaty-making power; for in many cases a treaty cannot go into effect without the passage of a law or appropriation, in which the lower house would necessarily have to concur. Hence, he conceives the constitutional doctrine to be "that though the President and Senate have the general power of making treaties, yet wherever they include in a treaty matters confided by the Constitution to the three branches of Legislature, an act of legislation will be requisite to confirm these articles, and that the House of Representatives, as one branch of the Legislature, are perfectly free to pass the act or to refuse it, governing themselves by their own judgment whether it is good for their constituents to let the treaty go into effect or not." The quotation is taken from a letter to Monroe, of March 21, 1796, and is in effect the doctrine of the Blount Resolutions, which it anticipates by some two weeks. The resolutions were motivated by the discussion in the House over certain aspects of Jay's treaty; and it is of Jay's treaty Jefferson is thinking, both here and in a similar passage addressed to Giles, December 31, 1795. The question had occurred to him, however, four years earlier, when an Algerian treaty was proposed in the cabinet which would have required an appropriation to carry out its terms. The position he takes is consistent throughout, and is identical with that which has become settled American practice.[15]

As to the force and validity of treaties, Jefferson changes his position considerably. In 1790, indignant over Hamilton's proposal to abrogate the French treaty on the ground that it had

---

[14] Anas, *Writings*, I, 408.

[15] To Monroe, Mar. 21, 1796, *ibid.*, IX, 329; cf. to Giles, Dec. 31, 1795, *ibid.*, p. 315; Anas, *ibid.*, I, 294 ff. (Mar. 11, 1792), 305 ff. (Apr. 9, 1792); see also *Annals of Congress*, 4 Cong., 1 sess., pp. 426-772, *passim.*

been entered into with the no longer reigning house of Bourbon, he wrote that a treaty "made by the President, with the concurrence of two-thirds of the Senate, is a law of the land, and a law of superior order, because it not only repeals past laws, but cannot itself be repealed by future ones"—a confusing and seemingly self-contradictory statement, to which is appended at a later date the following note: "Unless with the consent or default of the other contracting party. It may well be doubted, too, and perhaps denied, that the treaty power can control a law. The question here proposed was then of the first impression. Subsequent investigations have proved that the contrary position is the more general truth."[16]

Where there is a marked failure in the attainment of a desired end, it is for the legislative branch to determine wherein the failure lay, and what its remedy. After the acquittal of Aaron Burr on charges of treason, Jefferson laid before Congress the record of the case, with the comment: "You will be enabled to judge whether the defeat was in the testimony, in the law, or in the administration of the law; and wherever it shall be found, the legislature alone can supply or originate the remedy. The framers of our constitution certainly supposed they had guarded, as well their government against destruction by treason, as their citizens against oppression, under pretense of it; and if these ends are not attained, it is of importance to inquire by what means, more effectual, they may be secured."[17]

One defect in the law which Jefferson believed conducive to miscarriage of justice was the involved and technical language in which statutes were worded. In offering his draft of *An Act for Establishing Elementary Schools* to Joseph C. Cabell, he apologizes for having couched it in simple terms, devoid of legal jargon. "You, however, can easily correct this bill to the taste of my brother lawyers, by making every other word a 'said' or 'aforesaid,' and saying everything over two or three times, so that nobody but we of the craft can untwist the diction, and find out what it means; and that, too, not so plainly but that we may conscientiously divide one half on each side."[18] Where sovereignty rests with the people, the law must be intelligible to the masses.

The foregoing account is a more or less idealized discussion of what, in Jefferson's opinion, the legislative branch of a representative government ought to be; and his steady faith in its ultimate practicability is the more marked when we consider that he was under no illusions as to its actual workings. There is a passage in which he describes the membership of the House which passed on the national bank as consisting of bank directors, holders of bank stock, stock jobbers, blind devotees, ignoramuses, and those who, comprehending, were yet too lazy to examine or censor.[19] And after the failure of the Non-Importation Bill in the Senate, he wrote of that body that it "was intended as a check on the will of the Representatives when too hasty. They are not only that, but completely so on the will of the people also." All these evils, he thinks, can be avoided by the simple panacea of placing the officeholders under the control of a more frequent recurrence to the will of their constituents.[20]

II

The executive, or president, is responsible for the administration of the laws enacted by the legislative branch. But the peculiar form his office has taken in America is to considerable extent, at least, due to a misconception. Montesquieu and Blackstone both assumed that the king is the administrative head of the British constitution, and the American framers, with the career of George III before them, copied this mistake.[21] Since the revolution of 1688, the Parliament had been in fact supreme, and the growth of the ministerial system had made the prime minister rather than the king the actual head of the English government, to whom the American president would most nearly correspond. Jefferson, however, never doubts the paral-

---

[18] To Cabell, Sept. 9, 1817, *ibid.*, XVII, 418.

[19] *Anas, ibid.*, I, 345.

[20] To Madison, May 15, 1794, *ibid.*, IX, 288-89.

[21] Oliver Wendell Holmes, *Collected Legal Papers* (London and New York, 1920), p. 263.

lel between president and king in function; and it is his experience with kings that prompts a warning. "In a government like ours, it is the duty of the Chief Magistrate, in order to enable himself to do all the good which his station requires, to endeavor by all honorable means, to unite in himself the confidence of the whole people. This alone, in any case where the energy of the nation is required, can produce a union of the powers of the whole, and point them in a single direction, as if all constituted but one body and one mind, and this alone can render a weaker nation unconquerable by a stronger one."[22] The executive, further, must assume full responsibility for his acts. "Responsibility is a tremendous engine in a free government."[23]

The term of office of the executive, like that of members of the legislature, should be short. Jefferson comes to this conclusion rather through observation of existing dictatorships than through a reasoned analysis of the alternatives. When the American constitution was still under consideration, he wrote: "What we have recently read in the history of Holland, in the chapter of the Stadtholder, would have sufficed to set me against a chief magistrate eligible for a long duration, if I had ever been disposed towards one; and what we have always read of the elections of Polish Kings should have forever excluded the idea of one continuable for life."[24] He seems never to have suspected the chaos resultant upon rapid changes of administration and policy, or the practical impossibility of constructive legislation over a period of years on the part of a government whose only element of continuity is the vague and shadowy mass of the nation.

Jefferson first suggested a seven-year term for the president, making him thereafter ineligible, in place of the four years with reëligibility proposed in the draft of the American constitution; but experience brought him to modify his stand in favor of even greater brevity. "My opinion originally was that the Presi-

[22] To J. G. Jefferson, June 25, *Writings*, 1810, XII, 353-54.
[23] To A. Stuart, Dec. 23, 1791, *ibid.*, VIII, 277.
[24] To Col. Smith, Nov. 13, 1787, *ibid.*, VI, 372.

dent of the United States should be elected for seven years, and forever ineligible afterwards. I have since become sensible that seven years is too long to be irremovable, and that there should be a peaceable way of withdrawing a man in midway who is doing wrong. The service for eight years, with a power to remove at the end of the first four, comes nearly to my principle as corrected by experience."[25]   Some eight years later he declares himself to be for "responsibilities at short periods, seeing neither reason nor safety in making public functionaries independent of the nation for life, or even for long terms of years. On this principle I prefer the Presidential term of four years, to that of seven years, which I myself had at first suggested, annexing to it, however, ineligibility forever after; and I wish it were now annexed to the second quadrennial election of President."[26]

Among the peculiarly executive functions, he names nomination to office, and the transaction of business with foreign powers. The Senate, to be sure, may confirm or refuse to confirm a nomination, but its power in this regard he would limit strictly to "advice and consent." To give the nominating power itself to the legislative would be a "violation of the principle of the separation of powers. It swerves the members from correctness, by temptations to intrigue for office themselves, and to a corrupt barter of votes; and destroys responsibility by dividing it among a multitude. By leaving nomination in its proper place, among executive functions, the principle of the distribution of powers is preserved, and responsibility weighs with its heaviest force on a single head."[27]   Similarly, relations with other states are wholly executive; and though the Senate may decline to confirm an individual appointed on a foreign mission, they have no authority to negative his grade. Of the five acts involved: choice of destination, grade of envoy, nomination, ap-

[25] To Taylor, Jan. 6, 1805, *ibid.*, XI, 56-57; cf. to Short, Sept. 20, 1788, *ibid.*, VII, 145-46.

[26] To James Martin, Sept. 20, 1813, *ibid.*, XIII, 381-82.

[27] To Kercheval, July 12, 1816, *ibid.*, XV, 37.

pointment, and commission, the consent of the Senate should be necessary only in the case of appointment.[28]

Of greater importance is the executive veto on measures passed by the legislature, which may be overruled by a two thirds majority of both houses. As a lawyer, however, Jefferson was of the opinion that a judicial veto would be of higher value. He writes of the constitution that "I like the negative given to the Executive, conjointly with a third of either House; though I should have liked it better, had the judiciary been associated for that purpose, or invested separately with a similar power."[29] His vigorous objection when Marshall exercised such a power was due more to the fact that he regarded it as unconstitutional usurpation, than to any belief in its inherent wrongness; and it is unquestionable, too, that his views on the matter were colored by party and personal differences with the Chief Justice.[30]

The executive must also be considered as enjoying certain immunities foreign to the ordinary citizen. When threatened with a subpoena in the Burr trial, Jefferson wrote that he could not regard the president as subject to judicial orders, since the three branches of the government were coördinate, and distinct from each other. He held in this case, that possible benefit to one individual should not be used to force the executive to abandon, even for a time, his duties toward the whole.[31] Had the summons been tendered by any justice other than John Marshall, Jefferson's response might perhaps have been more cordial; but then, no other justice would have thought of ordering to the witness stand the president of the United States.

The president is to be assisted in the work of administration by a cabinet, composed of the heads of various executive departments, chosen by himself with the approval of the Sen-

[28] Official Papers, *ibid.*, III, 15 ff.
[29] To Madison, Dec. 20, 1787, *ibid.*, VI, 387.
[30] Randall, *Life of Jefferson*, II, 36 ff., 364-65; Henry Adams, *History of the United States* (9 vols. New York, 1889-1891), I, 194; A. J. Beveridge, *Life of John Marshall* (4 vols. Boston and New York, 1916-1919), III, 398 ff.
[31] To George Hay, June 20, 1807, *Writings*, XI, 240 ff.

ate. The precise function of the cabinet as a body is not, however, exactly clear in Jefferson's writings. During his own administration, he regarded it as being in the nature of an executive council. "For our government, although in theory subject to be directed by the unadvised will of the President, is, and from its origin has been a very different thing in practice. The minor business in each department is done by the Head of the department, on consultation with the President alone. But all matters of importance or difficulty are submitted to all the Heads of departments composing the cabinet, sometimes by the President's consulting them separately and successively, as they happen to call on him; but in the greatest cases, by calling them together, discussing the subject maturely, and finally taking the vote, in which the President counts himself but as one. So that in all important cases the executive is, in fact, a directory, which certainly the President might control; but of this there was never an example, either in the first or in the present administration."[32] Yet some fourteen years earlier, he had been surprised and a little hurt that, after a cabinet discussion, Washington should have decided the question at issue by a "mere majority, including his own vote."[33]

There is no doubt that Jefferson's cabinet was more harmonious than Washington's had been, and as long as its members consistently inclined toward his own views, Jefferson had no occasion to disregard their advice. That he would have done so, had occasion arisen, is probable on the evidence of a later opinion, perhaps his most mature statement on this question, which occurs in a letter to Destutt de Tracy. Here he argues against the plural executive advocated in de Tracy's commentary on Montesquieu, holding that, although in America many had favored an executive council, and it had even been tried during the recess of Congress in 1784, when it immediately fell into schism and discord, the experience of the French Directory was deemed proof of the impracticability of such a form. Citing the

---

[32] To Short, June 12, 1807, *ibid.*, p. 227; cf. to Samuel Dexter, Feb. 20, 1801, *ibid.*, X, 208.   [33] *Anas*, *ibid.*, I, 351-52.

dissensions in Washington's cabinet, which, without the supreme executive head, must have produced complete inaction, he points out that the single executive gives unity to the government and renders departmental clashes abortive.[34]

For representatives to give orders to cabinet officials directly rather than through the president, and after consulting him, is an usurpation of executive power on the part of the legislative. But Jefferson is none the less willing that the executive should, if emergency arises, presume on the power of the legislature. During Washington's administration, acting in collaboration with Hamilton, he authorized the purchase of a quantity of saltpetre larger than that for which Congress had voted funds; and again, during his own incumbency as president, the secretary of the navy was granted authority to purchase timber for one hundred gun-boats, together with quantities of saltpetre and sulphur, on the presumption that Congress would sanction it.[35] Still more pointed is the case of Louisiana; but that has been reserved for more particular consideration in another connection.

The office of vice-president Jefferson held to be "constitutionally confined to legislative functions";[36] and from this attitude American practice has never had occasion to depart.

The appointive power given to the executive provides opportunity for an almost unlimited system of official patronage; and however he may have inveighed against it in his more detached moments, Jefferson was unable to avoid the spoils system altogether when in office. In 1820 he characterizes it as introducing into the government "a principle of intrigue and corruption"; and while occupying the presidency, he wrote that "every officer of the government may vote at elections according to his conscience; but we should betray the cause committed to our care, were we to permit the influence of official patronage to be used to overthrow that cause."[37] The fact remains, how-

---

[34] To de Tracy, Jan. 26, 1811, *ibid.*, XIII, 15 ff.

[35] Anas, *ibid.*, I, 375, 475; see chap. 8, sec. IV, below.

[36] To Gerry, May 13, 1797, *Writings*, IX, 382.

[37] To Levi Lincoln, Oct. 25, 1802, *ibid.*, X, 340; cf. to Madison, Nov. 29, 1820, *ibid.*, XV, 294 ff.

ever, that on assuming the presidency, and finding the offices filled with Federalists of Adams's appointing, he proceeded to clean house. Some of the removals he justifies on the ground of illegal or improper conduct, others because the appointments were made after the result of the election was known;[38] while of the whole procedure, he writes that it "seems but common justice to leave a successor free to act by instruments of his own choice."[39] The storm of criticism which followed these removals seems hardly justified by the facts. Jefferson actually displaced for political reasons less than twenty officeholders; and when he had occasion to name his own first set of appointees, the bankruptcy commissioners under the act of 1801, republican and federalist were represented with commendable impartiality.[40] He never gloried in the power of office for its own sake; and did in fact actually sacrifice one quarter of the patronage of the federal government when he decided in 1801 to dispense with the system of internal revenue.[41] He was not, however, wholly unprepared for the abuse his opponents heaped upon him. Almost five years before he had himself assumed the presidency, he had written of it: "I know well that no man will ever bring out of that office the reputation which carries him into it. The honeymoon would be as short in that case as in any other, and its moments of ecstasy would be ransomed by years of torment and hatred."[42]

In the main, Jefferson follows the interpretation of executive powers set forth in the *Federalist*. And by his failure to appreciate the close fusion of executive and legislative functions in the British system, he lent his support to the perpetuation of an unfortunate distribution of powers. For an American president may continue in office, even though he lose his majority in the legislature. As de Tocqueville points out, this is not his

[38] See letters to Giles, Mar. 24, 1801, *ibid.*, X, 238 ff.; to Rush, Mar. 24, 1801, *ibid.*, pp. 241 ff.
[39] To Abigail Adams, June 13, 1804, *ibid.*, XI, 29.
[40] Channing, *History of the United States*, IV, 251 ff. See also Channing, *The Jeffersonian System* (New York and London, 1906), p. 17.
[41] *Ibid.*, p. 32.
[42] To Edward Rutledge, Dec. 27, 1796, *Writings*, IX, 353.

strength, but his weakness. He can neither obstruct the passage of a law, nor avoid executing it, and is completely subject to the legislative branch.[43]

III

The third—in American experience, perhaps the dominating —branch in the elaborate system of checks and balances we call government, is the judiciary. And Jefferson was fully cognizant of its importance, although he was unwilling to grant to it the final voice in interpreting the constitution. The judiciary occupied a commanding place in his mind as early as the first groping steps towards forming an independent government in America; and within a few days of the *Declaration*, he outlined his views to his old law teacher, George Wythe:

"The dignity and stability of government in all its branches, the morals of the people, and every blessing of society, depend so much upon an upright and skillful administration of justice, that the judicial power ought to be distinct from both legislative and executive, and independent upon both, that so it may be a check upon both, as both should be checks upon that. The judges, therefore, should always be men of learning and experience in the laws, of exemplary morals, great patience, calmness and attention; their minds should not be distracted with jarring interests; they should not be dependent upon any man or body of men. To these ends they should hold estates for life in their offices, or, in other words, their commissions should be during good behavior, and their salaries ascertained and established by law.

"For misbehavior . . . the house of representatives should impeach them before the governor and council, when they should have time and opportunity to make their defense; but if convicted, should be removed from their offices, and subjected to such other punishment as shall be thought proper."[44]

The passage refers, of course, to the state courts, since no attempt had yet been made to create a federal judicial body; but it

[43] Alexis de Tocqueville, *Democracy in America* (2 vols. New York, 1898), I, 159-60.

[44] To George Wythe, July, 1776, *Writings*, IV, 258-59.

lays down the broad pattern to which the Supreme Court was ideally to conform. Ten years later Jefferson outlined the relation he believed should obtain between state and federal jurisdictions. The proposition having been made to let Congress negative the acts of the state legislatures, he replied that it "fails in an essential character; that the hole and the patch should be commensurate. But this proposes to mend a small hole by covering the whole garment." He offers a judicial substitute: "Would not an appeal from the State judicature to a federal court, in all cases where the act of Confederation controlled the question, be as effectual a remedy, and exactly commensurate with the defect?"[45] He would have gone, however, further than American practice has followed, and allowed Congress in its turn to exercise a restraining power over the court. The judicial branch of the federal government will thus exercise jurisdiction over all cases arising under the constitution, and will serve as a court of appeals from the states. And it will also, in some measure at least, be an international tribunal. While secretary of state, Jefferson had been struck by the inadequacy of the courts to handle certain cases involving runaway slaves, and had urged provision for similar questions "by enlarging the jurisdiction of the courts, so that they may sustain indictments and informations on the public behalf, for offenses against the law of nations."[46]

As early as 1801, when the Judiciary Act was repealed and impeachment proceedings were brought against Pickering and Chase, Jefferson had begun to question the course of the judiciary; and in his later years of retirement, his disapproval was outspoken. He had seen it grow, under the skillful guidance of John Marshall, from an inoffensive third in the governmental scheme of things into a powerful and dominating first. And lawyer though he was, with a lawyer's respect for legal institutions, he saw in the attitude of the court a threat to the coördination of powers. If the three branches are to be equal and inde-

---

[45] To Madison, June 20, 1787, *ibid.*, VI, 132-33.
[46] Official Papers, *ibid.*, III, 212 ff.

pendent, one cannot overrule the others. So he attacks the judiciary with more than appropriate bitterness, and denies the "right they usurp of exclusively explaining the Constitution." To consider the judges as the final arbiters of constitutional questions is "a very dangerous doctrine indeed, and one which would place us under the despotism of an oligarchy."[47]

This interpretation seems not wholly justified. The negative of the court can be overruled by constitutional amendment; and Jefferson himself had advocated frequent revision of the basic law. Further, he had declared in favor of a judicial rather than an executive veto upon legislation, although it may be presumed that he intended it should be nullified by the legislative two-thirds, as in the case of the executive power. It has earlier been suggested that the American system might have resembled much more closely the parliamentary government of England, but for a misunderstanding on the part of the framers of the constitution. No single member of the Philadelphia convention seems to have realized the implications of a written constitution, or grasped the significance of the party system, with its logical consequence, the responsible ministry. The American Congress was designed to check the power of the president as Parliament was conceived to check the king, rather than to coöperate with him in carrying out a given program as Parliament did coöperate with the prime minister.

Jefferson seems never fully to have appreciated the essential difference between the two types of legislative body. His view of the judiciary function is prompted by a supposed parallel with the British Parliament, whereby any measure passed in due form is law, and if it conflicts with any previous enactment, the earlier law is automatically repealed. The office of the judge is not to decide the validity of the law, but the subsumption of the specific case under the law. When legislative and judiciary are alike bound by the terms of a written constitution, however, the office of the judge may well come, in strict logic, to include the

[47] To William Jarvis, Sept. 28, 1820, *ibid.*, XV, 277; cf. to Judge Spencer Roane, Mar. 9, 1821, *ibid.*, XV, 326.

interpretation of its provisions. Had Jefferson followed more closely the decisions of the state courts under the confederation, he must have been not altogether unprepared for the decision in Marbury *vs.* Madison. The doctrine of judicial review had been definitely foreshadowed in New Jersey in 1780 in the case of Holmes *vs.* Walton, in Virginia two years later in Commonwealth *vs.* Caton, and in the still more famous Rhode Island case of Trevett *vs.* Weeden in 1786. In each of these cases, a state judiciary body had declared, either openly or by implication, that certain acts of the state legislature were unconstitutional, and therefore null and void.[48] The Virginia court of appeals was given specific power by the constitution of the state to pass on the validity of legislative acts.[49]

Jefferson charges the court also with usurping the powers of the states. "It has long . . . been my opinion . . . that the germ of dissolution of our federal government is in the constitution of the federal judiciary; an irresponsible body, (for impeachment is but a scarecrow,) working like gravity by night and by day, gaining a little today and a little tomorrow, and advancing its noiseless step like a thief, over the field of jurisdiction, until all shall be usurped from the States, and the government of all be consolidated into one."[50] Yet a measure of unity is necessary, if the whole is to endure; and he had himself suggested the appeal from state to federal courts.

IV

The first great principle of the constitution is the division of its powers among the several branches of government, each checked by the others from passing beyond its assigned sphere of activity. But it would be only an instrument of oppression without an express declaration of rights to stand between the

---

[48] See A. C. McLaughlin, *The Confederation and Constitution* (New York and London, 1905), pp. 151-53, 250-51; Beveridge, *op. cit.*, III, 611; Commonwealth *vs.* Caton, 4 Call 5-21, Trevett *vs.* Weeden, in Chandler, *American Criminal Trials*, II, 269-350.

[49] Channing, *History of the United States*, III, 438.

[50] To Hammond, Aug. 18, 1821, *Writings*, XV, 331-32; cf. to Ritchie, Dec. 25, 1820, *ibid.*, p. 297; to Roane, Mar. 9, 1821; *ibid.*, p. 326.

freedom of the individual and the authority of the state. It is a corollary of the natural rights doctrine, and follows from the premise that government exists for the people rather than the people for the government. "It had become an universal and almost uncontroverted position in the several States, that the purposes of society do not require a surrender of all our rights to our ordinary governors; that there are certain portions of right not necessary to enable them to carry on an effective government, and which experience has nevertheless proved they will be constantly encroaching on, if submitted to them; that there are also certain fences which experience has proved peculiarly efficacious against wrong, and rarely obstructive of right, which yet the governing powers have ever shown a disposition to weaken and remove. Of the first kind, for instance, is freedom of religion; of the second, trial by jury, habeas corpus laws, free presses."[51] A bill of rights puts into the hands of the judiciary a legal check on the powers of legislative and executive, for the protection of the people.[52]

Jefferson's early opposition to the federal constitution was based primarily on its omission of a bill of rights, "providing clearly, and without the aid of sophism, for freedom of religion, freedom of the press, protection against standing armies, restriction of monopolies, the eternal and unremitting force of the habeas corpus laws, and trials by jury in all matters of fact triable by the laws of the land, and not by the laws of nations."[53] His other objections to the instrument, such as its abandonment of the principle of necessary rotation in office and its centralization of power, he dropped on mature consideration. "It is a good canvass, on which some strokes only want retouching"; but until it was certain that a bill of rights would be immediately offered in the form of amendments, he was dubious as to the advisability of supporting it.[54]

[51] To Noah Webster, Dec. 4, 1790, *ibid.*, VIII, 112-13.
[52] To Madison, Mar. 15, 1789, *ibid.*, VII, 309.
[53] To Madison, Dec. 20, 1787, *ibid.*, VI, 387.
[54] To Madison, July 31, 1788, *ibid.*, VII, 96; cf. to Washington, Dec. 4, 1788, *ibid.*, pp. 36-37; to A. Donald, Feb. 7, 1788, *ibid.*, VI, 425-26, *et passim.*

It was not enough for Jefferson that the rights he named as being reserved to the people are implicitly so reserved in the body of the constitution. Wilson had argued that in the case of the general government all is reserved which is not given, while in the particular ones, all is given which is not reserved. But Jefferson replies that this is "surely a *gratis dictum*, the reverse of which might just as well be said; and it is opposed by strong inferences from the body of the instrument, as well as from the omission of the clause of our present Confederation, which had made the reservation in express terms. It was hard to conclude, because there has been a want of uniformity among the States as to the cases triable by jury, because some have been so incautious as to dispense with this mode of trial in certain cases, therefore, the more prudent States should be reduced to the same level of calamity. It would have been much more just and wise to have concluded the other way, that as most of the states had preserved with jealousy this sacred palladium of liberty, those who had wandered, should be brought back to it; and to have established general right rather than general wrong. . . . I have a right to nothing, which another has a right to take away; and Congress will have a right to take away trials by jury in all civil cases. Let me add, that a bill of rights is what the people are entitled to against every government on earth, general or particular; and what no just government should refuse or rest on inference."[55]

It is no doubt true that a bill of rights will not always accomplish the purpose for which it is intended; but "though it is not absolutely efficacious under all circumstances, it is of great potency always, and rarely inefficacious. A brace the more will often keep up the building which would have fallen, with that brace the less. There is a remarkable difference between the characters of the inconveniences which attend a declaration of rights, and those which attend the want of it. The inconveniences of the declaration are, that it may cramp the government in its useful exertions. But the evil of this is short-lived, mod-

---

[55] To Madison, Dec. 20, 1787, *ibid.*, pp. 388-89.

erate and reparable. The inconveniences of the want of a declaration are permanent, afflicting and irreparable."[56] Similarly,
there may be desirable exceptions to some of the rules laid down
in the bill of rights; "yet if the exceptions cannot be agreed on,
the establishment of the rules, in all cases, will do ill in very
few."[57]

The importance Jefferson attached to the bill of rights cannot be overestimated. He ranks it, together with a representative legislature, as one of the two "essentials constituting
free government";[58] and in a very definite sense the whole
governmental fabric is woven out of these reserved rights.
They will therefore repay more detailed analysis.

Freedom of religion is dictated by Jefferson's own broad
tolerance in matters of faith, by a deep distrust of the power of
an established church, and by a conviction that men will be free
in fact only when they are spiritually and mentally free. The
declaration, however, "that religious faith shall be unpunished,
does not give impunity to criminal acts, dictated by religious
error."[59] Monopolies are barred because they give to the one
economic advantages denied to others; but they "may be allowed to persons for their own productions in literature, and
their own inventions in the arts," for a given term of years,
these being in the nature of advantages earned by superior talent
or ingenuity. Jefferson fathered the American copyright and
patent laws. His bill of rights also shows scant respect for brass
buttons. Military strength does not presuppose a standing
army; and he looks upon professional soldiers as superfluous.
Not only are the people to be spared the duty of quartering
troops without their consent; they are to be relieved as far as
possible from the burden of supporting armies at all.[60]

More important are freedom of speech and of the press.
"The people shall not be deprived of their right to speak, to

[56] To Madison, Mar. 15, 1789, *ibid.*, VII, 311.
[57] To Madison, July 31, 1788, *ibid.*, p. 98.
[58] To Dupont de Nemours, Feb. 28, 1815, *ibid.*, XIV, 255.
[59] To Madison, July 31, 1788, *ibid.*, VII, 98.
[60] To Madison, Aug. 28, 1789, *ibid.*, pp. 450-51.

write, or *otherwise* to publish anything but false facts affecting injuriously the life, liberty, property or reputation of others, or affecting the peace of the confederacy with foreign nations." Time and again Jefferson has expressed his conviction that where common sense has fair play, things cannot go far wrong; but common sense can never make itself felt unless the great mass of the people are free to express their own opinions, and to read and hear the opinions of others. Speech and thought are beyond the domain of government. Jefferson waxes warmly indignant that anyone should presume to censor books;[61] and a free press is more important than government itself. "I am persuaded myself," he writes, "that the good sense of the people will always be found the best army. They may be led astray for a moment, but will soon correct themselves. The people are the only censors of their governors; and even their errors will tend to keep these to the true principles of their institution. To punish these errors too severely would be to suppress the only safeguard of the public liberty. The way to suppress these irregular interpositions of the people, is to give them full information of their affairs through the channel of the public papers, and to contrive that those papers should penetrate the whole mass of the people. The basis of our governments being the opinion of the people, the very first object should be to keep that right; and were it left to me to decide whether we should have a government without newspapers, or newspapers without a government, I should not hesitate to prefer the latter. But I should mean that every man should receive those papers, and be capable of reading them."[62]

The function—nay, the duty—of the press is to speak the will of the people; and it is upon the will of the people that government ultimately rests. To bridle the press in any way is therefore to subvert to the uses of the privileged few the power that belongs to all. "No government ought to be without censors; and where the press is free, no one ever will. If

---

[61] To N. G. Dufief, Apr. 19, 1814, *ibid.*, XIV, 127 ff.
[62] To Carrington, Jan. 16, 1787, *ibid.*, VI, 57-58.

virtuous, it need not fear the fair operation of attack and defense. Nature has given to man no other means of sifting out the truth, either in religion, law, or politics."[63] The people, if only they can be given true and adequate information, are the best guardians of their liberties. Despite this exalted view of the destiny of the press, Jefferson was fully aware that editorial opinion was not always uplifting, and that newspaper dispatches were not always true. But he views the evil as one that will right itself, and expresses complete confidence that "the public judgment will correct false reasonings and opinions, on a full hearing of all parties; and no other definite line can be drawn between the inestimable liberty of the press and its demoralizing licentiousness."[64]

The final safeguards of the individual against the power of the state are habeas corpus laws and trial by jury. The former will render confinement without trial as brief as possible, enforcing the dictum that every man is innocent until proved guilty; the latter will make the people their own judges in matters of fact.[65]

v

The doctrine of state rights, with which Jefferson's name is often associated, is itself only an element in a larger principle: the rights of the individual. He would secure the sphere of the state against the encroachments of the federal authority because he believes the smaller unit better adapted to preserve the liberty of individuals, and more likely to promote their happiness—the self-realization which is the only legitimate end of government. He reasons that the smaller the unit, the greater the responsibility of the individual citizen, and the greater his opportunity for self-government; the larger the unit, the less is the likelihood of widespread dissension, or of a false principle gaining the upper hand. To preserve the virtues of both, the state should be organized as an hierarchy of political groups,

[63] To Washington, Sept. 9, 1792; *ibid.*, VIII, 406; cf. to Col. Yancey, Jan. 6, 1816, *ibid.*, XIV, 384.
[64] Second Inaugural Address, *ibid.*, III, 382; cf. Anas, *ibid.*, I, 353.
[65] To Madison, Aug. 28, 1789, *ibid.*, VII, 451.

each retaining certain functions for its own exercise, while delegating others to the higher units in the scale. The arrangement is essentially feudal in its conception; and it does not avoid the principal weakness of the feudal order, namely, that any given unit, when it deems its strength sufficient, may disavow the authority of those above it. The doctrine was carried in America, as it had been in Europe, to the brink of disaster.

At the top of the hierarchy stands the federal government, which may in theory cover an indefinite extent of territory, and rule over numbers limited only by its resources. Its activities are defined, as its powers are declared, in the constitution; and while certain functions may be exercised in varying degrees by more than one member of the hierarchy, foreign relations and national defense are exclusive concerns of the federal unit. "To make us one nation as to foreign concerns, and keep us distinct in domestic ones, gives the outline of the proper division of powers between the general and particular governments."[66] Both may levy taxes, through their duly constituted legislative organs, to meet their own needs; although Jefferson had earlier doubted the advisability of letting the federal Congress go beyond imposts as a means of raising revenue.[67]

Next in the descending scale come the states; and these are, historically, the starting point of Jefferson's system. He was satisfied with the various distinct colonial administrations, until the necessity of presenting an united front in the war for independence led him to conceive them as organized under a federal head; and it was only considerably later that he realized the possibilities of the further subdivision of the states into counties, and finally into wards or townships.

The size of the states cannot, of course, be precisely determined; but Jefferson suggests that new territory be divided into sections of moderate size, say 30,000 square miles. Larger divisions he feels will eventually crumble into smaller, and will

[66] To Madison, Dec. 16, 1786, *ibid.*, VI, 9; cf. to Carrington, Aug. 4, 1787, *ibid.*, p. 227, *et passim.*
[67] To Carrington, Dec. 21, 1787, *ibid.*, p. 395.

at the same time be opposed to the wishes of the people.[68]
When Congress adopted a different plan, proposing to make
the western states fewer and larger, he objected that this "is
reversing the natural order of things. A tractable people may
be governed in large bodies; but, in proportion as they depart
from this character, the extent of their government must be
less. We see into what small divisions the Indians are obliged
to reduce their societies."[69] He does not offer a population
unit: to do so would mean progressive dissection of the states,
which could only result in confusion and disorder.

The relation between state and federal governments is in
part one of coördination, in part one of subordination of the
former to the latter. "Comparing the two governments together, it is observable that in all those cases where the independent or reserved rights of the States are in question, the two
executives, if they are to act together, must be exactly coördinate;
they are, in these cases, each supreme head of an independent
government. In other cases, to wit, those transferred by the
Constitution to the General Government, the general executive
is certainly preordinate."[70] While the country was still governed under the Articles of Confederation, he had opposed the
land office plan for dividing the new lands among the states to
be sold, on the ground that it "separates still more the interests
of the States, which ought to be made joint in every possible
instance, in order to cultivate the idea of our being one nation,
and to multiply the instances in which the people shall look up
to Congress as their head."[71]

The distinction between the powers of the state and those
of the union he sums up briefly: "To the united nation belongs
our external and mutual relations; to each State severally the
care of our persons, our property, our reputation, and religious
freedom. This wise distribution, if carefully preserved, will
prove, I trust from example, that while smaller governments

[68] To Monroe, July 9, 1786, *ibid.*, V, 259-60.
[69] To Madison, Dec. 16, 1789, *ibid.*, VI, 9-10.
[70] To Monroe, July 11, 1801, *ibid.*, X, 267.
[71] To Monroe, July 17, 1785, *ibid.*, V, 13-14.

are better adapted to the ordinary objects of society, larger con-
federations more effectually secure independence and the preservation of republican government."[72]   Well enough, as far
as theoretical reasoning goes.   But is the distinction capable of
preservation? and if so, how?   Writing in regard to the advisability of revising the Virginia constitution, Jefferson declares
that he wishes "to preserve the line drawn by the federal constitution between general and particular governments as it stands
at present, and to take every prudent means of preventing
either from stepping over it.   Though the experiment has not
yet had a long enough course to show us from which quarter
encroachments are most to be feared, yet it is easy to foresee,
from the nature of things, that the encroachments of the State
governments will tend to an excess of liberty which will correct
itself, . . . while those of the General Government will tend
to monarchy, which will fortify itself from day to day, instead
of working its own cure, as all experience shows.   I would rather
be exposed to the inconveniences attending too much liberty,
than those attending too small a degree of it.   Then it is important to strengthen the State governments; and as this cannot
be done by any change in the federal constitution . . . it must
be done by the States themselves, erecting such barriers at the
constitutional line as cannot be surmounted either by themselves
or by the General Government.   The only barrier in their power
is a wise government.   A weak one will lose ground in every
contest."[73]

So real does he believe the danger of encroachment by the
federal government on the rights of the states to be, that he
advocates as a last resort the weapon of nullification by the
states, if the central authority oversteps in their opinion the
limits prescribed to it by the constitution.   With the exercise
of wisdom and forbearance by both parties, however, these conflicts can be largely avoided.   "I have always thought that
where the line of demarcation between the powers of the Gen-

[72] To the General Assembly of Rhode Island, May 26, 1801, *ibid.*, X, 263.
[73] To Stuart, Dec. 23, 1791, *ibid.*, VIII, 276-77.

eral and State governments was doubtfully or indistinctly drawn, it would be prudent and praiseworthy in both parties, never to approach it but under the most urgent necessity."[74]

The state governments are to be organized along the same lines as those laid down in the federal constitution, with tripartite division into legislative, executive, and judiciary branches. But for more intimate details of administration, the state is divided into counties, each with its court of law, and with its special duties to perform; and the basis on which the whole structure ultimately rests is a final division of the county into still smaller units, or wards, characterized by Jefferson as the "most fundamental measure for securing good government, and for instilling the principles and exercise of self-government into every fibre of every member of our commonwealth."[75]   The ward will serve at once the double purpose of giving to every citizen a direct share in the conduct of his government, and of performing efficiently the more minute, and consequently more important, administrative functions.

"Divide the counties into wards of such size that every citizen can attend, when called on, and act in person.   Ascribe to them the government of their wards in all things relating to themselves exclusively.   A justice, chosen by themselves, in each, a constable, a military company, a patrol, a school, the care of their own poor, their own portion of the public roads, the choice of one or more jurors to serve in some court, and the delivery, within their own wards, of their own votes for all elective officers of higher sphere, will relieve the county administration of nearly all its business, will have it better done, and by making every citizen an acting member of the government, and in the offices nearest and most interesting to him, will attach him by his strongest feelings to the independence of his country, and its republican Constitution.   The justices thus chosen by every ward, would constitute the county court, would do its judiciary business, direct roads and bridges, levy county and

[74] To Cabell, Jan. 17, 1814, *ibid.*, XIV, 83-84.
[75] *Ibid.*, p. 70.

poor rates, and administer all the matters of common interest to the whole county. These wards, called townships in New England, are the vital principle of their governments, and have proved themselves the wisest invention ever devised by the wit of man for the perfect exercise of self-government, and for its preservation. We should thus marshal our government into, 1, the general federal republic, for all concerns foreign and federal; 2, that of the State, for what relates to our own citizens exclusively; 3, the county republics, for the duties and concerns of the county; and 4, the ward republics, for the small, and yet numerous and interesting concerns of the neighborhood; and in government, as well as in every other business of life, it is by division and subdivision of duties alone, that all matters, great and small, can be managed to perfection. And the whole is cemented by giving to every citizen, personally, a part in the administration of the public affairs."[76]

The organization of the wards seems to have been first conceived as part of Jefferson's plan for education, but its significance for other purposes of government could not long be overlooked. It not only gives solidarity to the citizen body, but affords a sure means of making immediately effective that intangible but all-powerful force known as public opinion. "A general call of ward meetings by their wardens on the same day throughout the State, would at any time produce the genuine sense of the people on any required point, and would enable the State to act in mass." The gradation of authorities, too, forms in a very real sense a system of fundamental checks and balances. In the ward, if nowhere else, will the individual achieve a sense of oneness with the whole; a sense of individuality, too, in that he has his part to play in the drama, and with it a measure of self-realization. "Where every man is a sharer in the direction of his ward-republic, or of some of the higher ones, and feels that he is a participator in the government of affairs, not merely at an election one day in the year, but every

[76] To Kercheval, July 12, 1816, *ibid.*, XV, 37-8; cf. to Adams, Oct. 28, 1813, *ibid.*, XIII, 400; to Cabell, Feb. 2, 1816, *ibid.*, XIV, 422.

day; when there shall not be a man in the State who will not be a member of some one of its councils, great or small, he will let the heart be torn out of his body sooner than his power be wrested from him by a Caesar or a Bonaparte."[77]

Here again Jefferson rests his case on the assumption, historically unjustified, that government is everybody's affair; and that the common man, if only he be given an opportunity, can and will manage the public concerns wisely and efficiently. It is seldom indeed that the common man will allow social responsibilities to interfere with private ends. But the fact that, now and again, some great spirit sprung from the masses has achieved the heights—the fact that the way lies open to all who have the courage, the talent and the will—may in itself be sufficient justification of democracy.

[77] To Cabell, *ibid.*

CHAPTER VII

THE FUNCTIONS OF GOVERNMENT

I

THE FUNCTIONS of government may be broadly divided into repressive and productive: into those which restrain the few for the protection of the many, and those which open the way to the larger life. The first are necessary if the independent existence of the state is to be preserved; the second are essential if the state is to achieve as its end the happiness of the mass of its citizens. Although Jefferson never explicitly made such a distinction, he fully appreciated its implications, and included both functions among the duties he assigned to the government. Repressive functions, in his system, extend to police power and national defense—the protection of the individual or the group from internal or external infringement of guaranteed rights. Productive functions include the regulation or encouragement of agriculture, commerce and industry, public works, education, and in general all that the twentieth century knows as social legislation. Finance is a necessary correlative of any form of state activity; and the relation of the state to property, public and private, also falls under both heads. In so far as the state protects private property, it is a repressive function; but it goes beyond this negative attitude, as we shall see, and concerns itself with the just distribution and use of property as well as its security.

Local policing and its administration in the courts properly belongs to local and lesser members of the governmental hierarchy. Each is to determine its needs, create its organization, and devise its own method of finance. With this phase of the police power, Jefferson does not concern himself. With national defense, however, he was forced to come to grips; and if his attitude was to a considerable degree unpopular, he may be credited with the more sincerity in taking it. The maintenance of armed land and naval forces not only adds a tremendous item to the national budget, but adds measurably to the danger of war as well. Give one child in a group a stick, and he will immediately use it on one of his fellows; give a nation a large and well-equipped fighting force, and national honor becomes surprizingly touchy, national interests suddenly discover previously unnoticed threats. So Jefferson writes, "I am for relying, for internal defense, on our militia solely, till actual invasion, and for such a naval force only as may protect our coasts and harbors from such depredations as we have experienced; and not for a standing army in time of peace, which may overawe the public sentiment; nor for a navy, which, by its own expenses and the eternal wars in which it will implicate us, will grind us with public burthens, and sink us under them."[1] He finds the maintenance of armed harbors inconsistent with his republican principles, and goes so far as to doubt the constitutionality of establishing a military academy.[2]

Jefferson was essentially a man of peace. But he had seen too much of war to believe peace could be maintained without creating a reputation for strength. His opposition to a standing army and navy is based on the conviction that national power depends on something deeper than a show of military force. If he believes there should be no army, it is because he would make every citizen a potential fighting man. "This was the case with the Greeks and Romans, and must be that of every free State. Where there is no oppression there will be no pauper hirelings. We must train and classify the whole of our male citizens, and make military instruction a part of collegiate education. We can never be safe till this is done."[3]

In this statement there is perhaps a belated tribute to the courage and determination of the minute men of the revolution;

[1] To Gerry, Jan. 26, 1799, *Writings*, X, 77.

[2] *Anas*, *ibid.*, I, 409 ff.; see also Seventh Annual Message, *ibid.*, III, 447.

[3] To Monroe, June 18, 1813, *ibid.*, XIII, 261; cf. to Kosciusko, Feb. 26, 1810, *ibid.*, XII, 365 ff.

but there is a note of anxiety, too. He is writing in 1813, with
a war in progress—a war fought on American soil, and one in
which the American defense was directed with singular ineffi-
ciency. It would be an unwarranted invasion of the rights of
private property, however, to guard against such contingencies
in the future by forcing the people to maintain a standing army
sufficiently large to protect a sprawling, thinly settled nation,
bordered by none too friendly foreign powers on two sides, by
a wilderness on a third, and on the fourth by more than a
thousand miles of undefended and all but indefensible seacoast.
It is the duty of the state to protect the property of its citizens,
not alone from foreign intruders, but also from the tax burden
necessarily consequent upon the maintenance of a sizable army.
In a democracy, the people are the state; let the people, then,
protect their own property in cases which demand greater dis-
play of force than the militia can give. So might Pericles have
argued in rallying the Athenians to defend their homes against
Spartan invaders.

II

Although property is not regarded by Jefferson as a natural
right, it is of paramount importance to the society, and its preservation is one of the principal objects of government, just as it
is one of the primary reasons for entering into the social compact. But "preservation of property" does not imply preservation of inequality in the distribution of property. Just as
Jefferson went beyond Locke's theory of rights, he goes beyond
his theory of property—and beyond that of Adam Smith, too.

Locke had declared that the "supreme power cannot take
from any man any part of his property without his own consent,"[4] a dictum typical of the eighteenth-century attitude, and
one which was already a commonplace by the time Locke gave
it caste. It means that the law of the economic world is the
survival of the fittest; or in the more classic formulation of
Adam Smith, that the individual best promotes the interest of

---

[4] *Of Civil Government,* II, xi, 138; cf. Tawney, *Religion and the Rise of Capitalism,* pp. 257 ff.

society by following his own interest. The sphere of the state does not extend into the economic realm in which its citizens live and move and have their being. The result of this system, as Karl Marx was in due course to point out, is the concentration of property and wealth in the hands of a small and ever diminishing group, while the great mass of the people are being progressively dispossessed. It is then inevitable that the group possessing economic power will tend to dominate the councils of the state to the exclusion of those who are without resources.

That Jefferson saw these results clearly may well be doubted; but he had at least followed the general line of reasoning far enough to be convinced that the power of the state must be used to eliminate the more extreme inequalities of property, for the social good. His draft of the Virginia constitution of 1776 provides for the distribution by the state of all unappropriated or forfeited lands, so that "Every person of full age neither owning nor having owned fifty acres of land, shall be entitled to an appropriation of fifty acres or to so much as shall make up what he owns or has owned fifty acres in full and absolute dominion. And no other person shall be capable of taking an appropriation."[5] The abolition of primogeniture is a means of breaking up large estates, and providing against a class of disinherited younger sons; and Jefferson's bill to abolish entails[6] was the first effective blow at the landowning aristocracy of Virginia. But in a letter written in 1785, he clearly implies that the power of the state to interfere with private property should go even farther than this.

"I am conscious that an equal division of property is impracticable, but the consequences of this enormous inequality producing so much misery to the bulk of mankind, legislators cannot invent too many devices for subdividing property, only taking care to let their subdivisions go hand in hand with the natural affections of the human mind. The descent of property of every kind therefore to all the children, or to all the brothers and sisters, or other relations in equal degree, is a politic meas-

---

[5] *Writings* (Ford Edition), II, 25.   [6] *Ibid.*, pp. 103 ff.

ure and a practicable one. Another means of silently lessening the inequality of property is to exempt all from taxation below a certain point, and to tax the higher portions of property in geometrical progression as they rise. Whenever there are in any country uncultivated lands and unemployed poor, it is clear that the laws of property have been so far extended as to violate natural right. The earth is given as a common stock for man to labor and live on. If for the encouragement of industry we allow it to be appropriated, we must take care that other employment be provided for those excluded from the appropriation. If we do not, the fundamental right to labor the earth returns to the unemployed. It is too soon yet in our country to say that every man who cannot find employment, but who can find uncultivated land, shall be at liberty to cultivate it, paying a moderate rent. But it is not too soon to provide by every possible means that as few as possible shall be without a little portion of land. The small landholders are the most precious part of a state."[7]

We have here an organic conception of society, in opposition to Locke's individualism. The state is a whole, of which the component individuals are parts, and the property rights conceded to each are conditional on their compatibility with the good of the whole. Such a view was not altogether unheard of in Jefferson's day. Before the middle of the eighteenth century, Francis Hutcheson, one of Adam Smith's predecessors in the chair of moral philosophy at Glasgow, had subjected the rights of property to a social limitation; and Priestley, at the time Jefferson is writing, advanced the principle that the society has a right to use for the common good all property found or acquired within its territorial limits.[8] Jefferson enjoyed the personal friendship of Priestley after the English chemist's removal to America in 1794, but it is hardly likely that he knew his theory earlier than that date. It is however reasonable to

[7] To the Rev. James Madison, Oct. 28, 1785, *Writings*, XIX, 17-18.

[8] Paschal Larkin, *Property in the Eighteenth Century* (London and New York), pp. 96 ff., 126; see Francis Hutcheson, *A System of Moral Philosophy* (2 vols. London, 1755), I, 319 ff.

suppose that he had read Hutcheson's writings early enough to have been influenced by them, even though there is no evidence that he was actually so influenced. There is also a property limitation in Harrington, who, as we have seen, was known to Jefferson, and the ancient Spartan division of land is detailed in Thucydides, one of his favorite writers. But whether he got it from any one of these possible sources, or developed it independently, the doctrine itself is well in advance of his day: so far in advance that Adam Smith, in terms of it, is reactionary.[9]

Nor is this theory of property the product of a momentary gleam of insight on Jefferson's part, to be put by and forgotten when the circumstances evoking it had passed. The draft of the Virginia constitution, and the bill to abolish entails date from 1776; but in 1807 he was still seeking to limit, on the authority of the state, the property rights of individuals for the social advantage of the whole. The embargo of that year he conceived to be motivated by this principle, which seems entirely consistent with his political philosophy as a whole. Still later, in 1816, he speaks of the law of "equal inheritance to all in equal degree" as a safeguard against the "overgrown wealth" of a few individuals; and if, at seventy-three, he believes it sufficient in itself, it is presumably because he has found it so in practice, after forty years of its operation in Virginia.[10] It is rather for a later generation, which has seen the steady increase of unemployment in the midst of plenty, to push the principle to its indicated end.

III

The individualistic theory of property as held in eighteenth-century England regarded education also as a private enterprize; but in Jefferson's philosophy, both go overboard together. Among the productive functions of government, he places education foremost, with an emphasis on which too much insistence cannot be placed. And he is altogether consistent in doing this. If the end of government is the happiness of the mass of its citizens in the broadest sense; if the ultimate purpose

[9] Cf. Larkin, *op. cit.*, pp. 97-98.   [10] See sec. V, below.

of the state is to make possible for the individual the abundant life, which sets spiritual above material values; then education for all in the highest degree to which each is capable of assimilating it is surely an essential means to that end. "No other sure foundation can be devised, for the preservation of freedom and happiness."[11]

There is no better foundation, either, for the maintenance of peace and order. "And say, finally, whether peace is best preserved by giving energy to the government, or information to the people. This last is the most certain, and the most legitimate engine of government. Educate and inform the whole mass of the people. Enable them to see that it is their interest to preserve peace and order, and they will preserve them. And it requires no very high degree of education to convince them of this. They are the only reliance for the preservation of our liberty."[12]   And if education is the most legitimate engine of government, it is also the most certain bulwark of the people against oppression in the name of government. Jefferson is convinced that "to open the doors of truth, and to fortify the habit of testing everything by reason, are the most effectual manacles we can rivet on the hands of our successors to prevent their manacling the people with their own consent."[13]

He accordingly proposes in one of his presidential messages to Congress that education should be assumed as an object of public care, and that a national establishment for that purpose be endowed.[14]   At a later date he prepared in minute detail an *Act for Establishing Elementary Schools*, the provisions of which compass a complete system of universal public education.[15]   The *Act* relates specifically to the state of Virginia, but it is such as could be applied without change to any territorial unit of whatever size, and Jefferson no doubt entertained the

[11] To Wythe, Aug. 13, 1786, *Writings*, V, 396.

[12] To Madison, Dec. 20, 1787, *ibid.*, VI, 392.

[13] To Judge Tyler, June 28, 1804, *ibid.*, XI, 34.

[14] Sixth Annual Message, *ibid.*, III, 423-24; see also A Bill for the More General Diffusion of Knowledge, *Writings* (Ford Edition), II, 220.

[15] *Writings*, XVII, 418 ff.

lingering hope that it would be so applied. It provides first for the division of the state into wards, of such size as to be able to raise a company of militia: five or six square miles, he estimates;[16] with the establishment in each ward of a school, in which is to be taught "reading, writing, numerical arithmetic and geography." At this school "shall be received and instructed gratis every infant of competent age who has not already had three years' schooling. And it is declared and enacted, that no person unborn or under the age of twelve years at the passing of this act, and who is *compos mentis*, shall, after the age of fifteen years, be a citizen of this commonwealth until he or she can read readily in some tongue, native or acquired."

The *Act* then provides for the establishment of colleges in each of the nine districts into which the state was to be divided, comprising in each district about eighty square miles,[17] in which would be taught the "Greek, Latin, French, Spanish, Italian and German languages, English grammar, geography, ancient and modern, the higher branches of numerical arithmetic, the mensuration of land, the use of the globes, and the ordinary elements of navigation." And the culmination of the system is an university or central college, which shall offer courses in "history and geography, ancient and modern; natural philosophy, agriculture, chemistry and the theories of medicine; anatomy, zoölogy, botany, mineralogy and geology; mathematics, pure and mixed; military and naval science; ideology, ethics, the law of nature and of nations; law, municipal and foreign; languages, rhetoric, belles lettres, and the fine arts generally."

The Visitors, or governing body of the ward schools will make what seems to be an annual selection from each school of the pupil who has shown greatest promise after three years of training,[18] and whose parents are too poor to afford a college course, and will send him before the Visitors of his collegiate district. These latter will select the two most promising of the applicants, who will then attend college for five years at the

---

[16] To Adams, Oct. 28, 1813, *ibid.*, XIII, 399.

[17] To Cabell, Sept. 9, 1817, *ibid.*, XVII, 417.

[18] To Adams, Oct. 28, 1813, *ibid.*, XIII, 399; Randall, *Life of Jefferson*, I, 225.

public expense. After this period is over, the same Visitors will choose between the two the one who has proved himself most worthy, and send him for three more years to the University. Jefferson prefaces his *Act*, in a letter to Joseph C. Cabell, with the characteristic comment that "no matter how wrong, experience will amend it as we go along, and make it effectual in the end."[19]

Noteworthy among the principles embodied in the document is the educational qualification for citizenship. The child is not to be forced to attend school against the will of its parents; but education is offered, free to all who will avail themselves of it, and those who neglect the privilege are disfranchised. The notion seems first to have been suggested by a similar provision in a proposed Spanish constitution, the value of which Jefferson was quick to appreciate, saying of it that "there is one provision which will immortalize its inventors. It is that which, after a certain epoch, disfranchises every citizen who cannot read and write. This is new, and is the fruitful germ of the improvement of everything good, and the correction of everything imperfect in the present constitution. This will give you an enlightened people, and an energetic public opinion which will control and enchain the aristocratic spirit of the government."[20] It is a long step in advance for democratic theory when it recognizes an educational qualification for the suffrage.

It will be readily seen that the college of Jefferson's plan is not at all the institution we designate by that name, but is rather an intermediate school of the type of the French lycée. It is meant to include, not only subjects preparatory to the university course, but technical and vocational training as well, for those who cannot, or do not care to go further.[21]

Jefferson's own primary interest in the educational field centered around the university, and the last years of his life were devoted to making his ideal a reality in the organization of the

---

[19] To Cabell, Sept. 9, 1817, *Writings*, XVII, 418.
[20] To Chevalier Luis de Onis, Apr. 28, 1814, *ibid.*, XIV, 130.
[21] To A. Coray, Oct. 31, 1823, *ibid.*, XV, 487-88; cf. to Peter Carr, Sept. 7, 1814, *ibid.*, XIX, 211 ff.

University of Virginia. A few of the features he incorporated in it are of sufficient interest to be mentioned here. The general scheme of the university is utilitarian: to teach "all the branches of science useful *to us,* and *at this day.*"[22] But it includes more than this. It includes the basis of that broad culture which alone renders civilization tolerable. Religious freedom is, of course, fundamental; and theology is specifically excluded. Students may attend any religious service they desire, or none if they prefer, although moral instruction will be deemed essential.[23]

The university is to be divided into eight groups, or schools, and the student is left perfectly free to attend any he may choose.[24] Nor will courses be prescribed for him to follow. "We shall, on the contrary, allow them uncontrolled choice in the lectures they shall choose to attend, and require elementary qualification only, and sufficient age. Our institution will proceed on the principle of doing all the good it can without consulting its own pride or ambition; of letting every one come and listen to whatever he thinks may improve the condition of his mind."[25] The only instance of a dogmatic prescription of any kind is in the selection of "text and documents" for the school of law as relates to government. The texts are Locke's second *Treatise,* and Sydney's *Discourses;* and the documents are the *Declaration of Independence,* the *Federalist,* the *Virginia Resolutions* of 1799, and Washington's *Farewell Address.*[26] And in this choice there is perhaps an element of pardonable pride. Two of the documents are the work of Jefferson himself; and the *Federalist* was in part written by Madison, who served with Jefferson on the board of Visitors, and succeeded his friend as its secretary.

It is also worthy of notice that the university included a dis-

---

[22] To Dr. Thomas Cooper, Aug. 25, 1814, *ibid.,* XIV, 173; see also to Cooper, Oct. 7, 1814, *ibid.,* XIV, 200.

[23] Minutes of Board of Visitors, etc., *ibid.,* XIX, 413 ff.

[24] *Ibid.,* p. 443.

[25] To George Ticknor, July 16, 1823, *ibid.,* XV, 455.

[26] Minutes, etc., *ibid.,* XIX, 460-61.

pensary, where "all *poor*, free persons, disordered in body, topically or generally, and applying for advice, shall receive it *gratis*," and others at a nominal fee. All were to receive free vaccination, and were encouraged to do so.[27] This implicit recognition of the responsibility of the state towards its poor is another corollary of its utilitarian end. If the state were perfect, there would be no poverty; but since no state can ever attain more than a small measure of perfection, it must make up, as best it can, for its defects. Poor relief has already been specified as among the functions of the ward organization.

Nor is public education limited to the operation of a public school system. The general circulation of books and papers is equally important. Thus during his first administration, Jefferson advocated the abolition of postage on newspapers, "to facilitate the progress of information";[28] and in 1809, well before the outline of the school system had matured, he proposed the establishment in each county of a circulating library.[29]

While schools were still a luxury and education the privilege of the few, Jefferson proposed universal elementary training at the public expense; and while the older colleges were still dominated, each by the dogma of its own theology, he built a liberal university dedicated to freedom of thought and investigation. He knew that the democratic state can prosper only in proportion to the intelligence and integrity of its citizens, and he sought to impress this truth, by word and by example, on the statesmen of his day. Nor were his labors without their due reward. America came at length to acknowledge its responsibility for the intellectual well-being of its children, and though of slow growth, a public school system closely resembling Jefferson's plan has been evolved. Through the *Notes on Virginia* his influence was exerted in France on the foundations of a system that was to reach its fruition under the Third Republic,[30] and the scheme of the university attracted the interest of Goethe in remote Weimar.

[27] *Ibid.*, p. 489.
[29] *Ibid.*, III, 322.
[28] Randall, *op. cit.*, II, 681.
[30] Chinard, *Thomas Jefferson*, p. 98.

IV

Jefferson lived and wrote in a period which saw the national state climbing rapidly towards its greatest development; and the national state is necessarily founded on economic self-sufficiency. Prosperity, therefore, depends on a balance between agriculture, manufactures, and commerce. "An equilibrium of agriculture, manufactures, and commerce, is certainly become essential to our independence. Manufactures, sufficient for our own consumption, of what we raise the raw material (and no more). Commerce sufficient to carry the surplus produce of agriculture, beyond our consumption, to a market for exchanging it for articles we cannot raise (and no more). These are the limits of manufactures and commerce. To go beyond them is to increase our dependence on foreign nations, and our liability to war."[31] He reasons with incisive logic that the necessity of protecting a far-flung commercial activity brings in its train imperialism and war, and he would reduce the danger as much as possible by keeping commerce within reasonable bounds. But when he has gone so far, he has acknowledged that the state is no longer self-sufficing. Like the Greek city-state, the national state was outgrown even before it reached its zenith.

And there is a further implication, namely, that the self-sufficient state is ill-adapted to fulfill the end of securing to its citizens the greatest degree of happiness. For Jefferson himself had observed that in general, "it is a truth that if every nation will employ itself in what it is fittest to produce, a greater quantity will be raised of the things contributing to human happiness, than if every nation attempts to raise everything it wants within itself."[32] Here is a plain enough admission that the state must look beyond its own boundaries if it is adequately to fulfill its ethical end.

Jefferson was the early and outstanding advocate of "free commerce with all nations, political connection with none"; but

[31] To Gov. James Jay, Apr. 7, 1809, *Writings*, XII, 271; cf. to Thomas Leiper, Jan. 21, 1809, *ibid.*, p. 238.

[32] To M. Lasteyrie, July 15, 1808, *ibid.*, pp. 91-92.

free commerce does not mean unregulated commerce. It is free only in the sense that one citizen is as free to engage in it as the next. Some form of commercial regulation by Congress is necessary, or wars will be inevitable.[33] And where he believed, in 1800, that the merchants would manage commercial enterprises the better the more they were left free to manage for themselves, he was convinced, by 1816, that his country faced the necessity of choosing between two alternatives: "1, licentious commerce and gambling speculations for a few, with eternal war for the many; or, 2, restricted commerce, peace, and steady occupations for all."[34] Commercial wars with France and England during his own administration, together with the difficulties experienced in his attempt to enforce the embargo, served to dampen materially his ardor for free commerce; and the issue was finally forced by the war of 1812, which led the younger republican leaders to go over to the side of protection.

The function of government in the fields of commerce and industry, however, is limited to regulation. The enterprizes themselves are to be carried on by individuals. The reason is two-fold. They will be better managed by those who seek a profit from them; and it is material "not to abstract the high executive officers from those functions which nobody else is charged to carry on, and employ them in works which are going on abundantly in private hands."[35] This is not to say that the state should not take a paternal interest in the development of its resources to the uttermost, where the greater good of its citizens may result; but the state is to play the rôle of patron, rather than that of initiator. Jefferson believes mutual coöperation between individuals for the improvement of knowledge and methods is the surest way to advancement, in agriculture and commerce no less than industry and the arts; and it is on

[33] To Monroe, June 17, 1785, *ibid.*, V, 16 ff.; to Adams, July 7, 1785; *ibid.*, pp. 31 ff.; cf. to Gerry, Jan. 26, 1799, *ibid.*, X, 77.

[34] To Crawford, June 20, 1816, *ibid.*, XV, 29; cf. to Gideon Granger, Aug. 13, 1800, *ibid.*, X, 168.

[35] To R. W. Bibb, July 28, 1808, *ibid.*, XII, 108; cf. to W. C. C. Claiborne, July 17, 1808, *ibid.*, p. 97.

this principle that he suggested a state-wide system of agricultural societies, organized in county units, to aid in the dissemination of agricultural knowledge, improvement of methods and introduction of new crops. It is an idea familiar enough, both in theory and in practice, to the American farmer of today.

It will be remembered, also, that the policy of internal improvements at government expense was inaugurated by Jefferson, and included a coast survey, river and harbor improvements, and the construction of roads and canals. At the suggestion of Gallatin, Ohio was admitted to the union in 1803[35a] with the provision that one-twentieth of the net proceeds from the sale of lands within the state should be applied to the building of roads from the Atlantic seaboard to the Ohio valley; and in 1806 Congress appropriated $30,000 for the Cumberland Pike, which was to be only a beginning. Public works, the benefit of which would be felt by large numbers of citizens, were within the scope of governmental activity as Jefferson conceived it, even though they might be of doubtful constitutionality; and he sought, as Madison and Monroe sought later, to put the improvement program beyond question by constitutional amendment.[36]

Jefferson stands at the vague line of demarcation separating one era from another; and though he lived too early to conceive of the large-scale industrial and agricultural enterprizes of today, he felt unmistakably the unrest and uneasiness preceding the birth pangs of a capitalistic industrialism. There is a note of real regret in his letters as he looks down from his quiet retreat at Monticello and sees the old physiocratic order disintegrating. His ideal would have been a society built up on a plantation basis, with the family as the central unit; a society of landowners, with each establishment as nearly self-sufficing as possible, producing its own food, timber, and raw materials, with home industry replacing manufacture. He would have

[35a] *United States Statutes at Large*, II, 175.—The Enabling Act was passed April 30, 1802, but territorial government was still in effect until March 1, 1803.
[36] Channing, *History of the United States*, V, 6-7, 317.

imported only luxuries, for those who could afford them, and in general even these he would have discouraged.[37]

He knew, however, that a system admirably adapted to Virginia could not be carried out successfully in New England. He followed and approved the manufacturing and commercial ventures of his northern countrymen; and through the influence of Gallatin, came to regard them with increasing favor towards the close of his administration.[38] After the opening of the nineteenth century, it was no longer possible to deny with Quesnay that industry and commerce as well as agriculture were sources of national wealth. Adam Smith's arguments were not to be ignored, even by so staunch an agrarian as Thomas Jefferson. His only recorded objection to the *Wealth of Nations* is that the book is too long and too dull to suit its purposes;[39] and he endorsed without reserve the less cumbersome summaries of J. B. Say and Destutt de Tracy. Nor was he satisfied with mere lip service to the gods of the new industrialism. He had himself studied the application of steam to manufacture and transportation, and had been foremost among his contemporaries in applying the new forces in his chosen province, that of agriculture. Even while clinging fondly to the old agrarian order, he helped prepare the way for the industrial revolution in America.

What Jefferson feared above all was the growth of a capitalistic class; and he failed to realize that industry could proceed only by the investment of increasingly large sums of money. The embargo of 1807 gave the first impetus to large-scale production in America, and the war of 1812 served to establish the factory system. While commerce was at a standstill, capital formerly invested in shipping was turned to the manufacture of products once supplied by Great Britain, the total investment in New England increasing from half a million dollars when the embargo was laid to forty millions at the close of the war seven years later.[40] The same period saw fourteen

---

[37] To John Melish, Jan. 13, 1813, *Writings*, XIII, 207 ff.
[38] Channing, *The Jeffersonian System*, p. 257.
[39] To Joseph Milligan, Apr. 6, 1816, *Writings*, XIV, 460.
[40] Allen Johnson, *Union and Democracy* (Boston and New York, 1915), pp. 234-35.

steamboats plying the western rivers, while steam was rapidly replacing water power in manufacture. It was in 1814 that Lowell introduced the power loom at Waltham, Massachusetts, and consolidated in one plant all the processes of cotton manufacture.

To these developing enterprizes the peace was disastrous. For English manufacturers seized the opportunity to flood the market at low prices with their accumulated goods, which even import duties failed to restrain. Lord Brougham explained the policy to Parliament with engaging frankness. "It was well worth while," he argued, "to incur a loss upon the first exportation, in order, by a glut, to stifle in the cradle those rising manufactures in the United States which the war had forced into existence, contrary to the natural course of things."[41] And before the close of the year 1815 most of the New England textile mills had been forced to shut down. Relief from the government was demanded; and Jefferson, watching from his retirement the crumbling of the old agricultural order, conceded its necessity. He had reached at length the conclusion that "to be independent for the comforts of life, we must fabricate them for ourselves. We must now place the manufacturer by the side of the agriculturalist."[42]

Congress responded in 1816 with a protective tariff. Webster supported the measure to the extent of advocating protection for existing industries; but Calhoun spoke for the new age when he demanded encouragement for future enterprizes as well. "Neither agriculture, manufactures, nor commerce, taken separately, is the source of wealth. It flows from the three combined and cannot exist without each."[43] The average duty was raised by the tariff of 1816 from the seven and one-half per cent of 1789 to thirty per cent, committing the country to a policy in which industrial needs were placed above revenue. So far had the republicans gone on the road towards nationalism that, less than a decade after the retirement of Jefferson, the

[41] *Ibid.*, pp. 235-36.
[42] To Benjamin Austin, Jan. 9, 1816, *Writings*, XIV, 391.
[43] *Annals of Congress*, 14th Cong., 1st sess. 1815-1816, pp. 1329-36.

policy of the party in power had merged with that of the older federalist opposition; and even the aged leader looked down from his mountain-top not altogether disapprovingly.

v

Running the machinery of a state is not a business, although it may be a profession; and its financial system is not designed to create a profit for those in charge of it, but exists only to meet the legitimate expenses of government. Expenses, however, there must be; and some system of revenue, so adjusted that its burdens fall as equitably as possible upon the citizens, is a first essential. Jefferson would add that it is equally essential the people should understand the system of finance. "The accounts of the United States ought to be, and may be made as simple as those of a common farmer."[44]

Now there are only two ways of raising revenue, in a state which is forbidden to enter the industrial lists on its own account: by some form of taxation, or by borrowing; and since money borrowed must ultimately be repaid, no system of state finance can be soundly based on any principle other than taxation. This therefore is the basis Jefferson advocates. His theory of taxation is explained in detail in a letter intended as a preface to an American edition of Destutt de Tracy's *Treatise on Political Economy*:

"The taxes . . . class themselves readily according to the basis on which they rest. 1. Capital. 2. Income. 3. Consumption. These may be considered as commensurate; Consumption being generally equal to Income, and Income to the annual profit of Capital. A government may select either of these bases for the establishment of its system of taxation, and so frame it as to reach the faculties of every member of the society, and to draw from him his equal proportion of the public contributions; and, if this be correctly obtained, it is the perfection of the function of taxation. But when once a government has assumed its basis, to select and tax special articles from either

44 To Madison, Mar. 6, 1796, *Writings*, IX, 324.

of the other classes is double taxation. For example, if the system be established on the basis of Income, and his just proportion on that scale has been already drawn from every one, to step into the field of Consumption, and tax special articles in that, as broadcloth or homespun, wine or whisky, a coach or a wagon, is doubly taxing the same article. For that portion of Income with which these articles are purchased, having already paid its tax as Income, to pay another tax on the thing it purchased, is paying twice for the same thing; it is an aggrievance on the citizens who use these articles in exoneration of those who do not, contrary to the most sacred duties of a government, to do equal and impartial justice to all its citizens.

"How far it may be the interest and duty of all to submit to this sacrifice on other grounds, for instance, to pay for a time an impost on the importation of certain articles, in order to encourage their manufacture at home, or an excise on others injurious to the morals or health of the citizens, will depend on a series of considerations of another order. . . .

"To this a single observation shall yet be added. Whether property alone, and the whole of what each citizen possesses, shall be subject to contribution, or only its surplus after satisfying his first wants, or whether the faculties of body and mind shall contribute also from their annual earnings, is a question to be decided. But, when decided, and the principle settled, it is to be equally and fairly applied to all. To take from one, because it is thought his own industry and that of his fathers has acquired too much, in order to spare to others, who, or whose fathers have not exercised equal industry and skill, is to violate arbitrarily the first principle of association, 'the *guarantee* to every one a free exercise of his industry, and the fruits acquired by it.' If the overgrown wealth of an individual be deemed dangerous to the State, the best corrective is the law of equal inheritance to all in equal degree; and the better, as this enforces a law of nature, while extra-taxation violates it."[45]

Such is the theory of taxation; but there are still certain

[45] To Joseph Milligan, Apr. 6, 1816, *ibid.*, XIV, 464 ff.

empirical qualifications to be added to it. Jefferson sees grave
danger in making a government, when in power, independent
of its revenue;[46] and accordingly lays down the principle that
no tax "should be yielded for a longer term than that of the
Congress wanting it, except when pledged for the reimburse-
ment of a loan."[47] He has also some remarks to make on the
equalization of taxes on articles of consumption, declaring that
"the government which steps out of the ranks of the ordinary
articles of consumption to select and lay under disproportionate
burdens a particular one, because it is a comfort, pleasing to the
taste, or necessary to health, and will therefore be bought, is,
in that particular, a tyranny. Taxes on consumption like those
on capital or income, to be just, must be uniform. I do not
mean to say that it may not be for the general interest to foster
for a while certain infant manufactures until they are strong
enough to stand against foreign rivals; but when evident they
will never do so, it is against right, to make the other branches
of industry support them."[48]

To the borrowing of money by the government, Jefferson
objects on principle, chiefly because, deprived of the power, war
could not be declared without the consent of the states.[49] He
is willing to concede, however, that power to borrow money
may at times be necessary; and when it is so, it is a duty on the
part of the citizens to lend what they can. But he adds the
usual safeguard. "It is a wise rule, and should be fundamental
in a government disposed to cherish its credit, and at the same
time to restrain the use of it within the limits of its faculties,
'never to borrow a dollar without laying a tax in the same in-
stant for paying the interest annually, and the principle within
a given term; and to consider that tax as pledged to the creditors
on the public faith.' On such a pledge as this, sacredly observed,
a government may always command, on a *reasonable interest*,
all the lendable money of their citizens, while the necessity of

[46] To ———, Aug. 13, 1776, *ibid.*, IV, 276.
[47] To John W. Eppes, Sept. 11, 1813, *ibid.*, XIII, 355.
[48] To Gen. Samuel Smith, May 3, 1823, *ibid.*, XV, 432-33.
[49] To John Taylor, Nov. 26, 1798, *ibid.*, X, 64-65.

an equivalent tax is a salutary warning to them and their constituents against oppressions, bankruptcy, and its inevitable
consequence, revolution. But the term of redemption must be
moderate, and at any rate within the limits of their rightful
powers."[50]

The limit which will prevent the creation of a perpetual
debt is prescribed by the law of nature. He argues that the
world belongs, for their use, to those who live in it, and the
will of a man must expire with his life. Estimating from Buf-
fon's tables that of all the adults living at a given moment, one
half will be dead in eighteen years, eight months, the conclusion
follows that "at nineteen years . . . from the date of a contract,
a majority of the contractors are dead, and their contract with
them." No public debt, then, should be contracted without
providing for its full payment in not more than nineteen
years.[51]

To the federal government alone, as the highest central
authority, belongs the right to issue circulating money; and
Jefferson was inclined, in the early years of the republic, to
question even its power to make paper money good as legal
tender.[52] He had passed through a period of crazy speculation
and uncontrollable inflation, and had lived to see the bottom
drop out. It is no wonder that he was skeptical of anything but
gold. And it might be added that his philippic against the
bubble of paper finance would sound strangely familiar to
modern ears.[53]

[50] To Eppes, June 24, 1813, *ibid.*, XIII, 269.
[51] *Ibid.*, pp. 269 ff.
[52] To Taylor, Nov. 26, 1798, *ibid.*, X, 65; see also to Eppes, June 24, 1813, *ibid.*,
XIII, 269.
[53] See letter to Yancey, Jan. 6, 1816, *ibid.*, XIV, 379 ff.

BOOK III

THE REIGN OF LAW

... For the letter killeth, but the spirit giveth life.

—PAUL TO THE CORINTHIANS

CHAPTER VIII

THE NATURE OF LAW

I

LIKE SO MANY of the dominating figures in the formative period of American institutions, Thomas Jefferson was a lawyer of considerable ability. A poor speaker, his success at the bar and in public office was largely due to broad scholarship, clear reasoning, and a compelling force of diction in stating an argument. He won cases as he won partisans, through a genius for formulating and vitalizing the principles upon which decisions were to be made. He never stated a conclusion without explaining the premises from which he drew it; and by piecing together these principles, expressed in various cases, public utterances, and private correspondence, it is possible to reconstruct a fairly complete philosophy of law—a philosophy which has more adherents today than it had when Jefferson propounded it.

Jefferson's jurisprudence does not follow the natural law theory as closely as one would be led to expect, considering his advocacy of the natural rights doctrine. Although he starts from the natural law premise of an intimate connection between law and morals, he goes beyond this more or less restricted view in the direction of socialization of the law. The ultimate end of law is abstract justice, an ethical concept; but law is also an instrument of social control. Although certain "natural" principles which are ascertainable by reason establish bounds beyond which it cannot go, and it is thus in a sense "discovered," law is also made, to provide means of accomplishing specific ends.[1] Positive laws are merely declaratory of universal moral principles; but those principles may be so declared as to achieve constructive social results.

[1] To Gallatin, Aug. 11, 1808, *Writings*, XII, 122.

Jefferson holds, with Montesquieu, that there is a necessary inner connection between the forms of the state, and law. His own experience had taught him that however nature and reason may have given universal principles of right to men, man himself must make his laws to fit his own requirements; and he must not hesitate to change them when they no longer serve their end. Law is not to be externally imposed on the members of a given society, without reference to their needs, but is rather to be molded and adapted to the peculiar character of the people.

The Jeffersonian state is essentially a legal state, and the equality of men is in the end an equality before the law. The principle is laid down in the *Declaration of Independence* in the same sense in which it appears in the Roman law: men are equal, not in wealth, or talent, or intelligence, but they are equal in the eyes of the law. The law is the common factor in the state which affects all men in the same way. In the legal state, the natural rights of man become the civil rights of citizenship: the rights guaranteed to men under the law.

The democratic form of the state brings with it certain consequences with respect to its legal institutions. For, if the sovereignty belongs to the people, and the people alone choose their own lawmaking body, the consent of the people will be the ultimate sanction of law.[2] Jefferson's divergence from the legal theory implicit in the political philosophy of Hobbes, which has come down to us through Austin as analytical jurisprudence, is thus fundamental. In so far as Jefferson is capable of classification at all, he presents a compound of philosophical and social utilitarian legal thinking: he has gone beyond the former, but is not ready to go all the way with the latter. Although Austin, who was the actual founder of the analytical school, did not receive his appointment as professor of jurisprudence in the University of London until the year of Jefferson's death, the doctrine of the school is old enough to be treated as contemporary with the development of American legal thought. It was the theory on which Parliament acted in pre-

[2] To Edmund Randolph, Aug. 18, 1799, *ibid.*, X, 126-27.

cipitating the American revolution. It is based on the assumption of Hobbes that sovereignty is force, and through Bentham it arrived at the complete separation of jurisprudence and morals. The law as given was to be studied analytically, and the function of the jurist went no further. Law had no meaning unless translated into terms of action. Ethics belongs to legislation; but the making of law and its application and administration were regarded as functions of distinct branches of government, with no overlapping. Jefferson was too much a physiocrat to accept the divorce of morals from legal philosophy; and though he took over, even emphasized, the separation of powers, he never carried the dogma to the point of affirming one and only one source of interpretation for the law. Neither could he have accepted the dictum that power to enforce a given law is its only sanction. Law, like government itself, rests for Jefferson on the consent of the people, and on its own inherent reasonableness.

The "just mean" between a weak and relaxed government like that under the Articles of Confederation, and a monarchy, is "a government of laws addressed to the reason of the people and not to their weaknesses."[3] It will protect their interests by guaranteeing their rights; it will give them freedom by protecting them from arbitrary control, and by placing them under the rule of a law of which their own will is the sanction and their own reason the judge.

Law is not static and immutable, but growing, changing, expanding as man's horizon widens. And if it can furnish principles of right, valid for all time and every place, the rules of law themselves must vary as societies vary, must adapt themselves to the needs of a given people and the physical and economic conditions of a given state. So Jefferson points out that because, in the America of his day, horses were easy to steal and of great value to their owners, the law punished horse-stealing severely; while in Europe, where the crime was difficult and rare, the penalty was slight. On the other hand, it was in parts

[3] To T. M. Randolph, Jan. 7, 1793, *ibid.*, IX, 13.

of Europe a capital offense to steal fruit from the trees, while in America, where fruit was plentiful, it was not even a crime.[4]

Thus law serves an utilitarian end, dictated by the needs of the society; and where it defeats that end it is wrong. Jefferson suggests, for example, in a letter to Lafayette, that land tenure in France should follow the English model and grant a lease for three lives rather than for one. "But I am told the laws do not permit it. The laws then, in this particular, are unwise and unjust, and ought to give that permission."[5] The law defeats itself when its rules prevent the attainment of useful ends. It must be rational, just and impartial; and it must change as changing forces in the social life present new ends, new interests, new points of view. He cites the old law under which a Jew, as alien, could not sue, and speaks of its modification having been brought about through commerce. "Now commerce has taught the world more humanity."[6]

It would, hovever, be a mistake were the law to change too rapidly. Regarded as a means of social control, law will be effective only to the extent that the people have faith in its dependability; hence the old common law maxim that it is better for a law to be certain than for it to be just. There is grave danger, where a duly constituted lawmaking body exists, that statutes will multiply so rapidly as far to outstrip the agencies for making them effective. Jefferson recognizes the danger, and offers a solution. "The instability of our laws is really an immense evil. I think it would be well to provide in our constitutions, that there shall always be a twelvemonth between the engrossing a bill and passing it; that it should then be offered to its passage without changing a word; and that if circumstances should be thought to require a speedier passage, it should take two-thirds of both Houses instead of a bare majority."[7]

Mention has already been made of Jefferson's insistence on

---

[4] Observations on Article États Unis, etc., *ibid.*, XVII, 79-80.
[5] To Lafayette, Apr. 11, 1787, *ibid.*, VI, 108.
[6] *Commonplace Book*, p. 320.
[7] To Madison, Dec. 20, 1787, *Writings*, VI, 393.

the argument that one generation has no right legally to bind the next. The basis of this relativism he states in a letter to Madison. "I set out on this ground, which I suppose to be self-evident, that the *earth belongs in usufruct to the living; that the dead have neither powers nor rights over it.*" He reasons from this, as we have seen, that one generation cannot contract debts greater than it can itself pay off; and on similar ground "it may be proved, that no society can make a perpetual constitution, or even a perpetual law."[8] This principle is especially significant for Jefferson's philosophy of law in the light of a parallel assertion on the part of one of the leading exponents of the sociological or functional theory: as Dean Pound phrases it, "the average life of a statute is one generation."[9] Although not actually repealed, laws are seldom invoked after the period of their usefulness is past.

II

Like Montesquieu, also, and like Aristotle before him, Jefferson profited by an historical study of laws and institutions, and his debt to the English law is great. So also is the debt of America. Holding the growth of the law to be a process of progressive summation, and shearing away of outworn rules, Jefferson sees the laws of England as divided in their development into four distinct stages, at the conclusion of each of which a general review is made of what has gone before. The first of these summations is Bracton's *De Legibus Angliae;* the second, Coke's *Institutes;* the third, the *Abridgment of the Law* by Matthew Bacon; and the fourth, Blackstone's *Commentaries.* Bracton and Coke, noteworthy for their subjection of king and Parliament alike to the law, still stand as monuments in English legal evolution, but Bacon's work is now virtually forgotten, perhaps deservedly. It is totally different in character from the institutional works of Bracton, Coke, and Blackstone, which were

---

[8] To Madison, Sept. 6, 1789, *ibid.,* VII, 454 ff.; cf. to Washington, Apr. 25, 1794, *ibid.,* IX, 284; to Cartwright, June 5, 1824, *ibid.,* XVI, 48.

[9] *Evolution of Legal Rights,* Messenger Lectures, 1931 (unpublished); cf. *Interpretations of Legal History* (Cambridge and New York, 1923), p. 13.

in the nature of texts, but is one of the first attempts at combining a digest of the law with commentary, and is designed for the lawyer rather than for the student. Most of the *Abridgment* is simply a publication of the incomplete manuscripts of Lord Chief Baron Gilbert, which Bacon seems to have lacked energy or scholarship to revise.[10]

As for Blackstone, Jefferson finds that the *Commentaries,* although stylistically superior, is, like Justinian's *Institutes,* only an elementary work, making it still necessary to refer to the original writings of which it is a summary.[11]   He has no love for Blackstone on any ground, charging that his book, "although the most elegant and best digested of our law catalogue, has been perverted more than all others, to the degeneracy of legal science."   And in another passage, he avows that "Blackstone and Hume have made tories of all England, and are making tories of those young Americans whose native feelings of independence do not place them above the wily sophistries of a Hume or a Blackstone."[12]   Other legal writers who figure prominently in Jefferson's background are Lord Kames, the Scottish philosopher and jurist, whose *Historical Law Tracts* are abstracted in the *Commonplace Book;* and Sir John Dalrymple, whose *History of Feudal Property in Great Britain* follows next in order in Jefferson's notes.   Still more important was Beccaria, from whom he quotes at length, and who seems to have been responsible for most of the Virginian's views on criminal law.[13]

In colonial America, the English common law had been widely accepted by the courts, and by the time of the Revolution, it had gained so firm a hold that independence did not materially alter its status.   It was many years before American statute law was at all adequate to deal with such questions as might

---

[10] Matthew Bacon, *Abridgment of Law and Equity* (3 vols. London, 1736; 7th edition, 8 vols. 1832). Cf. P. H. Winfield, *Chief Sources of English Legal History* (Cambridge, 1925), pp. 242-43, 249-50.

[11] To Dr. Thomas Cooper, July 16, 1814, *Writings,* XIV, 54 ff.

[12] To Spafford, Mar. 17, 1814, *ibid.,* p. 120; see also to Judge Tyler, June 17, 1812, *ibid.,* XIII, 166 ff.

[13] *Commonplace Book,* pp. 557-69, 569-85, 806-32.

arise, and the judges found the common law system a convenient tool to consolidate their power. So the common law was treated by the courts as a part of American law, without legislative adoption, the doctrine being first announced by Chief Justice John Jay in charging the national grand jury at Richmond, May 22, 1793.[14] Such a doctrine, in the hands of a federalist bench, proved a powerful factor in party politics; and Jefferson made it an issue in the republican battle for control. To assume that the common law has validity in federal courts, he contended, would make possible the closing of the state courts altogether, since citizens of the same state could then sue under federal jurisdiction.[15] The common law was, however, conceded to be in force in those states which had adopted it as such; for the Judiciary Act of 1789, better known as the Conformity Act, declares that "what is law in any State shall be the rule of decision in their courts, as to matters arising within that State," except where controlled by federal statutes.[16] It was not until 1812 that the Supreme Court finally put an end to the doctrine that federal courts could sustain indictments under the English common law, where no American statute covered the case.[17]

It may be seriously questioned whether the common law has been or can be adopted apart from English statutes;[18] and Jefferson was unwilling to accept English statute law. A line must be drawn somewhere, and a point marked off, after which the English law no longer has validity in America. "The general assembly of Virginia," Jefferson writes in the *Notes on Virginia*, "was constituted . . . by letters-patent of March 9th, 1607, in the fourth year of the reign of James the first. The laws of England seem to have been adopted by consent of the settlers, which might easily enough be done whilst they were few and living all together. Of such adoption, however, we have no

---

[14] Beveridge, *Life of John Marshall*, III, 24-25.
[15] To Edmund Randolph, Aug. 18, 1799, *ibid.*, X, 125 ff.
[16] To Dr. John Manners, June 12, 1817, *ibid.*, XV, 125-26.
[17] United States *vs.* Hudson, 7 Cranch 32; see also Beveridge, *op. cit.*, III, 28.
[18] See Pope, "The English Common Law in the United States," *Harvard Law Review*, XXIV, 6.

other proof than their practice till the year 1661, when they were expressly adopted by an act of the assembly, except so far as 'a difference of condition' rendered them inapplicable. Under this adoption, the rule in our courts of judicature was, that the common law of England, and the general statutes previous to the fourth of James, were in force here; but that no subsequent statutes were, *unless we were named in them,* said the judges and other partisans of the crown, but *named or not named,* said those who reflected freely."[19]

Jefferson's knowledge of legal systems was too extensive, and his experience too wide, for him to commit himself to any single body of law; and if he cites the English law in one case to prove his point, he denies its validity in another on grounds of common sense. For example, he argues on the basis of the common law that debts due the soldiers of Virginia and North Carolina should be paid directly to the claimant rather than to any intermediary who may have bought the claim, such claims being non-transferable in common law.[20] While on the question as to whether American citizens and British subjects, born before the revolution, could be aliens to one another, he quotes Coke in Calvin's case, only to disagree with him, holding that "in this question, fictions of law alone are opposed to sound sense."[21] He had some familiarity, too, with Roman and French law, and did not hesitate to call on both for precedent.[22]

The civil code, Jefferson believes to be superior to the common law code, but objects to the incorporation of the two into a single body, which would be "like Nebuchadnezzar's image of metals and clay, a thing without cohesion of parts." And he expresses the opinion that the "only natural improvement of the common law, is through its homogeneous ally, the chancery, in which new principles are to be examined, concocted and digested. But when, by repeated decisions and modifications, they are rendered pure and certain, they should be transferred by statute to

[19] *Writings,* II, 182-83; cf. C. H. McIlwain, *The American Revolution,* p. 77.
[20] Official Papers, *Writings,* III, 21 ff.
[21] To Adams, Feb. 7, 1786, *ibid.,* V, 276-77.
[22] See the Batture at New Orleans, *ibid.,* XVIII, 1-132.

the courts of common law, and placed within the pale of ju-
ries."[23]

III

It is of highest moment that the law be wisely administered
and rigorously enforced. "The execution of the laws is more
important that the making of them."[24] It must be within reach
of all, and it must be applied in all cases with equal impartiality.
Hence, "the public security against a partial dispensation of
justice, depends on its being dispensed by certain rules. The
slightest deviation in one circumstance, becomes a precedent
for another, that for a third, and so on without bounds."[25] Yet
these rules of law must be interpreted by their judges with fair-
ness and common sense. Jefferson has no use for the technical-
ities so often used, in his day as in our own, to defeat justice. So
he declares that "whenever the words of a law will bear two
meanings, one of which will give effect to the law, and the
other will defeat it, the former must be supposed to have been
intended by the Legislature, because they could not intend that
meaning, which would defeat their intention, in passing that
law; and in a statute, as in a will, the intent of the party is to
be sought after."[26] And again, he writes that "where the words
of a statute will admit of two constructions, the one just and the
other unjust, the former is to be given them."[27] Cases which,
though within the letter of the law, are not within its intention,
are relievable by "an equitable exercise of discretionary power."[28]

Jefferson had affirmed that it "is not honorable to take a
mere legal advantage, when it happens to be contrary to justice";[29] and a specific case in which he was interested will serve
to illustrate the point. The case has to do with a patent granted
to a Mr. T. C. Martin, whose description of a "wheat-thrashing

---

[23] To Judge Tyler, June 17, 1812, *ibid.*, XIII, 166.
[24] To l'Abbé Arnould, July 19, 1789, *ibid.*, VII, 423.
[25] To George Joy, Mar. 31, 1790, *ibid.*, VIII, 10.
[26] To Gallatin, July 9, 1808, *ibid.*, XII, 110.
[27] To Isaac McPherson, Aug. 13, 1813, *ibid.*, XIII, 326.
[28] To Gallatin, Oct. 18, 1808, *ibid.*, XII, 173.
[29] Official Papers, *ibid.*, III, 25.

machine" had been recorded and the patent made out, when he thought of a further improvement, which he tried to have incorporated in the description without paying the fee for a second patent. Jefferson, as his attorney, writes of the matter to John Taylor: "I practiced a little art in a case where honesty was really on our side, and nothing against us but the rigorous letter of the law. . . ."[30]

He is consistent, too, in his principle that the law must give equal and impartial justice to all, high as well as low, and protests against what he considers a violation of it in England: the intended trial of Warren Hastings in special court (he was tried before the House of Lords), instead of King's Bench. "If he is cited before another court, that he may be judged, not according to the law of the land, but by the discretion of his judges, is he not disfranchised of his most precious right, the benefit of the laws of his country, in common with his fellow citizens?"[31] Those who sit in the high places are not above the law; and it would equally defeat the end designed if the poor man, simply because he was poor, could not secure from the courts equal protection with the rich. So he boasts that "by the laws of this country every individual claiming a right to any article of property, may demand process from a court of justice, and decision on the validity of his claim."[32] Jefferson also affirms the common doctrine that "ignorance of the law is no excuse in any country. If it were, the laws would lose their effect, because it can be always pretended."[33]

Administration of the law is essentially a pragmatic process in Jefferson's view. For the law is a means to an end. It is the end that is important, and the law is to be so applied as best to accomplish its purpose in a given case. The point is aptly illustrated in a letter from Jefferson, then governor of Virginia, to governor Thomas Sim Lee of Maryland, dated from Richmond, February 1, 1787. "Joseph Shoemaker is a

---

[30] To Taylor, June 4, 1798, *ibid.*, XVIII, 205.
[31] To William Rutledge, Feb. 2, 1788, *ibid.*, VI, 417.
[32] To Genet, June 17, 1793, *ibid.*, IX, 129-30.
[33] To Limozin, Dec. 22, 1787, *ibid.*, VI, 401.

citizen of this state and has been an active mischievous traitor. The dangers of escape on the road from Baltimore to this place, and from this place, where since our removal from Williamsburgh no public jail has been yet erected, are so great as to induce me to suggest to your Excellency the trial and punishment under your laws, should he have committed any depredation within your State which they would punish capitally; and in this case I will on intimation from your Excellency furnish you with proofs of his citizenship authenticated in any way in which your laws shall require. Should he not be amenable to justice under your laws, or should he be acquitted on trial, I will on information thereof take immediate measures for having him received, and brought hither."[34] This is, of course, an extraordinary case; but it serves to show the lengths to which Jefferson was willing to go to adapt the administrative machinery of the law to a specific set of circumstances.

He does not, to be sure, visualize the social-utilitarian ideal of adjusting the punishment to the individual offender, but under the stimulus of Beccaria, to whom he makes numerous footnote references in his early Virginia *Bill for Proportioning Crimes and Punishments*,[35] he goes far beyond the excesses of the criminal law of his day. Too far beyond, in fact, for his colleagues to follow him, who accordingly rejected his bill. Nor was he quite sure of its merits himself, but for a different reason. Of the bill he writes to Wythe that he has "strictly observed the scale of punishments settled by the Committee, without being entirely satisfied with it. The *Lex Talionis* . . . will be revolting to the humanized feelings of modern times. An eye for an eye, and a hand for a hand, will exhibit spectacles in execution whose moral effect would be questionable."[36] Punishment not proportioned to the offense is, he contends, unjust; and capital punishment is the "last melancholy resource" against the antisocial. The death penalty, further, removes one who may become an useful citizen, thereby weakening the state, and

[34] *Ibid.*, IV, 350.
[35] *Ibid.*, I, 218 ff.; in Ford's edition, II, 203 ff.
[36] *Writings*, I, 217.

at the same time depriving the state of his labor and of his example. In general, "cruel and sanguinary" laws defeat their own end; for the sympathies of men are enlisted to resist them by smothering testimony, or hearing it with bias.

Treason, defined as levying war on the commonwealth from within, or giving aid to her enemies from without, is to be punished by hanging; but must be proved by "two sufficient witnesses" or by confession. The lands and goods of the traitor are forfeit to the commonwealth. Petty treason, murder of wife by husband, parent by child, or child by parent, are to be punished by hanging, and the body is to be delivered to the anatomists for dissection. Murder by poison shall suffer death by poison. Murder by duel shall be punished by hanging, and if the challenger, his body shall be gibbeted. Any other form of murder shall incur death by hanging. But here is the unique provision of the bill: in all cases of petty treason and murder, half the lands and goods of the offender shall go to the nearest kin of the person killed, and the other half to his own heirs; except where the slain be the challenger in a duel, in which case none of the slayer's goods shall go to the kin of the slain, but instead a moiety to the commonwealth.

Manslaughter, for the first offense, shall incur a penalty of seven years at hard labor, one half the property going to the kin of the slain, and the rest being sequestered by the state, with a reasonable part of the income going to the family of the slayer. The second offense shall be considered murder. Involuntary homicide resulting from attempted trespass or larceny shall not be deemed such, but shall be punished according to intention. Execution for treason or murder shall take place on the next day but one after the sentence has been passed, unless that day be Sunday, when it shall be done the Monday following. Imprisonment for debt, if based not on unwillingness to pay but on inability to do so, is absurd, repugnant to the plainest principles of law, and serves no good end.[37] The practice re-

---

[37] *Commonplace Book*, citing Kames, *Historical Law Tracts*, 11; cf. Channing, *History of the United States*, V, 191 ff.

mained, however, in America as it did in England, until well into the nineteenth century. Jefferson would also withdraw the ancient "benefit of clergy," which had enabled many a guilty man, because he could read, to escape the consequences of his crime.

One example will suffice to show Jefferson's attitude towards law enforcement. The law, one gathers, should be swift and certain, but even the law should be humane. Having been informed that certain citizens had been guilty of acts amounting to high treason, or misprision of treason, he writes that such persons "it is indispensibly necessary to punish for their crimes by way of example to others and to disable from doing mischief." But he charges his agent "that you single out only those who have been foremost or most daring in their offenses, and that even these be treated by those into whose hands they shall be committed with no insult or rudeness unnecessary for their safe custody."[38]

The final and firmest bulwark of liberty in the legally ordered state is the right of every man to be tried by a jury of his peers. Ordinarily the judge decides cases of law, the jury cases of fact; but for the greater protection of the individual, this division should lie at the discretion of the jury. "And if the question relate to any point of public liberty, or if it be one of those in which the judges may be suspected of bias, the jury undertake to decide both law and fact. If they be mistaken, a decision against right, which is casual only, is less dangerous to the State, and less afflicting to the loser, than one which makes part of a regular and uniform system. In truth, it is better to toss up cross and pile in a cause, than to refer it to a judge whose mind is warped by any motive whatever, in that particular case. But the common sense of twelve honest men gives still a better chance of just decision, than the hazard of cross and pile."[39] Jefferson is here making a radical departure from what has come

---

[38] To Col. James Innes, May 2, 1781, *Writings*, IV, 419 ff.

[39] Notes on Virginia, *ibid.*, II, 179-80; cf. to l'Abbé Arnould, July 19, 1789, *ibid.*, VII, 322-23.

to be settled English practice in regard to law and fact; and his view has gained some popularity in this country. The precedent goes back to the trial of William Penn in England, where the jurymen were imprisoned for their verdict, and to the ever-memorable Zenger trial in New York in 1735—both cases involving the issue of personal liberty.

The jury system seems to have grown out of the "inquest," or prerogative right of the Frankish kings, brought to England at the time of the Conquest. Under this prerogative, a body of the oldest or most trustworthy men of a given neighborhood might be summoned, to answer upon oath such questions as might be put to them in regard to the affairs of their district.[40] Gradually this practice came to be introduced into criminal trials, the body of men called being at first themselves witnesses; but in the course of time their function became that of weighing evidence only. As early as the thirteenth century it seems to have been tacitly understood that jurors were to confine themselves to matters of fact rather than law. Judges, however, were loath to take their share of responsibility, and endeavored, so far as they could, to force an opinion under oath on the matter of law as well, until forbidden to do so by statute in 1285.[41] This division of law and fact was thus firmly established in England, and has been rigorously adhered to. In the United States, however, there has been a disposition to make the jury supreme as to both fact and law, the question having been raised during Jefferson's own term in the presidency, with Marshall upholding the radical view. The American jury may render a general verdict in which both law and fact as compounded in the issues submitted to them in the particular case may be determined. The duty is thus one of imperfect obligation, under which the jury may place its own interpretation on the terms and merits of the law involved.[42]

[40] Pollock and Maitland, *History of English Law* (2 vols. Cambridge, 1895), I, 140 ff.

[41] *Ibid.*, II, 629 ff.

[42] See Sparf and Hansen *vs.* United States, 156 U. S. 61.

IV

It has been urged that Jefferson regarded law as a means to an end; and he is entirely consistent in carrying out the consequences of this point of view. For it would follow that the end is more important than the means; and it would also follow that, in rare cases where the law would defeat its own purposes, or where there is no law adequate to the task at hand, it becomes a duty to proceed, for the time, by extralegal methods. This position was not taken, as Professor Chinard implies,[43] as a result of the Burr conspiracy, although that event called forth one of the clearest statements of it; but it goes back to the days of Jefferson's ministry in France. The first hint comes in 1785 in a letter to Adams, the American envoy in London, in which Jefferson encloses a draft of a treaty of commerce to be proposed to various European powers, and says of it: "I know it goes beyond our powers, and beyond the powers of Congress too; but it is so evidently for the good of all the States, that I should not be afraid to risk myself on it, if you are of the same opinion."[44]

The real test of the doctrine came with unexpected suddenness when Napoleon intimated to President Jefferson that he would be willing to sell Louisiana. Without waiting for legislative authorization, and without constitutional sanction, Jefferson bought the territory, saying of the purchase that "the executive in seizing the fugitive occurrence which so much advances the good of their country, have done an act beyond the Constitution. The Legislature in casting behind them metaphysical subtleties, and risking themselves like faithful servants, must ratify and pay for it, and throw themselves on their country for doing for them unauthorized, what we know they would have done for themselves had they been in a situation to do it."[45] The only means consistent with strict construction by which the purchase could be upheld was the passage of a constitu-

[43] Chinard, *Thomas Jefferson*, p. 438.
[44] To Adams, July 28, 1785, *Writings*, V, 42.
[45] To John C. Breckenridge, Aug. 12, 1803, *ibid.*, X, 411.

tional amendment specifically providing for the acquisition of the territory in question. Jefferson assumed that this program would be followed, and even went so far as to draft the necessary amendment; but his followers in the Senate received the proposal coldly, and he was forced in the end to accept a construction of the treaty-making power such as would cover the case.[46]

Jefferson was well aware that in buying Louisiana he was going beyond the constitution, but the act is by no means as arbitrary as has sometimes been charged. Livingston had been trying for weeks, with full legislative sanction, to buy New Orleans and West Florida,[47] and was joined by Monroe with similar instructions shortly before Talleyrand offered the whole territory for sale. To wait for an extension of their commission would have meant failure, and they did not hesitate long. Such opportunism as there was in the transaction was on the part of Livingston and Monroe rather than on that of the President; and in backing up their decision Jefferson was doing little more than Congress had authorized when the purchase of New Orleans and West Florida alone was contemplated. The sum voted for the original venture had been ten million dollars—only five million less than the price paid for all Louisiana. The constitution had not contemplated the addition of new territory to the Union, nor had Jefferson's political philosophy contemplated the situation in which the purchase placed him. He acted, therefore, on his own judgment, and revised his theory, as he sought to revise the constitution, to provide for such contingencies in the future.

The Louisiana affair gave Jefferson's opponents a tangible weapon, and the charge of inconsistency was loudly echoed from the housetops; for the outstanding exponent of strict construction had seemingly drawn from the constitution powers it did not grant. His defense was that the end justified the means;

[46] Henry Adams, *History of the United States*, II, 74 ff.; cf. to Breckenridge, Aug. 12, 1803, *Writings*, X, 411.

[47] *Ibid.*, I, 433 ff.; Channing, *The Jeffersonian System*, pp. 69 ff., and *History of the United States*, IV, 323.

and he went further, stating it as a general principle that the administrator was bound to go beyond the written law in those rare emergencies for which legislation had not provided. There is, however, a difference between Jefferson's action and that of Marshall in McCulloch *vs.* Maryland. Jefferson is not reading into the constitution what is not there. He frankly admits that the terms of the written law do not authorize his course, and makes no effort to explain it on constitutional grounds. He is acting for what he conceives to be the common good, and the issue is left squarely up to the sovereign people, to repudiate his act or to justify it by amending the law. That the accredited representatives of the people chose to do neither, but rather to follow the easier road of liberal construction, was no fault of Jefferson's. He had offered the choice, and he could do no more. In the case of Marshall's decisions, on the other hand, no choice was offered, and neither people nor popular representatives had any discretion in the matter. The court laid down the law, not as it was written but as the learned majority on the supreme bench agreed it should have been written; and from this judge-made law there was no appeal. Jefferson was not construing, but transcending, the constitution for the public good, and the means were at hand for the public to accept or reject his judgment. Marshall was subverting the constitution for an end which he knew in advance the people would reject were they given the opportunity.

In 1807, Jefferson writes that "on great occasions every good officer must be ready to risk himself in going beyond the strict line of law, when the public preservation requires it; his motives will be a justification as far as there is any discretion in his extralegal proceedings, and no indulgence of private feelings."[48] And the Burr conspiracy provokes the following: "Should we have ever gained our Revolution, if we had bound our hands by manacles of the law, not only in the beginning, but in any part of the revolutionary conflict? There are extreme cases where the laws become inadequate even to their own preserva-

---

[48] To Gov. Claiborne, Feb. 3, 1807, *Writings*, XI, 151.

tion, and where the universal resource is a dictator, or martial law."[49]

The end for the individual is happiness, but since he cannot exist out of society, his individual end must be merged to greater or less extent in the social end, or public good. And there are times when the means to this end must transcend the written law. Such is the substance of the doctrine, which is summarized by Jefferson himself. "A strict observance of the written laws is doubtless *one* of the high duties of a good citizen, but it is not *the highest*. The laws of necessity, of self-preservation, of saving our country when in danger, are of higher obligation. To lose our country by a scrupulous adherence to written law, would be to lose the law itself, with life, liberty, property and all those who are enjoying them with us; thus absurdly sacrificing the end to the means." He goes on to cite cases in which the "unwritten laws of necessity, of self-preservation, and of public safety, control the written laws of *meum* and *tuum*"; draws an hypothetical case anent Florida which parallels his own dilemma in regard to Louisiana; and refers to the Burr conspiracy. He concludes:

"From these examples and principles you may see what I think on the question proposed. They do not go to the case of persons charged with petty duties, where consequences are trifling, and time allowed for a legal course, nor to authorize them to take such cases out of the written law. In these, the example of overleaping the law is of greater evil than a strict adherence to its imperfect provisions. It is incumbent on those only who accept great charges, to risk themselves on great occasions, when the safety of the nation, or some of its high interests are at stake. . . . The line of discrimination between cases may be difficult; but the good officer is bound to draw it at his own peril, and throw himself on the justice of his country and the rectitude of his motives."[50]

The question here raised is one which every state must sooner

---

[49] To Dr. James Brown, Oct. 27, 1808, *ibid.*, XII, 183.
[50] To J. B. Colvin, Sept. 20, 1810, *ibid.*, pp. 418 ff.

or later face; and the solution Jefferson offers is perhaps the only possible one for a republic. Legislation can provide adequately for the events of normal political life, but no state can escape emergencies in which the operation of the ordinary machinery of law breaks down. In such cases, some form of dictatorship, such as that invoked in time of war by Presidents Lincoln and Wilson, is the only means of preventing complete breakdown of the agencies of government.

Jefferson's solution closely resembles that advanced by Cicero, with which he was doubtless familiar. The Roman statesman explains that "our people in the peaceful course of civil affairs command and even threaten the magistrates themselves, obstruct them, seek the aid of one against another, or carry an appeal from their decision to the centuries. But in war the people obey their magistrates as if they were kings, for their safety is of more moment than their mere whim."[51] Cicero goes on to propose an emergency dictatorship, following the Roman practice of his day. "When there shall be a serious war or civil uprising, if the senate so decree, one magistrate shall possess for not more than six months all authority which the two consuls normally possess. He shall be appointed with favorable auspices and shall be the master of the people."[52] And Rousseau, following Cicero and Roman custom, makes a similar provision, observing in the *Social Contract* that the "inflexibility of the laws, which prevents them from adapting themselves to circumstances, may, in certain cases, render them disastrous, and make them bring about, at a time of crisis, the ruin of the State."[53]

V

The significance of Jefferson's philosophy of law lies in its combination of an ethical basis with a point of view similar to that later developed by the sociological jurists. It is the familiar eighteenth-century natural law doctrine, refined by a semihis-

---

[51] *De Republica*, I, 40 (Sabine and Smith trans.).
[52] *De Legibus*, 3, 3, 9, quoted from Sabine and Smith, *Cicero on the Commonwealth*, 147 n.
[53] IV. 6.

torical, semipragmatic method, and broadened to incorporate elements from Madison's theory of interests.[54]   Jefferson's conception is of a law based on social needs and conditions, the ultimate purpose of which is justice.   In the ethical sense of right, law is inherent in nature and is discoverable by reason; but in the stricter sense, it is made, to meet specific demands from specific interests.   And above all, law is flexible.   It must grow as the society grows, and it must be administered, not as a body of immutable, ironclad rules, but as an instrument of social control.   The society is not created by law, but law by the society, to serve the supreme end of human welfare.

The conflict which this attitude involves between individual rights and social purpose is one which has far-reaching implications, to which we shall have occasion to refer in later chapters.   If law is considered with reference to the society as a unit, the state will be justified in limiting or even denying altogether the rights of the isolated individual for the sake of the larger good.   On this ground, for example, the right of the individual to bear arms has been consistently abridged in America; and the right of association and even that of free speech have more than once come under a temporary ban.   To admit a social interpretation of law is to admit that the purposes of the state as a whole are paramount to the welfare of any one individual or group; and it may well be questioned whether such an admission can be reconciled with an individualistic theory of democracy.

The difficulty thus raised in Jefferson's legal thinking is an outgrowth of a similar opposition earlier discussed in connection with his ethical beliefs.   While clinging to a doctrine of individual rights, he still sought to establish a social utilitarianism.   To do so, he was forced to admit that individual happiness is possible only in terms of the group, and that individual rights must, accordingly, yield to the social good.   Consistently applied, such a doctrine would be fatal both to the theory of state rights and to any positive individualism.   Jefferson saw nothing incon-

[54] *The Federalist,* No. 10.   Cf. Charles A. Beard, *Economic Interpretation of the Constitution of the United States* (New York, 1913), pp. 14 ff.

gruous, however, in asserting that men have no rights in opposition to their social duties, a point which he makes, in one form or another, so frequently that it cannot be discounted as a passing whim. These statements, taken in conjunction with the outstanding policies of his administration—reduction of the national debt, the Louisiana purchase, the embargo, all of them social in their purposes—lend some weight to the conclusion that his most characteristic position was nearer to social utilitarianism than it was to the individualism with which his name is apt to be associated.

CHAPTER IX

THE FAMILY OF NATIONS

I

JUST AS the state of Virginia or the state of Massachusetts has relations outside itself, and must be considered in many of its activities with reference to the larger national unit, so the nation itself must inevitably have contacts external to it. Simply because it shares a planet with other national states, its interests must at some point meet with theirs. Isolation, in any rigorous sense, means stagnation and death, both to the individual and to the state; and Jefferson would have been the first to protest against any such policy. When he asks for "peace, commerce, and honest friendship with all nations—entangling alliances with none,"[1] only the second phrase is negative, and it means no more than it says. Peace and commerce are both relations external to the individual states; and both presuppose for their maintenance some form of international organization—some system of international law. Both Jefferson's writings and his official acts testify to his belief that the intercourse of nations must be governed by some body of legal rules.

International law in the modern world begins with the publication in 1625 of the pioneer work of Grotius, *De Jure Belli ac Pacis*, which sets forth a code to govern the relations of independent states. It was a new conception of law, designed to meet the new problems of a changing political order; and it was based on a natural law theory which had also changed. Natural principles first assumed with Grotius the character of self-evident truths, from which a system of law could be deduced with all the rigor and precision of geometry. They were moral rules, to be sure; but they were rules which followed of necessity from the very construction of the universe.

[1] First Inaugural Address, *Writings*, III, 321.

For the next two centuries the "law of nations" enjoyed a period of optimistic growth, only to be blasted by the Napoleonic wars. A second period of development in international law covers the century between the Congress of Vienna and the fatal shot at Sarajevo; and a third era began with the Treaty of Versailles. Jefferson's work comes at the close of the first period, formulates the policy of the second, and anticipates some of the doctrines of the third.

The precise form international law took for him was determined in part by his legal and philosophical training, in part by experience in negotiating between nations. "The law of nations . . . is composed of three branches. 1. The moral law of our nature. 2. The usages of nations. 3. Their special conventions."[2] The special conventions of nations are more or less arbitrary, and are made to deal with special conditions as they arise. The usages of nations are rules gradually accumulated, which experience has shown to have utilitarian value. Both may be changed as need for change arises; but neither can transgress the moral law "to which man has been subjected by his creator, and of which his feelings or conscience, as it is sometimes called, arc the evidence with which his creator has furnished him." Justice is universal, and is the principal of intercourse between nations as it is between individuals. For "the moral duties which exist between individual and individual in a state of nature, accompany them into a state of society, and the aggregate of all the duties of all the individuals composing the society constitutes the duties of the society towards any other; so that between society and society the same moral duties exist as did between the individuals composing them, while in an unassociated state, and their maker not having released them from those duties on their forming themselves into a nation. Compacts, then, between nation and nation, are obligatory on them by the same moral law which obliges individuals to observe their compacts."[3]

Following the same analogy between men and states, Jef-

---

[2] Official Papers, *ibid.*, p. 228.   [3] *Ibid.*

ferson admits that in both cases there are circumstances under which contracts may be broken. "When performance, for instance, becomes *impossible*, nonperformance is not immoral; so if performance becomes *self-destructive* to the party, the law of self-preservation overrules the laws of obligation in others. . . . For the reality of these principles I appeal to the true fountains of evidence, the head and heart of every rational and honest man. It is there nature has written her moral laws, and where every man may read them for himself."[4] Of the degree and imminence of danger on grounds of which contracts may be voided, it is true that "nations are to be the judges for themselves; since no one nation has a right to sit in judgment over another, but the tribunal of our conscience remains, and that also of the opinion of the world. These will revise the sentence we pass in our own case, and as we respect these, we must see that in judging ourselves we have honestly done the part of rigorous and impartial judges."[5] In general, obligation "is not to be suspended till the danger is become real, and the moment of it so imminent that we can no longer avoid decision without forever losing the opportunity to do it."[6]

The nation is to be held as strictly to the moral code as is the individual. In refusing the offer of a certain "Mr. Hall," a British subject, to turn over to the United States government "for a price," certain documents of which he was the bearer, Jefferson declared that "moral duties were as obligatory on nations as on individuals, that even in point of interest a character of good faith was of as much value to a nation as an individual and was that by which it would gain most in the long run."[7] So essential does Jefferson believe honesty and fair dealing between nations to be, if the ultimate goal of human happiness is to be achieved, that the conduct of Bonaparte leads him to despair. "The total banishment of all moral principle from the code which governs the intercourse of nations, the melancholy reflection that after the mean, wicked and cowardly cunning of

---

[4] *Ibid.*, pp. 228-29.   [5] *Ibid.*
[6] *Ibid.*, p. 230.   [7] *Anas, ibid.*, I, 480.

the cabinets of the age of Machiavelli had given place to the integrity and good faith which dignified the succeeding one of a Chatham and Turgot, that this is to be swept away again by the daring profligacy and avowed destitution of all moral principle of a Cartouche and a Blackbeard, sickens my soul unto death."[8]

Since in terms of Jefferson's political philosophy the sanction of any law is the consent of the people, international law will be valid for a given state only to the extent that it is accepted by a majority of the citizens of that state. Treaties, agreements and other special conventions, since they are set up by legally constituted representatives of the people, are coordinate with municipal law, and are as binding on individuals as are local statutes. Any conflict between that part of the law of nations which rests on usage, and the municipal law of a given state, would have to be resolved, on Jefferson's principles, by special agreement, as was done in the consular convention with France of 1788.

II

It is not to be assumed that Jefferson went so far as to draw up any complete code of international law; he did no such thing. But there was no world tribunal in his day, and the power of the Supreme Court in international cases was limited. Principles were laid down and decisions made by the department of state; and in his capacity as secretary, Jefferson passed on a large number of questions of an international nature. It is mainly from his opinions expressed while in that office, together with other official acts and writings, that his theory as it will be reconstructed here is drawn. It is necessarily incomplete according to modern standards, because the number of points he was called upon to settle is insignificant in comparison with the possible extent of the subject matter of international law. The issues he did discuss, however, were most of them fundamental: and his opinions are backed by incisive logic, and wherever possible by the authority of other writers, such as Vattel, Grotius, Pufendorf, Wolff, and van Bynkershoek, although he did

[8] To Duane, Apr. 4, 1813, *ibid.*, XIII, 230.

not hesitate to create new precedent where he found the old not to his taste. Many of Jefferson's decisions were, in fact, new departures in international policy; for he was more than once called upon to pronounce judgment on questions which had not previously arisen. This is especially true as regards the law of neutrality.

First of all we must note a curious suggestion, for one who holds the law of nature to be universally applicable, to the effect that geographical conditions in America may call for a different code of natural law to govern relations with other nations.[9] Even in international law, Jefferson shows a tendency to break with the older natural law theory in favor of a sociological interpretation, having elements in common with Montesquieu's doctrine. This in 1800; and in 1816 he makes use of the *"jus gentium* of America," a principle foreshadowed in colonial days, to claim territory on the Pacific ocean. "If we claim that country at all, it must be on Astor's settlement near the mouth of the Columbia, and the principle of the *jus gentium* of America, that when a civilized nation takes possession of the mouth of a river in new country, that possession is considered as including all its waters."[10]

The principle did not apply, of course, in the case of Spain's occupancy of the mouth of the Mississippi; for the American claim to the upper waters of the river was well established, which raised another problem. In the dispute with Spain, he goes to considerable lengths to prove by the "law of nature and of nations" the doctrine that "different nations inhabiting the same river have all a natural right to an innocent passage along it, just as individuals of the same nation have of a river wholly within the territory of that nation."[11] And from this he deduces further rights. For it "is a principle that the right to a thing

---

[9] To Dr. Mitchell, June 13, 1800 (unpublished), quoted by Chinard in *Thomas Jefferson*, p. 398.

[10] To John Melish, Dec. 31, 1816, *Writings*, XV, 94; cf. Channing, *History of the United States*, I, 337.

[11] To Gallatin, July 4, 1807, *Writings*, XI, 257; cf. Official Papers, *ibid.*, III, 165 ff.

gives a right to the means, without which it could not be used, that is to say, that the means follow their end. Thus a right to navigate a river draws to it a right to moor vessels to its shores, to land on them in cases of distress, or for other necessary purposes, etc. This principle is founded in natural reason, is evidenced by the common sense of mankind, and declared by the writers before quoted."[12] His citations are from Grotius, Pufendorf, and Vattel. Needless to say, this argument was lost upon Spain. It was by no means established in that day that riparian states enjoyed a right of navigation to the sea through foreign territory. Citizens of Antwerp could not navigate the Scheldt to its mouth, and Spanish subjects themselves could not go down the Tagus past the Portuguese frontier.[13]

Natural law also dictates for Jefferson the right to possess and occupy uninhabited territory. So he argues that a society, "taking possession of a vacant country, and declaring they mean to occupy it, does thereby appropriate to themselves as prime occupants what was before common. A practice introduced since the discovery of America authorizes them to go further, and to fix the limits which they assume to themselves; and it seems for the common good, to admit this right to a moderate and reasonable extent."[14] But the practical situation in which Jefferson found himself forced a still further modification of his principle. "If the country, instead of being altogether vacant, is thinly occupied by another nation, the right of the native forms an exception to that of the newcomers; that is to say, these will have a right against all nations except the natives. Consequently, they have the exclusive privilege of acquiring the native right by purchase or other just means. This is called the right of preemption, and is become a principle of the law of nations, fundamental with respect to America. There are but two means of acquiring the native title. First, war; for even war may, some-

---

[12] Official Papers, *ibid.*, p. 180; he cites Grotius, 2. 2. 15; Pufendorf, 3. 3. 8; Vattel, 2. 129.

[13] See S. F. Bemis, "Thomas Jefferson," in *American Secretaries of State* (10 vols. New York, 1927-1929), II, 51; cf. Channing, *op. cit.*, III, 488.

[14] Official Papers, *Writings*, III, 18-19.

times, give a just title. Second, contracts or treaty."[15] This is an excellent example of a theory constructed to justify an act already done; for since the United States had already acquired its whole area from the Indians, it must needs be declared right they should have done so; and since war had frequently been the means, that too must be recognized as giving just title.

The only other important pronouncement of Jefferson's under the head of territory has also to do with Indian lands. The question having been raised as to the expediency of returning to the Indians certain lands acquired from them, he denied the power of the government to do so, on the ground that "by the law of nations it was settled that the unity and indivisibility of the society was so fundamental that it could not be dismembered by the constituted authorities, except, 1, where *all power* was delegated to them (as in the case of despotic governments), or, 2, where it was expressly so delegated"; and he found it not to be so delegated in the case in question.[16]

Jefferson was the first to fix the maritime jurisdiction at a sea league, or three miles, reserving, however, the right to extend it up to twenty miles if circumstances should warrant. In Grotius and the later writers on international law, the distance had been fixed at a cannon shot from the shore, which was too indefinite to be adequate.[17] The three-mile limit is now universally accepted, and the right of the United States to extend it to twelve miles has not been seriously questioned.

Under the head of individuals, Jefferson expressly recognizes the right of expatriation, presumably following Locke. "My opinion on the right of expatriation has been, so long ago as the year 1776, consigned to record in the act of the Virginia Code, drawn by myself, recognizing the right expressly, and prescribing the mode of exercising it. The evidence of this natural right, like that of our right to life, liberty, the use of our faculties, the pursuit of happiness, is not left to the feeble

---

[15] *Ibid.*; cf. Anas, *ibid.*, I, 340-41.

[16] *Ibid.*, p. 341.

[17] See T. W. Balch, "The United States and the Expansion of the Law Between Nations," *Pennsylvania Law Review*, LXIV, 131.

and sophistical investigations of reason, but is impressed on the sense of every man. We do not claim these under the charters of kings or legislators, but under the King of Kings. If he has made it a law in the nature of man to pursue his own happiness, he has left him free in the choice of place as well as mode. . . . I believe, too, I might safely affirm, that there is not another nation [except England], civilized or savage, which has ever denied this natural right. . . . How it is among our savage neighbors, who have no law but that of Nature, we all know."[18]

Here as elsewhere, Jefferson is apt to identify his own views with those of his country. Some twenty years before his statement just quoted was written, and twenty years after the Virginia Code referred to, Chief Justice Ellsworth had announced from the bench that "When a foreigner presents himself here, and proves himself to be of good moral character, well affected to the Constitution and Government of the United States, . . . if he has resided the time prescribed by law, we grant him the privilege of a citizen. . . . But this implies no consent of the government, that our citizens should expatriate themselves."[19] The right of expatriation involves the consent of two nations; that which receives the expatriate, and that which relinquishes its claim to his allegiance; and it must therefore be established by treaty. The right was not specifically recognized by the United States until the act of Congress of July 27, 1868, under which our present treaties were made; and the whole question has not yet been satisfactorily settled.[20]

On the same general ground of natural right, Jefferson goes on to propose a modification of the fourteen-year residence requirement for citizenship. The individual should have perfect freedom to choose the government to which he will give his allegiance, for the furtherance of his own happiness. Jefferson

---

[18] To Manners, June 12, 1817, *Writings*, XV, 124-25; to Wendover, Mar. 13, 1815, *ibid.*, XIV, 279; cf. Locke, *Of Civil Government*, II, 118.

[19] The Williams Case. See George Van Santvoord, *Sketches of the Lives and Judicial Services of the Chief Justices of the Supreme Court of the United States* (New York, 1854), pp. 267 ff.

[20] John Bassett Moore, *American Diplomacy* (New York and London, 1905), pp. 288 ff.; *Digest of International Law* (8 vols. Washington, 1906), III, 552 ff.

would have made America a refuge for the oppressed of the world.[21]

In regard to American nationals, he lays down the principle that "the persons and property of our citizens are entitled to the protection of our government in all places where they may lawfully go."[22] But a citizen residing in a foreign country is under the laws of that country while there. Speaking specifically of England, he adds that, in settling the case of an American citizen, the English judges should keep in mind the law of nations and the treaty of peace, "as making a part of the law of the land."[23] The extent of American jurisdiction over foreign subjects is set forth in the *Notes on Virginia*. Any controversy between foreigners of a nation allied to the United States—an allied nation here means a nation maintaining a resident consul in this country—is to be settled by their consul, or if both choose, by the ordinary courts of justice. If only one of the parties be foreign, the case is under the jurisdiction of the ordinary courts; but if instituted in a county court may be removed by the foreigner to the general court, who are to determine it at their first session. "In cases of life and death, such foreigners have a right to be tried by a jury, the one half of foreigners, the other of natives."[24] This is the jury *de medietate linguae,* an English institution, which was rejected by the framers of the American constitution, and was finally abolished in England in 1870.

Provision had been made in the constitution (Art. IV, sec. 2) for extradition of criminals from one state of the Union to another, but no power was granted for the return of malefactors to foreign countries until Congress passed legislation for this express purpose in 1793. Grotius and Vattel had held that one nation might legitimately request of another the return of fugitives from justice without treaty obligation;[25] but Jefferson

---

[21] First Annual Message, Dec. 8, 1801, *Writings,* III, 338.
[22] Official Papers, *ibid.,* p. 244.
[23] To Col. Forrest, Oct. 20, 1784, *ibid.,* V, 1.
[24] *Ibid.,* II, 182.
[25] See Moore's *Digest,* IV, 245 ff. for technical discussion.

maintained, as secretary of state, that the "delivery of fugitives from one country to another, as practiced by several nations, is in consequence of conventions settled between them, defining precisely the cases wherein such deliveries shall take place."[26] In the absence of any adequate precedent, he set forth his own views as to the content of any future agreements of this nature his government might make.

The matter of establishing such conventions presents difficulties, if the governments in question vary widely in the substance of their criminal law.[27] Hence, it is necessary for extradition treaties to enter into some detail. In general, Jefferson believes a nation has no right to punish a person who has not offended against it, such fugitives being regarded merely as strangers, who have a right of residence unless infectious. Exception is extended to dangerous criminals, namely, pirates, murderers, and incendiaries.[28]

Piracy he finds already adequately provided for by law, and he regards arson as too rare to be taken account of. "The only *rightful* subject then of arrest and delivery, for which we have *need*, is *murder*. Ought we to wish to strain the natural right of arresting and redelivering fugitives in other cases? . . . The punishment of all real crimes is certainly desirable, as a security to society; the security is greater in proportion as the chances of avoiding punishment are less." The fugitive from his country, however, does not escape punishment but incurs exile, placed by most as next to death. To the foreigner, of course, this is no punishment; but such cases are few, and "laws are made for the mass of cases." Jefferson concludes: "The object of a convention, then, in other cases, would be, that the fugitive might not avoid the *difference between exile and the legal punishment of the case*. Now in what case would this *difference* be so important, as to overweigh the single inconvenience of multiplying compacts?" He then goes on to discuss possible cases in the following order:

[26] To President Washington, Nov. 7, 1791, *Writings*, VIII, 253-54.
[27] To Pinckney, Apr. 1, 1792, *ibid.*, pp. 321-22.
[28] *Ibid.*, pp. 330 ff.

Treason is sufficiently punished by exile, because, though of greatest magnitude when real, most cases of treason are acts against the oppression of a government rather than against the government itself, and these are virtues. "The unsuccessful strugglers against tyranny, have been the chief martyrs of treason laws in all countries." For crimes against *property*, the punishment in most countries is highly disproportionate to the offense. "All *excess* of punishment is a crime. To remit a fugitive to excessive punishment is to be accessory to the crime." These cases, then, are sufficiently punished by exile. Forgery deserves more particular notice, but even here the fugitive is punished by exile and confiscation of whatever property he leaves; "to which add by convention, a civil action against the property he carries or acquires to the amount of the special damage done by his forgery. . . . The *carrying away* of property of another, may also be reasonably made to found a civil action." A treaty or convention, then, could be made, including forgery and the carrying away of property, under the head of *flight from debts.* "To remit a fugitive in this case, would be to remit him in every case. For in the present state of things, it is next to impossible not to owe something. But I see neither injustice nor inconvenience in permitting the fugitive to be sued in our courts."

The principal organ of the state for transacting foreign business is its executive head; in the American state, the president, directly or through his appointees, including the secretary of state, and ministers and consuls sent to foreign countries. These will deal with similar representatives of the powers in question. To maintain relations with another government implies a recognition of the legitimacy of that government; and the reception of a minister is, of course, such acknowledgement.[29] Jefferson takes the position, however, that recognition of a government *de jure* is not always necessary to carry on business with it. He writes to Gouverneur Morris, then minister at Paris, in 1792, that it "accords with our principles to acknowl-

[29] Official Papers, *ibid.*, III, 233.

edge any government to be rightful, which is formed by the will of the nation substantially declared. The late government was of this kind, and was accordingly acknowledged by all the branches of ours. So, any alteration of it which shall be made by the will of the nation substantially declared, will doubtless be acknowledged in like manner. With such a government *every kind* of business may be done. But there are *some matters* which, I conceive, might be transacted with a government *de facto;* such, for instance, as the reforming the unfriendly restrictions on our commerce and navigation."[30] This stand is manifestly dictated by expediency, and is another of the instances in Jefferson's career in which the practical man got the better of the theorist.

The tenure of a diplomatic envoy depends on the will of both states involved. "In fact, every foreign agent depends on the double will of the two governments, of that which sends him, and of that which is to permit the exercise of his functions within their territory; and when either of these wills is refused or withdrawn, his authority to act within that territory becomes incomplete."[31] So long, however, as he remains *persona grata* with the government to which he is sent, the diplomatic agent enjoys certain immunities. "Every person diplomatic *in his own right,* is entitled to the privileges of the law of nations. . . . Among these is the receipt of all packages unopened and unexamined by the country which receives him. The usage of nations has established that this shall liberate whatever is imported *bona fide* for his own use, from paying any duty. A government may control the number of diplomatic characters it will receive; but if it receives them, it cannot control their rights while *bona fide* exercised."[32] The serving a process on a diplomatic agent is a breach of privilege.[33]

Jefferson was, nevertheless, not wholly in sympathy with the immunities of the diplomatic code as it related to the lesser offi-

[30] *Ibid.,* VIII, 437.
[31] To Genet, Dec. 9, 1793, *ibid.,* IX, 264-65.
[32] To Gallatin, Oct. 18, 1805, *ibid.,* XI, 91.
[33] To van Berckel, July 2, 1792, *ibid.,* VIII, 385.

cials, or consuls, and even goes so far as to doubt the utility of maintaining them at all. In discussing a proposed revision of the consular convention with France, he held, among other things, that consuls are not immune from giving testimony in the courts under American law; and suggested that "Fewer articles, better observed, will better promote our common interest. As to ourselves, we do not find the institution of consuls very necessary." He thinks them of use only among uncivilized peoples, and finds that "all civilized nations at this day, understand so well the advantages of commerce, that they provide protection and encouragement for merchant strangers and vessels coming among them. So extensive, too, have commercial connections now become, that every mercantile house has correspondents in almost every port. They address their vessels to these correspondents, who are found to take better care of their interests, and to obtain more effectually the protection of the laws of the country for them, than the consuls of their nation can."[34]

The suggestion that commercial interests employ their own representatives to carry on the consular functions is entirely consistent with Jefferson's advocacy of individual initiative. It is consistent, too, with laissez faire economic theory; and business was already launched on the career that was to lead it in the course of another century to compete with government itself for power and influence. To John Jay, his predecessor as secretary of state, Jefferson details the changes he has effected in the consular convention with France:

"The clauses of the convention of 1784, clothing consuls with the privileges of the law of nations, are struck out, and they are expressly subjected to the law of the land.

"That giving the right of sanctuary to their houses, is reduced to a protection of their chancery room and its papers.

"Their coercive powers over passengers are taken away; and over those, whom they might have termed deserters of their nation, are restrained to deserted seamen only.

---

[34] To Count de Montmorin, June 20, 1788, *ibid.*, VII, 54 ff.

"The clause, allowing them to arrest and send back vessels, is struck out, and instead of it, they are allowed to exercise a police over the ships of their nation generally."[35]

Even of the value of carrying on international transactions by treaty, Jefferson is inclined to be skeptical, believing that "with nations as with individuals, dealings may be carried on as advantageously, perhaps more so, while their continuance depends on voluntary good treatment, as if fixed by contract, which, when it becomes injurious to either, is made, by forced constructions, to mean what suits them, and becomes a cause of war instead of a bond of peace."[36] And writing in 1815 to President Madison, Jefferson, speaking of commercial treaties, suggests that "Perhaps, with all of them, it would be better to have but the single article *gentis amicissimae,* leaving everything else to the usages and courtesies of civilized nations."[37]

III

It is on questions relative to the rights and duties of neutrals that Jefferson's contributions to international law are most significant; for the policy of neutrality declared by Washington in 1793 and carried through by Jefferson in his capacity as secretary of state, defined these rights and duties more clearly than had ever been done before.[38] His version of the law of war and neutrality is based on wide experience; for he had been governor of Virginia during two of the most trying years of the revolution, had served as secretary of state and later as president during a protracted squabble between France and England, and was an interested and close observer of the war of 1812. He was much influenced also by Vattel, whose authority in the later eighteenth century was preëminent, and who gives the best account of the law of neutrality. In general, Jefferson's views were, with a few notable exceptions, those upheld by

[35] Nov. 14, 1788, *ibid.,* VII, 165; cf. *ibid.,* pp. 171 ff.
[36] To Phillip Mazzei, July 18, 1804, *ibid.,* XI, 39.
[37] Mar. 23, 1815, *ibid.,* XIV, 293.
[38] See Balch, "The United States and the Expansion of the Law Between Nations," *Pennsylvania Law Review,* LXIV, 119.

most of the courts of his day, more or less weighted on the side of protection for commercial activity. Indeed, after the war of 1812 had become inevitable, and preparation for hostilities was actively going forward, Jefferson writes to Madison that he is "favorable to the opinion . . . that commerce, under certain restrictions and licenses, may be indulged in between enemies mutually advantageous to the individuals, and not to their injury as belligerents."[39] And in his list of "Instructions to the Ministers Plenipotentiary appointed to negotiate Treaties of Commerce with European Nations," in 1784, the following highly interesting passage occurs:

"4. That it be proposed, though not indispensibly required, that if war should hereafter arise between the two contracting parties, the merchants of either country, then residing in the other, shall be allowed to remain nine months to collect their debts and settle their affairs, and may depart freely, carrying all their effects, without molestation or hindrance; and all fishermen, all cultivators of the earth, all artisans or manufacturers, unarmed and inhabiting unfortified towns, villages or places, who labor for the common subsistence and benefit of mankind, and peaceably following their respective employments, shall be allowed to continue the same, and shall not be molested by the armed force of the enemy, in whose power, by the events of war, they may happen to fall; but if anything is necessary to be taken from them, for the use of such armed force, the same shall be paid for at a reasonable price; and all merchants and traders, exchanging the products of different places, and thereby rendering the necessaries, conveniences, and comforts of human life more easy to obtain and more general, shall be allowed to pass unmolested."[40]

He carries the same humanity into the actual conduct of war, as far as it is possible to do so. For example, writing to Patrick Henry, his predecessor as governor of Virginia, in regard to the arrangements made for quartering captured troops, Jefferson recommends that they be treated with all considera-

[39] Apr. 17, 1812, *Writings*, XIII, 140.   [40] *Ibid.*, XVII, 23 (May 7, 1784).

tion, adding that it "is for the benefit of mankind to mitigate the horrors of war as much as possible."[41] This does not deter him, however, from approving the strict confinement of the British governor, Hamilton, "on the general principle of national retaliation."[42] His attitude is clearly and vigorously expressed some two years later, in 1781, when he was himself in the governor's chair. Certain citizens of Virginia, having been taken prisoners when not under arms, and paroled, reported a threat of death if retaken in arms. The incident provoked the following letter, addressed to "Major-General Benedict Arnold, the Commanding Officer of the British force at Portsmouth":

"It suffices to observe at present that by the law of nations, a breach of parole (even where the validity of the parole is not questioned) can only be punished by strict confinement.

"No usage has permitted the putting to death a prisoner for this cause. I would willingly suppose that no British officer had ever expressed a contrary purpose. It has, however, become my duty to declare that should such a threat be carried into execution, it will be deemed as putting prisoners to death in cold blood, and shall be followed by the execution of so many British prisoners in our possession. I trust, however, that this horrid necessity will not be introduced by you and that you will on the contrary concur with us in endeavoring as far as possible to alleviate the inevitable miseries of war by treating captives as humanity and natural honor requires. The event of this contest will hardly be affected by the fate of a few miserable captives in war."[43]

Since the United States played the part of more or less interested neutral in wars and disputes involving France, England, and Spain, Jefferson was called upon to define and defend what he took to be the rights and duties of neutral powers. "Reason and usage have established," he says in the best statement of his general position, "that when two nations go to war, those

[41] Mar. 27, 1779, *ibid.*, IV, 54-55.

[42] To Sir Guy Carleton, July 22, 1779, *ibid.*, pp. 301 ff.

[43] Mar. 24, 1781, *ibid.*, pp. 399-400.

who choose to live in peace retain their natural right to pursue their agriculture, manufactures, and other ordinary vocations, to carry the produce of their industry for exchange to all nations, belligerent or neutral, as usual, to go and come freely without injury or molestation, and in short, that the war among others shall be for them as if it did not exist. One restriction on their natural rights has been submitted to by nations at peace, that is to say, that of not furnishing to either party implements merely of war for the annoyance of the other, nor anything whatever to a place blockaded by its enemy."[44]

Jefferson went so far as to hold, none the less, in a cabinet meeting of the first administration, against the opinions of Hamilton and Knox, that vessels of a belligerent might mount their own cannon in a neutral port, and might recruit their own citizens there. And, further, that a neutral might build and sell vessels to both parties of a quarrel, either in her own ports or by delivering them; denying the contention of Attorney-General Randolph that such ships, if attempt at delivery were made, could be seized as contraband.[45] His stand on this latter point, however, is reversed in the case of arms, although he continued to deny any breach of neutrality. In reply to a protest from the British Ambassador, he writes that American citizens "have been always free to make, vend and export arms. It is the constant occupation and livelihood of some of them. To suppress their callings, the only means perhaps of their subsistence, because a war exists in foreign and distant countries, in which we have no concern, would scarcely be expected. It would be hard in principle, and impossible in practice. The law of nations, therefore, respecting the rights of those at peace, does not require from them such an internal derangement of their occupations. It is satisfied with the external penalty . . . of confiscation of such portion of these arms as shall fall into the hands of any of the belligerent powers on the way to the ports of their enemies."[46]

[44] To Pinckney, Sept. 7, 1793, *ibid.*, IX, 221-22.
[45] Anas, *ibid.*, I, 372-73, 379.
[46] To George Hammond, May 15, 1793, *ibid.*, IX, 90-91.

He is clear that impartial justice must obtain in the relations of a neutral to the belligerents; and insists that the United States, as a neutral in the war between France and Great Britain, ought not to permit to one party acts forbidden by treaty to the other, even though the acts themselves are not unlawful. "We cannot permit the enemies of France to fit out privateers in our ports, by the 22nd article of our treaty. We ought not, therefore, to permit France to do it; the treaty leaving us free to refuse, and the refusal being necessary to preserve a fair neutrality."[47]   And the same attitude prevails, tempered with shrewd political wisdom, in his opinion as to the legality of troops of a belligerent marching across the territory of a neutral. When the question arose in the dispute between England and Spain over the possession of Nootka Sound, it seemed highly probable that the British would seek to move troops from Canada over American soil. So Jefferson writes that it is "well enough agreed, in the laws of nations, that for a neutral power to give or refuse permission to the troops of either belligerent party to pass through their territory, is no breach of neutrality, provided the same refusal or permission be extended to the other party."[48]   But in applying the doctrine, he is guided by principles of expediency, expressing his willingness to grant the permission lest, if it be refused, the troops would march without it, and his government should stand committed. "For either we must enter immediately into the war, or pocket an acknowledged insult in the face of the world; and one insult pocketed soon produces another." He suspects the part of wisdom to be to avoid giving an answer at all.

Blockade and contraband of war are the only two articles in the rights of neutral nations which war can abridge;[49] and Jefferson is inclined to doubt the ultimate validity of the principle of contraband. His views on the question change sufficiently, however, to render his position confusing. In July, 1793, he believes "it cannot be doubted, but that by the general

[47] Official Papers, *ibid.*, III, 248.   [48] *Ibid.*, p. 80; cf. Bemis, *op. cit.*, pp. 40 ff.
[49] To B. Stoddart, Feb. 18, 1809, *Writings*, XII, 250.

law of nations, the goods of a friend found in the vessel of an enemy are free, and the goods of an enemy found in the vessel of a friend are lawful prize."[50]   But in December of the same year he has virtually reversed his position, declaring the natural principle to be, as in the above passage, that *goods follow the owner*, but explaining that the "inconvenience of this principle in subjecting neutral vessels to vexatious searches at sea, has . . . rendered it usual for nations to substitute a *conventional* principle that *the goods shall follow the bottom*."[51] Still later, in 1801, he is no longer even convinced that natural law dictates the principle that the goods follow the owner, holding in substance that the practice of taking the goods of an enemy from the ship of a friend, though sanctioned by the usage of nations, is not so by the law of nature.   He now believes that national morality had never sanctioned the seizure of enemy goods in friendly territory; and the ship of a friend is to be regarded as his territory when on the high seas just as much as though in his harbor.   "We . . . perceive no distinction between the movable and immovable jurisdiction of a friend, which would authorize the entering the one and not the other, to seize the property of an enemy."[52]   He then goes on to justify the doctrine against the objection that "this proves too much, as it proves you cannot enter the ship of a friend to search for contraband of war.   But this is not proving too much. We believe the practice of seizing what is called contraband of war, is an abusive practice, not founded in natural right.   War between two nations cannot diminish the rights of the rest of the world remaining at peace."

IV

There are ways of settling the disputes of states less destructive and inhuman, and in the long run more effective than war, which is in fact the last resort, after other means of securing justice and safety have failed.[53]   "Friendly nations always nego-

---

[50] To Genet, July 24, 1793, *ibid.*, IX, 170.
[51] Dec. 20, 1793, *ibid.*, XVII, 348 ff.; cf. Randall, *Life of Jefferson*, II, 670 ff.
[52] To Livingston, Sept. 9, 1801, *Writings*, X, 277 ff., 280.
[53] To Sir John Sinclair, June 30, 1803, *ibid.*, X, 397; see also Anas, *ibid.*, I, 381.

tiate little differences in private. Never appeal to the world
but when they appeal to the sword." Arbitration of international disputes had barely begun in Jefferson's day, the first
arbitration agreement on record being that embodied in Jay's
treaty of 1794;[54] but he fully appreciated the value of the
judicial settlement there involved, as against the merely ad-
visory function covered by mediation. The authority of reason,
he declares, is "the only umpire between just nations."[55]

Although Jefferson could prosecute a war with vigor when
it could not be avoided, he was tireless in his efforts to make it
at least less frequent, and when it had become inevitable, to
render it as humane as possible. "Of my disposition to maintain
peace," he writes in 1817, "until its condition shall be made less
tolerable than that of war itself, the world has had proofs. . . .
I hope it is practicable, by improving the mind and morals of
society, to lessen the disposition to war; but of its abolition I
despair. Still, on the axiom that a less degree of evil is prefer-
able to a greater, no means should be neglected which may add
weight to the better scale."[56] War is a terrible thing, and it
must not be waged for petty causes. Jefferson offers a *reductio
ad absurdum* in opposing the use of force to restrain the *Little
Sarah*, a French prize fitted as a privateer in Philadelphia, "Because I would not gratify the combination of kings with the
spectacle of the two only republics on earth destroying each
other for two cannon."[57]

He went the length, also, of proposing a union of powers
for the preservation of peace, when he suggested concerted
action on the part of the states whose commerce suffered at the
hands of the Barbary pirates, to maintain a police force in the
Mediterranean.[58] World opinion, however, was not prepared
for that form of coöperation, and the question was only settled

[54] Balch, "The United States and the Expansion of the Law Between Nations,"
Pennsylvania Law Review, LXIV, 132.
[55] Fifth Annual Message, Dec. 3, 1805, *ibid.*, III, 387.
[56] To Noah Worcestor, Nov. 26, 1817, *ibid.*, XVIII, 298-99.
[57] Anas, *ibid.*, I, 368; cf. Randall, *op. cit.*, II, 157 ff.
[58] *Writings*, XVII, 145 ff.; cf. to Adams, July 11, 1786, *ibid.*, V, 364 ff.; to
Monroe, Aug. 11, 1786, *ibid.*, V, 385-86; Autobiography, *ibid.*, I, 97 ff.

by a series of wars, carried on individually by the interested nations. In this connection, it is possible to regard Jefferson's theory of the British empire, as set forth in the *Summary View*, as a contribution to the philosophy of international law, forming a background for a league or association of nations. For he visualizes a group of independent states, with possible conflicting interests, held together by an allegiance to a common administrative head, who has no actual power.[59]

When negotiation and arbitration fail, there are still compulsions that may be exercised without resorting to arms, and no one ever made better use of them than did Thomas Jefferson. He fully comprehended the value of economic pressure, and the tremendous force of "peaceable coercions." "War is not the best engine for us to resort to, nature has given us one in our commerce, which, if properly managed, will be a better instrument for obliging the interested nations of Europe to treat us with justice."[60]   And in March, 1793, when cargoes were in imminent danger of being denied entry into French ports, and irritation ran high, Jefferson had written apropos the possible convening of Congress to consider the question of war, and urged less violent measures. "But I should hope that war would not be their choice. I think it will furnish us a happy opportunity of setting another precious example to the world, by showing that nations may be brought to do justice by appeals to their interests as well as by appeals to arms. I should hope that Congress, instead of a denunciation of war, would instantly exclude from our ports all manufactures, produce, vessels and subjects of the nations committing this aggression, during the continuance of the aggression, and till full satisfaction is made for it. This would work well in many ways, safely in all, and introduce between nations another umpire than arms. It would relieve us, too, from the risks and horrors of cutting throats."[61]

[59] See Adams, *Political Ideas of the American Revolution*, especially 66 n.; and chap. 3, sec. IV, above.
[60] To Pinckney, May 29, 1797, *Writings*, IX, 389-90; cf. to Livingston, Sept. 9, 1801, *ibid.*, X, 281-82; to Paine, Mar. 18, 1801, *ibid.*, p. 223; to Logan, Mar. 21, 1801, *Writings* (Ford edition), VIII, 23.
[61] To Madison, Mar. 1793, *Writings*, IX, 33-34.

It is to be noted here that the embargo during Jefferson's administration proved a tremendously powerful weapon, and had the government been strong enough to secure its more rigid enforcement, might have averted the war of 1812. Recent researches in the French and British archives of the period reveal that it was far more effective than either its friends or its enemies realized at the time.[62]

The modern notion of arms limitation is another device for maintaining peace with which Jefferson was entirely familiar. In the negotiations with England over the fortifications on the Canadian line, Hammond, the British ambassador, had proposed an Indian buffer state between the two countries.[63] Jefferson countered with a proposal for limitation of armaments along the border; and Hammond ultimately offered a proposition to eliminate the forts entirely, to which Jefferson agreed with some enthusiasm.[64] The plan did not immediately bear fruit, but its monument today is four thousand miles of unfortified frontier.

Another means of compulsion is retaliation. Jefferson holds therefore, that while commerce ought to be free from every obstruction, if one nation erects barriers against another, such, for example, as tariff laws, the other must retaliate.[65] A nation has a right, also, to demand adequate satisfaction for injury sustained at the hands of another, but "to demand satisfaction *beyond* what is adequate is wrong."[66] This policy in the hands of John Hay a century later was fully to demonstrate the truth of Jefferson's assertion that a nation, "by establishing a character for liberality and magnanimity, gains in friendship and respect of others more than the worth of mere money."

After ample cause for war has arisen, Jefferson would still

[62] L. M. Sears, *Jefferson and the Embargo* (Durham, 1927), preface, *et passim.* Cf. F. W. Hirst, *Life and Letters of Thomas Jefferson* (New York, 1926), pp. 441 ff., for concurring English view. For critics of the Embargo, see Henry Adams, *History of the United States*, IV; Allen Johnson, *Jefferson and his Colleagues* (New Haven, 1921), chap. 8.

[63] Bemis, *op. cit.*, p. 30.   [64] Cf. Sears, *op. cit.*, pp. 40-41.

[65] To W. Seward, Nov. 12, 1785, *Writings*, V, 203.

[66] Official Papers, *ibid.*, III, 249, 406.

be not too precipitate in entering conflict. In regard to the seizure of the *Chesapeake* by the British, and other acts of aggression towards the end of his second term, he took infinite pains to avoid a rupture. "We act on these principles, 1. That the usage of nations requires that we shall give the offender an opportunity of making reparation and avoiding war. 2. That we should give time to our merchants to get in their property and vessels and our seamen now afloat. And 3. That the power of declaring war being with the Legislature, the executive should do nothing, necessarily committing them to decide for war in preference to nonintercourse, which will be preferred by many."[67]

The theory of the social contract which Jefferson advanced assumed the state of nature to be a state of peace; and in international affairs he sought to preserve this fundamental pacifism by every means in his power. If he never conceived, as Kant so clearly did,[68] a pacific world order based on a league of states, it was, perhaps, because the America of his day was too remote from Europe to make such a plan appear as within the range of possibility. Then, too, Kant had adopted Hobbes's conception of the presocial state as a war of each against all, in which peace could be preserved only by agreement to preserve it, backed by force; and had reasoned from analogy to postulate a similar agreement among national states. For Jefferson, peace was the natural, war the artificial state of man. If Kant's vision was of a world federation, in which war would not be tolerated, Jefferson's ideal was of a world democracy, in which cause for war would never arise.[69]

[67] To Clinton, July 6, 1807, *ibid.*, XI, 258; cf. to Bidwell, July 11, 1807, *ibid.*, p. 272.

[68] See *Zum Ewigen Frieden* (Leipsig, 1881, English translation by W. Hastie, Boston, 1914).

[69] Cf. Henry Adams, *op. cit.*, I, 146-47.

BOOK IV

THE DEMOCRATIC TRADITION

Unless its foundations be laid in justice the social structure cannot stand.

—HENRY GEORGE

CHAPTER X

RETROSPECT

I

THE POLITICAL philosophy of Thomas Jefferson rests on two basic assumptions, both of which are ethical: that the end of life is individual happiness, and that the purpose of the state is to secure and increase that happiness. Men are more important than institutions, and social good is to be reckoned in terms of human values. The ultimate end of government, like that of science, of art, of philosophy, is to further the material and spiritual well-being of men. And from this it follows that government must be responsible to the people, and relative to their will, expressed by a majority of voices; for the state is the creation and the creature of those who live in it. It is an instrument for the better attainment of the individual ethical end, to be altered or abolished when its usefulness is over.

Nature, which has planted in man the instinctive drive to seek happiness and avoid misery and pain, has endowed him also with the means for achieving this goal. Certain things are necessary to a happy life: liberty, security in the possession of material goods, freedom from arbitrary coercion by others. These are natural rights, attaching in equal degree to all, and carrying with them a duty on the part of each individual to respect them in his fellows. Men come together in society because they are essentially gregarious, and are so formed that no one is sufficient unto himself. He can be happy only in the companionship of others. And since in every group, men will be found who will overstep their rights to the injury of someone else, some form of government must be erected, having power to guarantee these rights by punishing those who transgress.

The social compact is a legal fiction, used to explain and to limit the power of the state; and its actual embodiment is the constitution, drawn up by representatives of the people, and sanctioned by the approval of the individuals who are to live under its rule. The constitution is in the form of a contract to which the several members of the society subscribe, setting up organs for making and enforcing the law, and machinery for carrying forward the welfare of the group. It is the fundamental law, constituting the form of the society and preserving it against too rapid change. The particular type of machinery thus brought into being will be dependent on the type of people to be governed by it, on the resources and character of the country, and on the demands likely to be made upon it.

But though there are many conceivable and practical forms of government, all soundly based states must, for Jefferson, follow broadly a general pattern. The best government is no government at all; only in a community in which there is no political coercion of any kind can the individual enjoy complete freedom. But in any except the smallest and most congenial groups, the total absence of government means anarchy, and in the end control by the stronger and more ruthless at the expense of the weaker. Next best is pure democracy, in which all the people have an equal share in carrying on the affairs of the state, meeting in common council to transact the public business; but this too becomes impractical when the state passes certain limits of area and population. The nearest approach to the ideal which can obtain in practice is the representative democracy, which Jefferson calls the republic. In it the functions of the state are carried on by individuals, elected by the people for short terms. Sovereignty belongs properly to the people themselves, but when their numbers are too great to permit them to exercise it effectively, they delegate it to certain individuals or groups to exercise for them.

These representatives of the people will be divided into three distinct branches: a legislature, consisting of two chambers, whose duty it is to make laws and to raise money for carrying them into effect; an executive, preferably an individual, who is responsible for the administration of the law; and a judiciary organ to judge and punish infractions of it, and to settle disputes between citizens. These branches of the government are coördinate, and are responsible to the people; and their authority is specifically limited by the constitution, or contract whereby their respective offices have been created. The constitution also includes various devices for preventing one department from encroaching on the province of any other; and a bill of rights to restrain any department from interfering in the sphere of the individual.

The duty of the individual citizen, however, extends much further than the mere election of representatives to carry on in his name the actual business of government. He must keep informed, through the press, books, the schools, on the issues of the day, the problems facing his representatives, the laws passed and their import. And he must exercise in person every function his qualifications will permit him to exercise. Government is equally the concern of all the men associated under it, and Jefferson would have declared as feelingly as Rousseau that "As soon as any man says of the affairs of the State *what does it matter to me?* the State may be given up for lost."[1] Every man is a potential ruler, and should be always ready to assume public office if his fellow citizens place that trust at his disposal; and every man, in office or in private life, should do his part in formulating the will of the group. Good government springs from a common interest in public affairs.

The larger the state, the more remote is the individual from the actual governing power; and there is consequently increasing danger that he will come to regard himself as impotent so far as the affairs of the nation are concerned, and lose interest in them. This danger Jefferson proposes to avoid by organizing the state into an hierarchy of self-governing units. The centralized federal republic is subdivided into states, each with its own executive, legislative, and judiciary organs; the state is made

[1] *Social Contract,* III, 15.

up of counties, with their own courts and administrative machinery; and the county itself is reduced to wards or townships,
of an area of some five or six square miles. In the ward, each
citizen is an acting member of the government, meeting in common council to carry on the business of the community. Thus
each man has a personal interest in the actual conduct of affairs,
either in his own ward or in one of the higher units of the
scale; and at the same time, the more minute details of administration, such as local roads and schools, are placed directly
under the supervision of those most concerned.

Jefferson believes, too, that this arrangement will enable the
functions of government to be carried on more effectively all
along the line. These functions are broadly divided into productive and repressive, the latter being necessary to the preservation of order, and extending to police power and national
defense; the former including education, regulation of business,
and promotion of agriculture and the arts, all of which follow
from the ethical end of the state. Of these, Jefferson necessarily places education foremost: for if government rests upon
the will of the individuals grouped under it, and if its end is the
ultimate well-being and happiness of those individuals, it becomes a primary duty of the state to educate them, provide them
with books and papers, and free them from censorship or control
in intellectual matters. It follows also that for the welfare of
the whole, the state may upon occasion be justified in restricting
the activities of the individual, by curtailing his commercial and
industrial ventures, or by limiting his property rights.

The instrument through which the will of the state becomes
articulate is law. Its ultimate sanction is the consent of the
people, and its end is the social good. But even the law must
not be absolute; the legislative power is limited by the inalienable rights of the individual—the constitutional bill of rights;
and is circumscribed by the law of nature—certain natural moral
principles inherent in the world order. Law is the element in
the state which affects all in the same way, and it is accordingly
the means of regulating the relations between individuals. In

like manner legal rules form the basis of intercourse between states. Some of these are dictated by usage, some by utility and the force of circumstances; but all are sanctioned by mutual agreement, and all derive their validity from the same moral law which validates individual conduct. In Jefferson's world, justice is immutable; and nations, like men, will be happy only as they are just, honest, fair. The principle of life and of the state is reason, which will, which must, triumph in the end.

II

One of the criticisms most often levelled at the democratic state is that by dividing the sovereignty among a multitude it destroys, or at least seriously impairs, the power of the state to act effectively. Such criticisms, however, can have little value, because the problem itself is a false one. The theory of sovereignty is neither metaphysical, as it has sometimes been called,[2] nor logical in the sense of necessary, but is a legal concept pure and simple; and for legal purposes the power of the state cannot be regarded as inhering in its members as discrete individuals, but rather in their collective or corporate capacity. The state acts through law, and its effectiveness depends, not on the agency which makes the law, but on that which administers it. There is thus no essential difference between the commands of a dictator and the deliberations of a parliament. Law is effective only to the extent that it is administered effectively, and in no state can this be done unless the bulk of the citizens are willing, or can be forced, to coöperate. In the democratic state, the coöperation must be voluntary; and it is precisely this which Jefferson means by popular sovereignty.

It is characteristic of the sovereign in the Austinian definition[3] that it should be outside the limits of positive law. It makes law, but is not itself restricted by law. If we try to localize the sovereignty as Austin did, this is a manifest absurdity. The voting citizens of the United States are very def-

---

[2] *E.g.*, A. C. McLaughlin, *The Confederation and the Constitution*, p. 222.
[3] John Austin, *Lectures on Jurisprudence* (2 vols. London, 1879), No. 6, I, 226.

initely subject to laws made by Congress; Congress is limited by the presidential veto, by the constitution, and by the Supreme Court's interpretation of the constitution; and the constitution, again, is limited by the people, who may amend it. Individual congressmen, further, may be and often have been defeated at the polls for failure to respond to pressure from their constituents; and in those states which have adopted the recall, an elected official may be removed from office by popular vote. There is no body or person in this country which owes no obedience somewhere.

This is not to imply that the notion of a legal sovereign is not useful, perhaps even necessary, in the administration of the government, but for this purpose it need include no more than the duly constituted legislative bodies and the machinery of the courts. The laws themselves must be sanctioned, as Jefferson held, by the approval of the people. Otherwise, the state is nothing more than organized force. Locke's distinction into nominal, legal, and political sovereignties[4] serves only to cloud the issue further. For other than legal purposes, a sovereign is unnecessary; and from the legal point of view, the fiction of the corporate or juristic personality of the state seems quite sufficient. A single indivisible, ultimate power is perhaps compatible with the philosophical monism of Hobbes and Kant, who inspired Austin; but an eclectic like Jefferson is under no such obligation to a self-imposed logic. The modern state is regulated and its activities are carried out by law; its sovereign, therefore, will be whatever force gives sanction to its legal acts. In the democratic state, this force is public opinion: a sovereignty the more useful because not confined within nationalistic bounds. Laws for regulating the intercourse between nations are sanctioned by the same power as that which makes effective the legal code of any given state.

The principle on which Jefferson's state rests must be the basal principle of every democratic society: that the government is created by the people, and is subject to be changed or

---

[4] *Of Civil Government,* Treatise II, secs. 149-51.

abolished at their discretion. And it is public opinion—the beliefs of a potential majority of the citizenry of any given state
or group of states—which dictates the course of political authority. On the long view, history bears out this thesis. No government has ever existed which has been able to defy public
opinion indefinitely; and with the spread of education and the
more general diffusion of knowledge the tenure of absolute states
becomes increasingly precarious. On such a theory the instruments for molding and expressing the popular will, the vehicles
for thrashing out differences and reaching the working compromises by which we live, are of supreme importance. No matter
what the occasion, the censorship of the press or the limitation
of popular discussion is a confession of failure. When any government deems the opposition to its policies so strong that to
allow it free expression, would endanger the fulfillment of
those policies that government has ceased to be legitimate.

Nor is the sanction of public opinion confined to the internal
acts of any specific state. It is the only pressure that can be
brought to bear to insure justice between nations; and though
of slower operation, it is in the end as sure. If this was so in
Jefferson's day, and he repeatedly affirmed that it was, how
much truer it is today, with London and Paris nearer to Washington than Baltimore was in 1800! On the Austinian theory,
there can be no such thing as international law, because there
is no single sovereignty to enforce it. Yet an international code,
based on nothing more than the phantom of world opinion, has
been in successful operation for three centuries.

It is no criticism of democracy to charge that it is incompatible with a theory of absolute sovereignty. Such a theory is
itself incompatible with the conditions and problems of actual
government, just as it precludes the possibility of international
harmony short of a superstate. Like all theories of absolutism
and all theories of imperialism, the notion of an indivisible sovereignty pushes morality outside the world and relegates individual liberty to the limbo of forgotten things. The Jeffersonian state is a specific denial of the assumption of Hobbes that

might is right, and the widespread acceptance of democratic ideas since Jefferson is a specific vindication of personal freedom.

III

From sophisticated New England John Adams wrote ironically to Jefferson: "Your taste is judicious in liking better the dreams of the future than the history of the past."[5] But the shaft did not strike home. Jefferson built upon ideals, to be sure, but he built also upon facts—facts of which Adams was only vaguely aware. For Adams had never known, as Jefferson and Jackson and Lincoln knew, the American frontier and the men it bred. A governing aristocracy might be possible in the wealthy coastal cities or among the alluvial plantations of the south; but beyond the rim of the mountains, where the wilderness lay still unconquered, there were no distinctions of class. There men were equal, and better, they were free, developing initiative and self-reliance in their westward march, and settling their own differences without appealing to the courts. Jefferson was himself the product of the first west in American history;[6] he loved the hardy independence of the pioneer, and sought to build something of the pioneer character into his philosophy of the state. Not wealth nor property nor class, but men form the basis of the political order: free men, in whom justice and fair dealing are instinctive; who labor together for the common good of all, in scorn of selfish aims.

The most fundamental criticism of democracy is perhaps the simple assertion that men are not like that. Jefferson preferred to believe, because of his own great love of freedom, that free men could not but be just, sincere, and true. For him the war of each against all is the abusive rather than the natural state of man: a product of civilization, which might still be eradicated by a wise and impartial government. He could not doubt that men, however corrupt they might become, were fundamentally rational and moral; he could not doubt the ultimate rightness of life. Like the Greek, he identifies the good man with the

---

[5] Aug. 9, 1816; *The Works of John Adams* (10 vols. Boston, 1850-1856), X, 226.
[6] W. E. Dodd, *Statesmen of the Old South* (New York, 1911), p. 23.

good citizen; and like the Greek, he holds evil to be error. If men do ill, it is because they do not know the good. The remedy is to teach them, give them free access to information about their affairs, encourage them to discussion.

Democracy has often been refuted, but it has never been silenced. Its difficulties are practical difficulties—it is slow, cumbersome, inefficient, blundering; its decentralization makes for waste and friction; the inexperience and multiplicity of its officers open the way for privilege and corruption. But all these have to do with its machinery rather than with its philosophy. The democratic state is not seeking an ideal of efficiency or of stability. For Jefferson the primary purpose of government is to promote the happiness, the self-realization of the individual. This democracy achieves, perhaps to a greater degree than any other form of government; and in so far as it does achieve this, it fulfills its ideal. The rest is of secondary importance.

The chief difficulty with Jefferson's political system is that of getting the individual into society without the use of force. He argues that some form of social organization is necessary to protect and enforce individual rights; and at the same time he bases morality on innate social instincts. Logically these two arguments are incompatible; for a consistent individualism cannot admit instinctive social desires, any more than a natural social order can leave room for unrestricted personal rights. Jefferson gets around the difficulty by putting a social limitation on the inherent rights of men. Rights and duties are in some sense related, and the individual can exercise his own rights only to the extent that they do not conflict with those of others. What results is a continuous compromise between the demands of the individual and the necessities of the society. No one gets all he wants, but everyone gets something; and the welfare of the group as a whole ultimately emerges as the real purpose of the state, the individual end being absorbed in the social end. Jefferson was not writing a philosophy of the state alone; he was helping to create and administer a government. His view was the view supported by Locke, it was upheld by the liberal thought of the age, and it was believed by the people to whom, in the end, the new state had to appeal for support. A perfect government would no doubt be perfectly logical; but the perfect government is as chimerical as the perfect man. In every state, as in every life, there is a measure of paradox, which may perhaps be strength as well as weakness.

Jefferson seeks to resolve the antagonism between individual and society in his treatment of liberty and equality; for it is only by making these two notions complementary that the compromise between personal and social ends can be carried out. Equality for Jefferson means simply that the state recognizes no distinction between its citizens; and liberty means the absence of external restraint. Now equality is itself a form of restraint; for I am free to act only to the extent that all others in the state may act in the same way, and I am the equal of others only to the extent that my liberty is so limited. Complete individualism implies freedom limited only by personal capacity; but where legal equality is recognized by the state, the restriction upon freedom becomes social rather than personal.

Liberty under these conditions is reduced to the absence of external restraint in so far as it is compatible with the welfare of the group, each individual in the society being regarded as equally free to act within these limits, and equally entitled to protection from the unlimited freedom of others. Since there is no sphere but that of the intellect in which the activity of one may not be injurious to others, freedom reduces in the end to intellectual freedom. Individual liberty means no more than liberty to think, to speak, to worship; liberty to read and write without censorship, and to associate with others for any legitimate purpose. But this is enough. Political growth and social change come slowly, through the introduction and gradual dissemination of new ideas; and the philosophy of democracy is simply a recognition of the fact that ideas will spread and change will come eventually, in spite of the opposition of intrenched privilege and class interest.

Jefferson's wisdom lay in his faith and his trust in men; and this alone is enough to explain the tremendous appeal and the almost irresistible force of democratic ideas in the modern world. For men in whom others believe come at length to believe in themselves; men on whom others depend are in the main dependable. Most of us do what we know is expected of us, be it good or ill. The objective of the democratic state is to secure the greatest possible happiness for all its citizens, and it assumes that this end is recognized and sought by the individuals concerned. It treats them, therefore, not as subjects, but as partners in a common enterprise; and it lifts them thereby from the ruck of serfdom to the level of human beings, breeding in them independence, initiative, and self-reliance.

The final test of any political philosophy is not the logical but the pragmatic test. The only criterion for judging any theory of the state is the measure of its practical success. The Jeffersonian state was built on the broad foundation of centuries of political theorizing to meet the conditions of a given time and place: to solve the problems of a pioneer people in a vast and undeveloped country. All this democracy accomplished, perhaps better than any other form of government could have done. Jefferson succeeded in both his immediate objectives—to justify a separation from Great Britain, and to create a government adequate to the people and the resources of America. But to build for the future is more difficult, and requires imagination and idealism such as few possess. Jefferson realized the futility of trying to fix in one generation political forms that should be valid for all time. He knew that a static society cannot endure, and his efforts were bent toward providing peaceable instruments for accomplishing the inevitable changes time must bring. His legacy is not his solution of the political problem, but his realization that the problem must be solved anew in each succeeding era. Our heritage is his faith that an informed and intelligent people can and will work out their own salvation.

IV

The Jeffersonian political philosophy exhibits two distinct tendencies, two divergent emphases, which are superficially incompatible. In affirming the best government to be that which governs least, Jefferson proclaims himself an individualist and commits himself to an economic theory of laissez faire; but he declares also that the welfare of the whole is the proper purpose of the state, and maintains the power of the government to curtail the activities of the individual for the common good. On the side of individualism, the society must be regarded as an aggregate, the members of which are free to seek their own ends as they see fit. On the other side, the group is an organism: the parts are equal, and are subject to such restrictions on their personal liberty as the health of the organism may require. The one emphasis leads to economic anarchy and philosophical isolation—to an "age of big business" and to Walden Pond. The other leads to a planned and controlled economy, and to a collective society—to state socialism and to Brook Farm.

It is not accident, or mere theoretical inconsistency, that brings Jefferson to the crossroads. The democratic and socialistic philosophies are closely linked, both historically and logically. The inconsistency is rather on the part of an age prone to regard them as at opposite poles. The seed of English socialism as it germinated in Mill and T. H. Green and blossomed in the Labor Party, was planted by Harrington and Locke; and the lineal ancestor of all modern proletarian movements is the democrat, Jean Jacques Rousseau. Both individualism and socialism go back, to be sure, to Greece, but for purposes of this study we need not delve so remotely into the past. The rise of individualism as a philosophical doctrine is traceable to the reformation, and as an economic dogma it is implicit in the Calvinist creed, which has stamped its impress ineffaceably on modern thought. It was economic individualism which brought in its train the revolt against absolutism and the rise of the democratic state.

Now it is this very economic individualism, tending to become more and more ruthless, that destroys at last the democratic order to which it gave rise. Democracy is a protest against political absolutism, which it ultimately replaces with an economic absolutism; and it is against this final consummation that socialist theory in its turn protests. Democracy, without an admixture of socialism, cannot survive the passing of an agricultural order; for the profits of commerce and industry are too large, and the power they give too great, to be compatible with the ideals of personal freedom and legal equality. If the power of the state must be checked, lest it be abused through sheer love of glory, how much more must the power of wealth be controlled, lest it be abused through the still more fundamental love of gain!

Democracy and socialism are alike motivated by the desire to free the individual from oppression, and to guarantee to each an opportunity for personal happiness, for self-realization, for practical liberty and spiritual freedom. Democracy is an attempt to distribute political power among the masses with the purpose of obviating once and for all the possibility of dictatorial control; socialism is a recognition of the fact that political and economic power must and will be identified.

The socialist, like the democrat, is attracted not by dreams of empire, but by the freedom, the emphasis on human values, the recognition of personal worth, which a highly mechanized civilization overwhelms.

The differentia of democracy is the sovereignty of the people, through public opinion, which is true of the socialist state alone among other forms of government. The only difference between the two is in fact a difference of emphasis; and unless both emphases are combined, as they were in Jefferson, neither form can hold its own. One is the natural corrective of the abuses of the other. If liberty be made basal, and logically followed, the result is a dictatorship by those who most successfully use their liberty to acquire economic power. If, on the other hand, equality be made the fundamental issue, the logical outcome is complete communism. If all men acted with

unselfish charity, there would be no political problem; but with
due allowance for human nature, it seems impossible to set up
an ethical code without authority behind it.   Since the reformation, and for some centuries before it, the authority of the church
has failed to enforce morality in a commercial world.   The alter-
native is an ethico-juristic code, established by public opinion operating through the channels of representative government,
and backed by the power of the state.   Liberty is restrained and
equality checked by law: law which is no mere arbitrary dictum
of organized force, but having a definite ethical content and a
specific social purpose.

Having gone so far, it becomes apparent that the individualistic and the socialistic tendencies in Jefferson—and in all
sound democratic theory—are no longer incompatible.   Both
follow from the initial premise of the democratic state: that the
purpose of government is to promote the personal happiness of
those who owe allegiance to it.   This end is impossible without a
measure of individual liberty; but it is also impossible if certain
persons or groups, through the attainment of economic power,
are allowed to coerce for their own ends other individuals or
groups.   The industrialist, the landowner, the labor leader, are
alike subject to regulation and control by the state whenever
their activities interfere with the right of others to the pursuit
of happiness.

These phrases are vague enough; but political society is
an elusive thing, and the rules must not be too rigidly defined,
lest they be rudely trampled underfoot as the game proceeds.
The exact point at which the power of the state must be exerted to curb individual enterprise, the precise line which marks
the social good, must be determined by expediency—by the possibilities of the given situation and the circumstances of the
hour.   When the population is small in comparison to the extent of the national domain, and vast natural resources are only
beginning to be exploited, there is enough for all, and individual initiative is the order of the day.   But where the proportion
of unemployed is large and distribution of economic goods in-

creasingly unequal, the balance of public opinion will swing towards the side of the dispossessed, and the social functions of the state will be emphasized. In general, the older and more densely peopled the country, the more socialistic it will become. The peculiar strength of the democratic philosophy lies in the very broadness of its principles, which makes possible adjustment to a changing social order within the familiar framework of the traditional governmental structure.

V

This double emphasis in Jefferson's thought has left to American democracy a dual tradition, the importance of which has been overshadowed by its association with sectional conflict. In the South, where society was organized on a plantation basis, the tradition tended more and more toward aristocratic individualism, worked out along the lines of the Greek democracy modified to conform to a vaster setting. John Taylor of Caroline selected from the Jeffersonian philosophy its agrarian bias, which he formulated in economic terms. Calhoun chose to emphasize the fiduciary nature of governmental authority; and with Alexander H. Stephens the terminable contract is made the ground for a legal defense of secession. All these men opposed centralized power, and took personal liberty as their ideal; but it was the liberty of a class which had replaced that of the whole. Rather than submit to a social limitation on the activities of every member of the group, Calhoun affirms the dogma of a superior race, and flatly repudiates the equality of men.

The social emphasis found its early expression in attempts like that of the Brook Farm group to establish collective societies, and was clothed in economic terms by Henry George, by Edward Bellamy, and by Thorstein Veblen. In the realm of practical politics social democracy first shows significant strength in the populist campaigns of the latter nineteenth century, and in the various "progressive" movements; while in the New Deal it has come into actual power. These two branches of the tradition will be examined more fully in the following chapters.

CHAPTER XI

DEMOCRATIC INDIVIDUALISM

I

JOHN TAYLOR of Caroline was a contemporary and close friend of the three great Virginians who formed the dynasty: Jefferson, Madison, and Monroe. But personal ambition never led him to seek the public stage, and he served his colleagues by word rather than by deed. Though he coupled unparalleled verbosity with a heavy and labored style, yet for all his literary sins, his close logic and his penetrating insight raised his pamphlets to the level of an official body of doctrine for the republican party. It is a doctrine singularly consistent in its championship of individualism, from his first attack on the bank in 1794 to his final philippic against the protective tariff some thirty years later. For Taylor was never called upon, as were his presidential friends, to make the compromises and modifications incident to the administration of high public office. He was able to follow his logic through to the end, unhampered by the dictates of political expediency. It was Taylor who suggested the Virginia Resolutions of 1799 to Jefferson;[1] and it was Taylor who sowed the seeds of nullification, for Calhoun to cultivate and for the South to reap.

The constitutional argument is formulated in Taylor's letter to Jefferson of June 25, 1798, and is expanded, with more or less relevant digressions, in his subsequent writings. The constitution, he contends, is a compact *between the states*, and the parties to it are the various ratifying conventions, these being in turn delegates of the people. It is therefore reserved for the states to determine whether or not the constitution is being infringed, and to declare null and void any unconstitutional act

---

[1] Taylor to Jefferson, June 25, 1798, *The John P. Branch Historical Papers*, II (June, 1908), 271-76.

of any branch of the general government. This thesis is most elaborately developed in the *Inquiry into the Principles and Policy of the Government of the United States,* published in 1814, and intended as a belated answer to the constitutional theory of the *Federalist,* and of John Adams's *Defense of the Constitutions of the United States.*[2] This instance alone will serve to show how rare was Taylor's consistency; for Jefferson, who had endorsed both the *Federalist* and the *Defense* in a day in which he had been no more disposed to accept central authority than he was in 1814, yet found no difficulty in taking Taylor's part against Adams.

It was largely the repeated insistence Taylor placed on popular sovereignty that gave him his commanding place in democratic councils. There is no doubt in his mind as to the literalness of delegated power, or the necessity of constant watchfulness on the part of the people lest it be abused. In the early stages of his attack on Hamilton's bank, *An Enquiry into the Principles and Tendency of Certain Public Measures,* published in 1794, Taylor summarizes the fundamental tenets of his creed. If political principles really exist, he argues, and if rights are to be more than mere words, it should be possible to select "a few simple axioms, beyond the reach of polemical artifice, and containing a degree of internal evidence, compelling indubitable conviction." These axioms are not embodied in the constitution, for that may be too readily interpreted by special interests. They are rather results of the constitution, which may be simply stated. The government is to be republican, "flowing from and depending on the people." The right of legislation resides in the people, and is periodically delegated by election to their representatives. The right of election is a substance and not a form, and a legitimate representation "implies an *existing operative* principle, in the representing, impelling them for the good of the represented." Whenever this principle ceases to exist, the government is converted into an usurpation.

[2] See Benj. F. Wright, "The Philosopher of Jeffersonian Democracy," *American Political Science Review,* XXII, 875 ff.; Henry H. Simms, *Life of John Taylor* (Richmond, 1932), pp. 133-44.

Here is individualism with a vengeance! The theory of the American constitution is not, as Adams and Madison had held, to balance interests or orders, but to unite the people in a single interest, and to divide political power between the people and their government, and between the states.[3] There is no room in the system for privilege of any kind. Legislation tending to give to any individual or group power denied to others is therefore unconstitutional. The effect of this principle is to reduce the functions of government to the lowest possible—to confine the activities of the state to those which have earlier been called "repressive" functions. For the moment the line is passed, and government goes beyond the mere preservation of order and liberty, a new source of privilege is created through patronage. The union is a confederation of the people of the various geographical units, and is in no sense a balance of classes or an accommodation of interests.

The three Virginia republicans who administered the government for a quarter of a century did much to carry out these principles, but none of the three went as far as Taylor, who filled the rôle of self-appointed critic during the first thirty-five years of the constitution. He regarded himself as a Jeffersonian, and Jefferson endorsed his writings without reserve. There are, however, various differences, which might easily go unnoticed by the two men themselves because overshadowed by their larger agreements. Both dreaded the power of capitalism, and fought against it as it manifested itself in the bank scheme and in the tariff, and both opposed the power of the Supreme Court to set aside acts of Congress. But in all these points Taylor's opposition is more thoroughgoing than Jefferson's. The latter accepted the tariff of 1816 on the ground that political independence demanded economic independence. Taylor remained agrarian to the end, holding that agriculture was the only primary and natural source of wealth.[4] He charged that to subsidize manufactures was to create a privileged class, and an

---

[3] *An Inquiry into the ... Government of the United States*, p. 161.
[4] *Arator* (Georgetown, 1813), preface.

artificial opposition of interests. To the doctrine of judicial review, Jefferson opposed constitutional interpretation by the accredited representatives of the people: the federal legislative and executive officers. Taylor offered as a substitute the contract theory of the constitution, and maintained the right of the contracting parties—the states—to refuse to carry out their constitutional obligations if the government overstepped its assigned limits.[5] Both denied the power of the Supreme Court to override the state courts, but Jefferson recognized the validity of an appeal on constitutional questions.

Taylor emphasizes one side of Jeffersonian democracy—the individualistic side; but he deserves none the less the first place in the tradition. His four most important works were published after Jefferson had retired from the presidency, and it was in those years of retirement that Jefferson himself was most inclined to emphasize individualism. It is possible to be more coldly logical and more rigorously consistent in the abstraction of the study than it is in the arena of politics; but it does not follow that the measures best designed to promote good government are those which conform most closely to the abstract principle. It is perhaps for this reason that, though Taylor is more consistent, Jefferson has been more enduring.

The economics of individualistic democracy is an uncompromising laissez-faire theory; and it is such a theory that Taylor expounds in his *Tyranny Unmasked* (1822), an elaborate argument against protection. The protective system creates a monopoly, the proceeds of which accrue to enrich the capitalists, a small minority, at the expense of the great mass of people who must pay more for their manufactured products. This is privilege, and is a plain perversion of the legal equality of the citizens. Moreover, an even greater blow will be struck at agriculture; for the farmer, in addition to paying more for the protected articles, will find the value of his own produce reduced in foreign markets by the restrictions on exchange. The unity of interest which Taylor held to be essential had already been

[5] *New Views on the Constitution of the United States* (Washington, 1823), p. 148.

undermined—if, indeed, it had ever existed—and his argument was soon to be echoed by a class as a weapon against the denial of its equal rights.

One further point in Taylor's writings must be discussed, because of its bearing on the later development of the individualistic thesis. In 1820 he published his *Construction Construed and Constitutions Vindicated,* which dealt at length with the two burning questions of the hour: the doctrine of liberal construction, as laid down by Chief Justice Marshall in McCulloch *vs.* Maryland; and the Missouri Compromise. In respect to the former, he reasserts the right of the states to hold the central government within its constitutional limits, and charges that because of the failure adequately to safeguard property against the encroachments of government, a monied class had arisen, and was steadily consolidating the central power at the expense of the community at large.[6] As to the Missouri Compromise, he holds that slavery was merely the excuse, and never the real point at issue. The real question involved was that of preserving the balance of power between the two great sections of the country. The ultimate result of this opposition of interests, he foresees clearly enough; for a balance of power between sections, like that between nations, can lead only to war.

Taylor stands as the link between the democracy of Jefferson and that of Calhoun. With the former, he champions the sovereignty of the people, and denounces class and privilege. With the latter, he regards the constitution as a compact between the states, of the terms of which the parties are to judge. Taylor's doctrine opens the way for nullification and secession just as surely as it was itself grounded on the *Declaration of Independence.*

II

Although the most productive period of his life was its last four years, 1820 to 1824, Taylor belonged, like Jefferson, to an earlier and a simpler age. The younger men who inherited the mantle of party leadership were faced with new conditions. The

[6] *Construction Construed,* p. 233.

industrial revolution had arrived; and with the changing social order in America, the economic realism of Calhoun succeeded the humanitarian idealism of the Virginia school. The
first meeting of the Twelfth Congress in 1811, saw the appearance in the House of Henry Clay, who had already won his
spurs in the Senate, and of John Caldwell Calhoun; while in
1813 Daniel Webster took his seat in the same body. It was
these three men, above all others, who determined the course
of American government for the next forty years.

It is with Calhoun, perhaps the greatest political thinker this
country has yet produced, that we are primarily concerned here.
Entering Congress when the country was in ferment and war
with England was only a few months away, it was probably
inevitable that he should have espoused the cause of nationalism, and he soon came to be the outstanding champion of the
war. In 1817, in recognition of his services in Congress, he
became Secretary of War in Monroe's cabinet, having just
passed his thirty-fifth birthday. Calhoun had not, however,
confined himself to military affairs. He had led in the fight
for internal improvements, and had gone with Clay to support
the so-called "American system"—the protective tariff. In 1816
there was no doubt a genuine need for moderate protection, the
manufacturing enterprizes which had sprung up in New England during the war being as yet unable to meet the competition
of the older British industrialism. But by 1828 the tariff burden
had begun to weigh heavily on the agricultural South. Taylor
had accurately forecast the outcome of the Missouri Compromise; and had presented the southern argument against the
tariff in the Senate in 1823, while Spencer Roane and Thomas
Cooper were actively agitating the question in the states.[7]

It was no longer possible for a southern statesman to hold
aloof; and sometime between 1823 and the tariff bill of 1828
Calhoun swung over to the opposition.[8] From that time until
his death in 1850 he was the acknowledged leader of the state

---

[7] Channing, *History of the United States*, V, 405 ff.

[8] W. M. Meigs, *Life of Calhoun* (2 vols. New York, 1917), I, 348 ff.

rights school, and the able champion of democratic individual-ism. The policy of this later period of Calhoun's intellectual maturity is extraordinarily consistent, bringing him to break party ties again and again, voting sometimes with the democrats, sometimes with the whigs, and not infrequently standing alone. He opposed any form of state subsidy to private enterprize, whether disguised as a tariff, or offered under the form of internal improvements; and he sought to divorce the government from any connection with privately controlled financial institutions. In opposing the recharter of the national bank, he offered as a substitute a bill to make the treasury independent, much as it has since come to be; and during the war with Mexico, he denounced the lavish expenditure on pensions. It was in 1832, however, that the lines were most sharply drawn, and the sectional issue was placed squarely in the center of the stage, where it was to remain until the echo of the guns of Sumter had died away in the smoke of Appomattox.

The steadily rising tariff reached its peak in that year; and with their hopeless minority in the House of Representatives, the southern states were impotent to stem the tide of wealth and privilege flowing under its provisions into the manufacturing states. After fruitless protest, the legislature of South Carolina, under Calhoun's leadership, passed an ordinance of nullification, refusing to permit the enforcement within the state of an act regarded as unconstitutional. President Jackson, though himself a South Carolinian, ordered troops to Charleston, and for a time coercion seemed inevitable; but love of union prevailed, and a substantial reduction in the tariff was agreed to in time to prevent military intervention.[9] The method of resistance, however, had been demonstrated successfully, and the tragedy of the Civil War had become all but inevitable.

Calhoun, like Taylor, regarded himself as a Jeffersonian, citing the Kentucky Resolutions of 1799, in which the very word was used, in support of nullification;[10] and as late as 1843 he identified the party divisions of his own day with the breach

---

[9] *Ibid.*, pp. 413 ff.   [10] *Ibid.*, pp. 445 ff.

between Jefferson and Hamilton.[11] Yet Calhoun had gone immeasurably beyond the sage of Monticello; for even while accepting the theory of democracy, he denied the very basis on which the Jeffersonian system had been reared. He too feared centralization; but he feared equally the dominance of the numerical majority. The escape from the former he found in the teaching of Jefferson; the escape from the latter involved a denial of that teaching. Against the dominance of numbers he erected the barrier of class, and based his democracy on a recognized inequality among individuals. Some were by nature inferior, and it was right that they should be held in slavery by those of the superior race.[12] Against the federalist doctrine of centralization he turned the state rights formula, refined and pushed to its logical extreme: nullification. It became in his hands a veto power to be exercised by the states on acts of the national government, and was in effect the germ of the referendum.[13] Sovereignty rests with the people, and the authority of government is a delegated authority. Its acts, therefore, are subject to review and repudiation by the people as the ultimate source of power.

But the "people" no longer means, as it meant for Jefferson, the great mass of those living in a given state. By Calhoun the term is restricted to those having a definite economic stake in the government: the citizen as distinguished from the slave. It is the ideal of the Greek democracy on which this defense of slavery is based; and it is not without its element of humanitarianism. For Calhoun believed, and perhaps rightly, that the life of the southern slave was easier and less brutalizing than that of the New England factory worker.

The most precious possession of the superior race is liberty, and Calhoun would guard it even more jealously than had Jefferson. It is not a thing to be preserved by a bill of rights,

<hr>

[11] *Ibid.*, II, 64-65.

[12] *Ibid.*, especially pp. 161-62; cf. *Disquisition on Government* (vol. I of *The Works of John C. Calhoun*, 6 vols. New York, 1851-56), pp. 54 ff.

[13] Cf. Calhoun's "Relation between State and Federal Governments," in *Speeches* (New York, 1843), p. 31.

but by something more fundamental. The two great threats to liberty are the abuse of delegated power and the tyranny of the stronger over the weaker interests.[14] The safeguard protecting from the first is the suffrage, and the state rights doctrine is the barrier against the second; for by nullification, the smaller groups or interests may compel a recognition of their rights from the larger. The conception is one of proportional economic representation, the suffrage alone determining the right of the numerical majority, while the vote through constituted organs, such as the legislature, determines the concurrent or constitutional majority, which regards interests as well as numbers.[15]

Calhoun's views are ably presented in his two posthumous works, the *Disquisition on Government,* and the *Discourse on the Constitution and Government of the United States.* The latter is a detailed defense of the contract theory of the constitution, and of the state rights doctrine. The former is a brilliant exposition of the philosophy of democratic individualism, which will amply repay more careful analysis.

III

The *Disquisition* was intended both as an independent contribution to political science and as an introduction to the commentary on the American constitution. It sets forth a concise theory of the origin and nature of the state, which is followed by an attempt to interpret the constitution to make it conform to the theory. If the construction is more or less labored, and at times not altogether convincing, it is no fault of the theory, but must be charged to the inadequate work of the convention of 1787. In his broader purpose, that of contributing to the philosophy of government, one must read the *Disquisition* to appreciate the measure of Calhoun's success.

The initial premise is Aristotelian: governments exist necessarily because man is a gregarious animal. His natural desires and inclinations compel him to enter into society, and universal experience shows that no society has ever existed without gov-

---

[14] *Works,* VI, 189-90.   [15] *Disquisition,* p. 28.

ernment. Society is logically prior to government, for its purpose is to preserve and perfect the race, while that of government is to preserve and perfect society; but both follow from the nature of man. The self-regarding are stronger than the social feelings, and the impulse to value one's own safety and happiness more highly than those of others leads inevitably to conflict, and hence to the necessity of some controlling power. This power is government, which, in turn, tends to disorder because administered by men, who are motivated by human selfishness. Their power to prevent injustice must therefore be safeguarded by the constitution or it will be perverted.

Constitution stands to government as government stands to society. Without government, the end of society would be defeated, and without constitution, the purpose of government could not be fulfilled. Government, however, is a matter of divine necessity, while constitution is the work of man. The problem he must solve is summed up in the question: "How can those who are invested with the powers of government be prevented from employing them, as the means of aggrandizing themselves, instead of using them to protect and preserve society?" To establish a power higher than government would be merely to transfer the tendency to abuse to this higher authority; to limit its powers so that they cannot be turned to evil would be to cripple it and defeat its purposes.

The government must be strong enough to command the entire resources of the state to resist external attack, yet must be sufficiently limited to prevent the abuse of this power. Many shrewd devices, such as religion, education, superstition, have been used for this purpose, but all of these Calhoun discards. His aim is to show "on what principles government must be formed, in order to resist, by its own interior structure"—its *organism*—"the tendency to abuse of power." This can be done only by furnishing the governed with the means of effectively resisting any unauthorized extension of the power of the governors: by making the rulers responsible to the ruled, through the suffrage.

The suffrage, although the "indispensible and primary principle in the *foundation* of a constitutional government," is not enough to prevent despotism. For the suffrage, by transferring the sovereignty from the government to the people, merely changes the seat of authority, without in any way altering the tendency of the government to the abuse of its powers. The suffrage is sufficient only if all the members of the community have the same interests. The more diversified these become, the more difficult it is to equalize governmental action with respect to them, and "the more easy for one portion of the community to pervert its powers to oppress, and plunder the others." Where government is controlled by the people, conflict arises between interests precisely as it does between individuals, each interest striving for power to further its own ends. Interests will combine to secure a majority, and party government results. So strong, indeed, is this tendency, that even were the community originally one of uniform interest and condition, competition for the perquisites of office alone would divide it into two hostile groups.

Solely by means of the taxing power, even if used only for normal purposes of revenue, one class may so disburse the proceeds as to be elevated to wealth and power while the other is reduced to abject poverty and dependence. And how much more so when the taxing power is perverted! That it will be so unless means are available to prevent it, follows from the nature of man. It is equally certain that the dominant majority for the time has the same tendency to oppression and abuse, and the same irresponsibility that the rulers would have, but for the suffrage. It makes no difference whether the power be wielded by a monarch, an oligarchy, or a numerical majority: the tendency derives from the nature of man, which is not changed by being multiplied. The only difference is that a minority may become a majority; yet this very uncertainty of tenure, combined as it is with party strife, will increase rather than diminish the tendency to oppression.

The suffrage cannot counteract this tendency without some

other provision; and it is this other provision, the most important and the least understood in the science of government, that *makes* the constitution in its strict sense. The problem is to prevent any interest or combination of interests from using the powers of government for selfish ends, by gaining exclusive control. This can be achieved only by taking the sense of each interest separately, and requiring the consent of all to put or keep the government in action. The organic structure must be such as will, "by dividing and distributing the powers of government, give to each division or interest, through its appropriate organ, either a concurrent voice in making and executing the laws, or a veto on their execution." The action of the government will depend on the concurrent consent of all the interests associated under it. As the suffrage prevents the ruler from oppressing the ruled, the concurrent veto prevents any interest or combination from oppressing others. From these two quarters only can abuse of power come, and these two principles together will serve to counteract it.

Suffrage and organism go hand in hand, the one collecting the sense of a majority of the community—the stronger interests or combinations—and the other taking the sense of each individual interest, the parties to which are adequately represented by their majority. There are thus two different majorities. One has regard to numbers only; but the other considers the state as made up of conflicting interests, and registers the will of each through its appropriate organ. This is the concurrent, or constitutional majority. Failure to distinguish these has led to confusing the numerical majority with the people, and accepting the will of the greater part for that of the whole. Since the numerical majority cannot give the sense of the whole, a government based on suffrage alone is not true self-government, but rule of a part by a part.

The misconception has still more fatal consequences; for it leads to the delusion that the restrictions imposed by organism on the will of the numerical majority are subversive and to be destroyed. Nor is the popular belief valid that a written constitution alone, suitably checked and balanced, is enough to restrain the tendency of the numerical majority to the abuse of its powers. Constitutional restraints are valueless without power to enforce them in the hands of those they are designed to protect. The party in power will seek to limit these restrictions by liberal construction, backed by its control of the governmental machinery, and in the end the constitution will be subverted, and the government turned into one of unlimited authority. Neither will the separation of powers help, because all branches are equally controlled by the numerical majority; unless, indeed, each division is the organ of a distinct interest, and has a negative on the others. But this is to substitute the concurrent for the numerical majority.

The concurrent majority is the negative of each interest on all the others—call it veto, check, nullification, or what you will —that makes possible resistance to the abuse of power. Without an effective negative, and this is the only effective one, there can be no constitution at all; for the constitution is the embodiment of the negative power as government is of the positive. It is the single power which makes absolute government, irrespective of the number exercising that power. The numerical majority is only the absolute form of the democratic state.

The distinction between governments is not that of the one, the few and the many, but is between the absolute and the constitutional. The principle which preserves the former is *force;* that which preserves the latter is *compromise,* which Calhoun calls the conservative principle. The absolute state can be resisted only by force, and must itself use force to curb resistance. In the constitutional forms, on the other hand, any interest can, by its negative, block all action tending to enrich others at its expense, thus forcing a choice between compromise and anarchy. And the necessity of avoiding anarchy is the same necessity which compels men to live in society.

Governments of the numerical majority are no exception to the rule of force in absolute states. The party system tends, as the struggle grows more and more bitter, to concentrate party power for the preservation of unity in fewer and fewer hands. Patronage becomes the reward of party service, and the actual power is vested in the hands of a small minority. Principle and policy then yield to cunning and deceit in the contest for place. Faction replaces party; and as the seekers of office outnumber the available places, the disappointed shift to the other side. This vibration continues until confusion, disorder and anarchy result. Revolution then overthrows the government and its form is changed. Such is the course of the government of the numerical majority.

The transition is more rapid as the population and wealth are greater, the climate and interests more diversified; and when the overturn comes, the reaction is usually in the direction of absolute monarchy. For when force intervenes, the leader of the successful faction has control, and the people are usually willing to accept his rule as a lesser evil than the incessant struggle of the past. The aristocratic government also terminates in monarchy, but of a less powerful form, because it is less fundamentally opposed to the military type. More broadly, constitutional governments of every form tend to degenerate into their absolute type, and all absolute governments tend to monarchy. This result is most likely in the democratic state, because in the aristocratic and monarchical forms, the orders are more jealous of their rights. Where class lines are most indistinctly drawn, they are most easily obliterated.

While the rule of the numerical majority tends inevitably to divide the community into two parties regardless of its internal unity, the government of the concurrent majority tends to unify the society regardless of its diversity of interests; and where the numerical majority corrupts and degrades, the concurrent majority strengthens and refines the moral fibres. For when knowledge, wisdom, patriotism are the surest means to political preferment, they will be cultivated; as will fraud and treachery in the like case.

The concurrent majority is also best calculated to achieve the end of government, namely, the protection and perfection of society. The mainspring of development is the desire of individuals to better their condition. Liberty and security are both essential to this end, but either extended too far curtails the other. It is the concurrent majority which preserves the proper balance between them. Power is necessary to secure to liberty the fruits of its exertions, and liberty repays by multiplying the gifts of civilization. The sphere of power must always include the means of internal and external protection, and the residuum belongs to liberty. The line between depends on various factors, geographical and economic as well as moral and intellectual, the principle operating to make liberty keep pace with moral and intellectual capacity. It follows that all people are not equally entitled to liberty. It is a reward for the deserving, and to be deprived of it is only justice to the ignorant and the degraded. Liberty and equality of condition are incompatible, and to insist on the latter would be to destroy both liberty and progress. It is the desire of the individual to better his condition that makes progress possible.

The best government is that which most adequately combines liberty and power, and this the concurrent majority does. It is best designed to secure liberty because it best prevents the abuse of power, and entrusts the liberty of the individual to those having like interests with himself. And the progress in civilization which comes from liberty contributes in turn to the development of power. In civilized society the elements of power are discipline, strategy, weapons, money, all of which are increased by the operation of liberty. So also will the concurrent majority operate to augment moral power, by cultivating a disposition to harmony and unanimity, and by giving office to the men best qualified to lead. For each interest, to advance itself, would have to conciliate all other interests; and would therefore select as its representatives men of wisdom, skill, and tact. The individual feelings would be enlisted on the side of the social.

IV

Calhoun's divergence from the Jeffersonian doctrine is fundamental, going back to the very roots of human nature. Man in the abstract is not rational and moral, but selfish and egoistic. Individualism is the primary state, and force alone can preserve the social order. Equality has gone by the board in anything more than a strictly legal sense, and a balance of interests has replaced the agrarian ideal. Calhoun spoke for the party of Jefferson; but it was a party no longer national in its scope. It no longer sought to secure for the individual his own greatest development, and the interest of an economic group had supplanted the dream of a classless society. Humanity was subordinated to cotton.

A more thoroughgoing Jeffersonian was Alexander H. Stephens, of Georgia. But like Calhoun, Stephens identified his philosophy with a lost cause, defending slavery on the ground of a necessary inequality of races. One of the most profound students of the constitution this country has produced, he too harked back to the strict construction view of the pre-Marshall era; and turned the Jeffersonian doctrine of a terminable contract into a legal defense of secession. Like Jefferson, he held the basis of good government to be the small democratic units comp_ized by the community, and measured the power of the state in terms of the loyalty and devotion of its citizens. He followed the older school, likewise, in his opposition to centralization and his advocacy of state rights, as well as in his insistence that true liberty is the ordered liberty of the legal state. But he too denied the equality of men, and championed the interests of a class rather than the welfare of the whole.

If the Jeffersonian philosophy developed on its aristocratic side through Calhoun and Stephens into a theory of class sovereignty which precipitated the Civil War, it developed also on its egalitarian side through Andrew Jackson. Lacking both the broad cultural background and the trained intelligence of Jefferson, as well as the class ties of Calhoun and Stephens, Jackson spoke for the western pioneer—for the hardworking and largely illiterate masses of laboring men, from which he had himself arisen. His equalitarianism recognized neither economic nor intellectual bounds, and this latter explains, perhaps, the distrust with which Jefferson had regarded him. Honest and inflexible, he belonged to an agrarian world, and could conceive of no other social order. Like Jefferson, he feared the dominance of an aristocratic class, and hated with all the force of his powerful nature the development of a capitalistic system. But where Jefferson had sought to replace the economic aristocracy with an aristocracy of talents, and in the Virginia dynasty had well-nigh succeeded, Jackson was content to substitute for the economic power of a class the numerical rule of the masses.

Jackson had been raised to office through an extension of the suffrage which gave the vote to large numbers of men without property—pioneer farmers in the West, and an urban proletariat created by the industrialism of the East. He reasoned that the source of power lay in the people, and that it was accordingly his duty to reflect their will. The capitalistic system enriched the few at the expense of the many; and since government was the instrument of the many, it must follow that the executive was bound to root out the "hydra of corruption" and to rid the state of capitalism. The National Bank was the only part of the system within his reach, the tariff being beyond his control, so Jackson contented himself with smashing the Bank, which he did with singular directness and remarkable thoroughness. In this he but reflected the will of the numerically superior group to which he owed his office; and it was also in deference to the known will of his constituents that he espoused the cause of nationalism, and scornfully rejected nullification.

A great natural leader, yet utterly without political or social philosophy; independent, honest, domineering, colorful, yet wholly untouched by the finer problems of economic theory; Jackson fired the imagination, and commanded the most devout loyalty of the lower classes, emphasizing in the democratic doctrine everything of which Jefferson and Taylor had sought to purge it. The Jackson era was noteworthy for vigorous administration and for violent quarrels, but left little constructive legislation.

Meanwhile the old federalism of Marshall and Hamilton proceeded under Webster and Clay to develop into a strongly nationalistic party, based on protection for industry and internal improvements at government expense. The Whigs, as they came to be called, learned from Jackson to appeal to the people for votes; but they made no pretence of sharing the perquisites of government with any but the economically dominant class. As Calhoun and Stephens reflected the sectional interests of the South, and Jackson of the West, Webster appealed to the industrial East. Party lines became more sharply geographical, as the clash of economic interests heaped fuel on the fires of party bitterness. The old democratic order was already a thing of the past when the last great Jeffersonian took command.

In a very real sense, Abraham Lincoln was the last great democratic liberal of the school of Jefferson. He too came from the frontier, and had inherited the easy freedom of a pioneer people. He too was the champion of the common man, above all humanitarian. Yet his vision transcended his class, and he saw in the conflict of sectional interests the end of American union. His rejection of the state rights formula followed the slowly maturing conviction that the best interests of the country as a whole could not be reconciled with sectionalism; but in all else he followed admittedly the lead of the great Virginian. In making himself the spokesman of the western farmers, Lincoln harked back to the agrarianism of Jefferson, even while admitting, as Jefferson himself had done, the necessity of manufactures and commerce to the life of the state; and it was from the industrial East as well as the agricultural West that he drew his support.

The Civil War marked the end of the Greek democracy of Calhoun and Stephens, the end of nullification as a corollary of state rights, and the end of the dogma of an inferior race. But it marked also the end of the Jeffersonian state. The planter aristocracy of the South went down to defeat, that government of the people, by the people, and for the people should not perish from the earth; but a hundred new and more powerful vested interests sprang to take its place. Four years after an assassin's bullet had placed the emancipator among the immortals, the railroads had pushed to the Pacific, and the age of big business had begun.

v

Democratic individualism is the political corollary, in a state boasting representative institutions, of the laissez-faire economic theory; and its most sacred belief is that private property is inviolable and beyond the power of government to question. It is the initial premise and the justification of capitalism. The history of political thought is shot through with paradoxes, not least of which is the fact that all the great American democrats of the individualistic school hated and feared the capitalistic system—the very thing their philosophy was designed to encourage. The key to the contradiction 's to be found in two circumstances. All of the men who have been discussed in this connection have thought, partially or wholly, in terms of an agrarian state; and all of them were southerners and slaveholders. The laissez-faire economy, when applied in an agricultural community, does not contribute to capitalistic development as obviously or as rapidly as it does in an industrialized society; and in the southern states of the American union it seemed the only argument that would justify the retention of slavery. For slaves were property, and as such could be placed beyond the interference of northern abolitionists by appealing to the individualistic doctrine.

This school of thought persisted and was pushed to its most extreme form in the South, because the South, before the Civil War, was to a great extent untouched by the tempo of the nineteenth century. Individualism was the child of an earlier age, and was well suited to a spacious world, where travel and communication were slow, communities were remote from each other, and men were dependent largely on their own exertions for the necessities of life, and for life itself. With the rapidly increasing population, and the growing industrialism and urbanization of the nineteenth century, however, the old philosophy served only to breed and to intensify the extremes of wealth and poverty. It was from this inequality of distribution that social democracy was born.

CHAPTER XII

SOCIAL DEMOCRACY

I

JEFFERSONIAN democracy had emphasized the social-utilitarian end of the state, and had, so far as the conditions of its origin warranted, so exercised the powers of government as to discourage great accumulations of property with their inevitable corollary of exploitation, while seeking at the same time the widest possible distribution of material goods and spiritual benefits. As the country became more populous, however, and its interests more diversified, the conflict between individual desires and social purposes became more harply defined, and from the original assumptions of democracy new principles of action were deduced, which came gradually to dominate the tradition.

Social democracy is necessarily a later growth than the individualistic form of the theory, for it places restrictions on liberty which will not be voluntarily accepted by the bulk of mankind until they can no longer be avoided. It is not surprizing, therefore, that the first efforts in this direction came from small and isolated groups, wholly outside the main stream of American political development; or that the first fairly widespread attempt at social coöperation should have come in a period of financial collapse. The first form was utopian socialism, varying widely as to theory and actualized in numerous communistic or semicommunistic settlements. Theirs were philosophies of perfection, at first spiritual, but later economic and political; and it was the perfectionist element in American democratic thought—the naïve faith in reason and in human nature—combined with a plenitude of land, and a pioneer people too busy with their own affairs to bother about their neighbors, that made them possible.

Utopias have been written by great humanitarians of all ages, from Plato's day to our own, but it was only in pioneer America, where social experiments were conducted on a lavish scale and the very immensity of the country seemed to invite superlatives, that any extensive effort was made to put utopian ideas into practice. The Jeffersonian philosophy was itself utopian in its ideals, and the establishment of communities where property and labor should be in common was but varying the means to hasten the end. Although not directly traceable to the diffusion of democratic ideas, the communistic experiments closely parallel the democratic movement in time, the utopians merging with the socialist-labor party when industrialism had won the day. Both groups built upon the equality of men, and both sought to create a classless society, the difference being mainly in tactics and in scope.

The earlier communities owed nothing to the Jeffersonian philosophy except the easy tolerance which gave them free rein and full legal protection for their activities; but in the course of their later development the utopian groups drew more and more heavily on the idealistic background of native democracy, sometimes incorporating imported liberalisms, sometimes modifying original importations with large injections of the American faith. Whatever their doctrinal beginnings, the utopian villages were governed, one and all, by popularly chosen assemblies, and were soundly based on the Jeffersonian foundation of liberty and equality, colored by reforming zeal. Their philosophies differed, from each other and from that which lay behind the American democracy, in various ways; but all alike shared the fundamental objective—the achievement of individual happiness and the balanced life. Because of their small numbers and their isolation it was possible for the utopias to curb more readily the self-interest inherent in individualism, and to emphasize more directly the social side of political organization.

During the nineteenth century, several hundred communal settlements existed in the United States, and the number of individuals participating in them at one time or another ran into the hundreds of thousands.[1] The earliest attempts to anticipate the millenium in this manner came from sectarian organizations, members of which were overwhelmingly German. These are of little importance for our purposes, however, because the motives which led to their origin were spiritual rather than political or social, and they were held together by religious ties.

More significant, though less successful, were the coöperative communities of the Owenite period. Robert Owen had succeeded in England in bringing about numerous reforms in factory legislation, and had created at New Lanark a model village for his workmen. But as his own views changed from philanthropic reform to full-fledged communism, he found himself powerless to make further progress against the rigid industrial system of his homeland, and he turned to democratic America as the natural field for his activities. He saw men everywhere held in bondage by a trinity of evils: private property, irrational religion, and a system of marriage based on these two; and it was to transcend this trinity that New Harmony, Indiana, was established in 1825. The community was planless from the start, and the eight or nine hundred settlers had been taken as they came, with no effort at selection. Almost immediately they fell out among themselves; and in the two years of its existence, New Harmony was governed under seven different constitutions. Its only achievement was in the realm of education, where the doctrines of Pestalozzi were put into practice.[2]

There were a few other Owenite villages, of still shorter duration but of similar history. The Yellow Springs community was established by a group of Cincinnati intellectuals, who had heard Owen lecture in 1824, and was successful enough until the novelty wore off, as it did in about six months. The Nashoba settlement in Tennessee, which was founded in 1825 by Frances Wright, included a group of mixed color, and had

---

[1] Morris Hillquit, *History of Socialism in the United States* (New York and London, 1903), p. 25.

[2] *Ibid.*, pp. 48-69.

as its avowed purpose the education of negro slaves to social and economic equality with whites. It, too, was successful for a short time, but rapidly declined after illness had forced its talented leader to forego her personal direction of the experiment, and was abandoned in 1828. Communities based on Owen's philosophy were also established in New York, Pennsylvania, and other parts of Ohio and Indiana, but were short-lived and unsuccessful.

Of a far different sort, however, were the associationist "Phalanxes," based on the social philosophy of Charles Fourier. Fourier was not a communist, and the ideal phalanx did not include community of property, but its activities were coöperative, and the distribution of returns was according to a fixed ratio. Each phalanx was to include 1500 to 2000 persons, who should live together in a great hall, or phalanstery, to which were attached dining rooms, workshops, and recreation parlors. Stock was to be issued for each association, four-twelfths of the total return going as dividends to the stock-holders, five twelfths as wages to labor, and three-twelfths to skill or talent. The same individual, however, might come in for a share under all three heads. The phalanx itself was the unit in a vast scheme of social reform which was ultimately to embrace the world.[3]

The doctrine was introduced into the United States by Albert Brisbane, an American who had studied philosophy under Cousin and Hegel, and had worked for two years with Fourier in Paris. Returning to his own country, he published in 1840 his *Social Destiny of Man*, a popular exposition of the theory, which won immediate success. Among others, Horace Greeley was converted by it, and from 1842 to 1844 Brisbane conducted a colume in Greeley's *Tribune* devoted to propaganda for the new system. The most able American writing on the subject, however, was Parke Godwin, associate editor of the *New York Evening Post*, and son-in-law of its editor, William Cullen Bryant. Godwin published in 1843 a thin pamphlet entitled

[3] *Ibid.*, pp. 70-108; John R. Commons, and Associates, *History of Labor in the United States* (2 vols. New York, 1921), I, 496 ff.

Democracy, Constructive and Pacific, in which he points out the the tendencies of capitalistic production, and anticipates the Marxian theory of the class struggle; and in the following year he contributed *A Popular View of the Doctrines of Charles Fourier.* As the movement grew in influence, it published its own periodicals. The *Phalanx,* edited by Brisbane, lasted from October, 1843, to the middle of 1845, and was succeeded by the *Harbinger,* emanating from Brook Farm, and numbering among its contributors George Ripley, John S. Dwight, Charles A. Dana, William Henry Channing, Henry James, James Russell Lowell, and Margaret Fuller. The *Present* was published by Channing, and there were other papers edited by the Fourierists of Wisconsin and Michigan.

The years of active propagation of the associationist doctrine coincide with the years of depression following the panic of 1837, and the movement rose and died within the decade 1840-1850. It was a period of intense economic stress, marked by social speculation and reforming zeal, when individualistic democracy was sorely tried. Abolition propaganda swelled in volume, and wage slavery was placed with chattel slavery by such eloquent agitators as Wendell Phillips. Fourierism seemed to offer a way out, and by 1844, when a national convention was held, adherents of the doctrine came in numbers from nine states. A national association was formed, of which George Ripley was elected president, the vice-presidents including Brisbane, Greeley, Godwin, and Dana. But the phalanxes which sprang up on every hand were not, like the communist utopias, small-scale indications of life in the perfect state. They were the perfect state; and their failure, with returning economic prosperity, meant the collapse of the doctrine.

The longest lived and most successful of these social units in a utopian world was the North American Phalanx, in Monmouth County, New Jersey, which lasted for twelve years. The members were mainly from New York City and from Albany, and were overwhelmingly men and women of culture and education. The Fourierist division of profits was adhered to, choice of occupation being free, and wages were varied according to the necessity and unpleasantness of the task. The average wage was from six to ten cents per hour, with room in the communal dwelling fixed at twelve dollars a year and meals proportionately cheap. The experiment was eminently successful until the whole movement of which it was a part lost impetus with the turn of the economic tide. Then enthusiasm waned, and dissolution became merely a matter of time. There were other reasonably successful phalanxes in Wisconsin and Michigan, the former being the only one to dissolve without financial loss; and many others, hastily started and quickly abandoned, in Pennsylvania, New York, Ohio, Iowa, and Illinois.

By far the most noted of the group, however, was Brook Farm, nine miles from Boston. Although it began in 1841 as the independent effort of a handful of New England intellectuals to achieve social democracy on a small scale, the Farm had strong resemblances to Fourierism from the start, and officially became a phalanx in 1844. Its members included Ripley, who conceived the scheme, Dana, Dwight, and Nathaniel Hawthorne; and among the numerous visitors, in sympathy with the experiment but hesitant to participate in its hardships, were Emerson, Channing, Margaret Fuller, Bronson Alcott, Theodore Parker, and Elizabeth Peabody. The community property was represented by shares of stock, and all the members were employed according to their tastes and abilities, at an uniform rate of wages. The maximum working day was ten hours. Free support was extended to those over seventy, and to children under ten, and education, medical attention, and the library were available to all without cost.

The administration was in the hands of four committees, concerned respectively with the general direction of the enterprize, and with agriculture, education, and finance. The school was the principal feature of the Farm, including all grades from the nursery to preparation for college, and covering a wide range of instruction in the arts and sciences. For the rest, there was only hard work and meagre financial return; but the whole was invested with a poetic glamour, lent by the personalities of the members and their friends, which still endures. The end came suddenly, in 1846, when the "Palace," barely completed, was destroyed by fire. Fourierist enthusiasm was already on the wane, and Brook Farm survived the disaster only a few months.[4]

The final phase of utopian socialism in America was the career of the Icarian communities, the last of which struggled on until 1895. The initiator of the movement, Etienne Cabet, had studied both medicine and law, and had successfully practiced the latter profession in his native Dijon before settling in Paris. There he became a revolutionist, and took a leading part in the upheaval of 1830 which brought Louis Philippe to the French throne. He soon fell out with the new ruler, however, and was banished for five years. In England, he wrote an utopian novel, *Voyage en Icarie*, which was published on his return to France in 1839, and was immediately successful. Thenceforth, his life was devoted to propaganda for his particular social reform, which included a progressive income tax, the abolition of inheritance, state regulation of wages, national workshops, agricultural colonies, and universal education. The economic distress preceding the revolution of 1848 brought large numbers of French workingmen to his standard; and in February of that year a colony of Icarians set out for Texas, where Cabet had contracted with a land company for a million acres.[5]

He had been roundly cheated by the Texas land agent, however; and when the vanguard arrived, worn with the hardships of the trip, they found it impossible to colonize the scattered sections allotted to them in time to make good their title. A new start was made from New Orleans, where Cabet himself joined the group, and in 1849 three hundred Icarians settled at Nauvoo, Illinois, which had been recently abandoned by the Mormons. For the next few years, the community prospered. One thousand acres of land were brought under cultivation,

---

[4] See Lindsay Swift, *Brook Farm, Its Members, Scholars, and Visitors* (New York, 1900).

[5] Hillquit, *op. cit.*, pp. 109-24.

mills, a distillery, and numerous shops were established, schools and a library maintained, and printing presses propagated the doctrine in English, French, and German. A constitution drawn up in 1850 placed the administration in the hands of six directors, one of whom was president, and the rest heads of departments, their acts being subject to the approval of an assembly consisting of all the men over twenty.

Cabet was consistently reëlected president; but as he grew old, he became more and more arbitrary. The assembly was in constant opposition, and an open rupture in 1856 resulted in the expulsion of the founder, together with 180 of the faithful. A week later Cabet died in St. Louis, and it was two years before his followers resumed communal life near that city; but the new settlement gradually disintegrated, and was dissolved in 1864.

Meanwhile, the group left behind at Nauvoo found themselves too shorthanded to till their fields and run their industries. In 1860 they removed to Iowa, where, after a long and bitter struggle with the wilderness, they emerged triumphant; and by 1868 they had doubled their numbers. Then they too split over the administration. They had taken into the fold many outsiders, who held more modern views. The International had united socialists the world over, and the Communist Manifesto had made utopianism a thing of the past. In 1878, at the instigation of the radicals, the community was dissolved by the courts, and a few years later the younger group moved to California, where they soon abandoned the Icarian faith. The older members maintained a semblance of communal life until 1895.

Taken as a whole, the utopian period in American social development was a conspicuous failure. Not a single one of the hundreds of communities established succeeded in solving, with any degree of permanence, the problems which had led to their inception, and their inadequacy served to discredit their method, once and for all. But whatever the shortcomings of American utopian experiments may have been, they served through half a century and more to call the attention of the thoughtful to the presence of an increasing maladjustment in the social system; and they offered a rich background, both practical and theoretical, for later attempts to solve the economic problem in terms compatible with a democratic form of government.

II

The nineteenth century had scarcely reached its meridian before Jefferson's prophecy began to be fulfilled. The farm yielded ground to the factory, and men crowded together in great cities, their corruption increasing with their numbers. The question of chattel slavery was settled in blood and destruction, but the problem of wage slavery only deepened with the years, and came in time to hold the center of the stage. Utopianism required an agrarian background. It failed to appeal to the growing legions of factory workers and other minions of the industrial system, because it could not solve their problem. The isolated, self-sufficing community was ideally suited to a semi-agricultural, semihandicraft culture; but a highly specialized machine civilization is necessarily dependent on a far-flung network of exchange, and the problem of the nineteenth century wage slave demanded the vaster setting of the International.

The associationists had been opposed from the outset by the workingmen's party, which presently developed a decided agrarian bias. Equality in land was proclaimed as a natural right in the old Jeffersonian sense; and men like George Henry Evans saw the solution of the industrial problem in the opening to free settlement of the public domain. The development of the American labor movement[6] was so far turned from its normal course by the presence of this vast unsettled area that it was not until 1890 that the land question definitely ceased to play a more or less important rôle. The first Industrial Congress in 1845 brought together such diverse types as Evans and his followers; Godwin, Brisbane, and Channing; and Robert

---

[6] Commons, and Associates, *op. cit.*, I, 522 ff., and II, *passim;* also, John R. Commons, "Labor Movement," in *Encyclopedia of the Social Sciences*, VIII, 682 ff.; and R. F. Hoxie, *Trade Unionism in the United States* (New York and London, 1917), chap. 4.

Owen; but the agrarians had the greater numbers and dominated both that and subsequent Congresses. The outcome of the agitation, as social democratic thought swung more definitely away from coöperation, was the Homestead Law of 1862;⁷ yet the results were not as satisfactory as Evans had predicted, and the failure of free lands to cure industrial ills led to two new and widely separated reform movements. Trade Unionism made a first hesitant bid to meet the conditions of a capitalism advanced to the technological stage, and broadened its scope to include in the Knights of Labor the entire working class; while agrarianism reached its apotheosis in the critique of Henry George. Both movements were ultimately to combine for political action in the People's Party.

Henry George accepts both the Jeffersonian ideal and the Jeffersonian method, only altering the emphasis from the political to the economic side. "It is not enough that men should vote," he declares, "it is not enough that they should be theoretically equal before the law. They must have liberty to avail themselves of the opportunities and means of life; they must stand on equal terms with reference to the bounties of nature."⁸ Like Jefferson, he has boundless faith in reason and in the inherent goodness of men; and he holds economics, as Jefferson had held politics, to be deducible from certain axiomatic "laws of nature," for which all that is necessary is an unbiassed mind and a clear head. The immutable basis of economics, like that of politics, is ethical; and behind human history and human achievement, behind individual aspiration and individual life lies the universal moral law. "Unless its foundations be laid in justice the social structure cannot stand."⁹

Like Jefferson, George took progress as a matter of course; and like Jefferson, he could not doubt the ultimate rightness of life. He could not, therefore, accept an economic theory which made poverty, misery, depravity, necessary correlatives of social growth. That progress and poverty went hand in hand

---

⁷ Commons, and Associates, *op. cit.*, I, 562-63.
⁸ *Progress and Poverty* (New York, 1915), p. 545.
⁹ *Ibid.*

could not be denied, but the cause must lie in social maladjust-ment—in the failure of men rather than in the failure of the moral law. So he reëxamines history, and reformulates the law of human progress. The incentive he finds in the desires inherent in man: animal, intellectual, sympathetic. It is through intellectual striving, through mental power, that we advance; but only through that part of mental power specifically devoted to progress—the residuum after deductions for maintenance and conflict.[10] The first essential is accordingly association, for the division of labor renders maintenance easier, and releases intellectual energy for other purposes; and the second essential is equality, which removes the cause of conflict. "Thus association in equality is the law of progress. Association frees mental power for expenditure in improvement, and equality, or justice, or freedom—for the terms here signify the same thing, the recognition of the moral law—prevents the dissipation of this power in fruitless struggles."[11] Men advance in proportion as they coöperate; stand still or retrogress as they provoke conflict or develop inequality of condition and power.

Aside from such external factors as climatic or geographical conditions, there are certain internal resistances to progress which go hand in hand with growth itself. As society becomes more and more complex, as functions become more highly specialized, social adjustments tend to lag, and inequality to spring up. For as association becomes integrated, the whole assumes proportions greater than the sum of the parts: a collective power arises which is apart from and superior to the individual powers involved, and which habit tends to concentrate in the hands of a small portion of the community. Inequality is born and begets greater inequality, its injustice being concealed under habitual social forms which have not kept pace with the growth of the community. So do patriarchs become princes and tribal chieftains kings.

Now the greatest of all inequalities is that involved in the distribution of land. Among primitive peoples the soil is the

---

[10] *Ibid.*, pp. 503-23.   [11] *Ibid.*, p. 505.

common heritage of all; but as the society grows, new lands are acquired by conquest, and partitioned as the private property of the conquering chiefs. Desire breeds greater desire, commons are enclosed, and a vested right to the land is set up in a class. As numbers increase, the value of the land increases, and an immense increment of wealth is concentrated in the hands of the landowners, without labor on their part, which enables them in time to become the masters of their fellows. Petrifaction then succeeds progress, and at last becomes retrogression. This is the history of all great civilizations, and will be the history of our own if we allow inequality in land to continue.

The solution of the problem George proposes is the confiscation by the state, for the common benefit, of economic rent— the public ownership of land. And in taking such a position, he believes he is simply pushing to its logical conclusion the ideal of American democracy. "What is it but the carrying out in letter and spirit of the truth enunciated in the Declaration of Independence—the 'self-evident' truth that is the heart and soul of the Declaration—*That all men are created equal; that they are endowed by their Creator with certain unalienable rights; that among these are life, liberty, and the pursuit of happiness.*'"[12] It is the Jeffersonian political philosophy formulated in economic terms, and broadened to include the broader horizon of a century of growth. "Political liberty, when the equal right to land is denied, becomes, as population increases and invention goes on, merely the liberty to compete for employment at starvation wages."[13]

For George, as for Jefferson, ethics, economics, and politics are bound up together. Liberty and equality are correlative terms, and only through their union can the objective of human welfare be achieved. In Jefferson's day, land seemed inexhaustible in comparison to population, and so he turned his attention primarily to securing political equality and political liberty. George had seen the tide of immigration reach the shores of the

[12] *Ibid.*, p. 542. George's italics.
[13] *Ibid.*. Cf. G. R. Geiger, *The Philosophy of Henry George* (New York, 1933), pp. 153-60.

Pacific, and had witnessed the appropriation of millions of acres of productive land, largely for speculative purposes. He had seen the Civil War and the panic of 1873, and all these factors combined to place his emphasis on the economic side of the doctrine.

Jefferson had argued that the earth is given as a common stock for man to labor and live on,[14] and for all his advanced reading on economic questions, he never wholly escaped the agrarian bias. It is the same bias which forms the cornerstone of the philosophy of Henry George, who differs only in carrying the principle to a more logical conclusion. If the earth is given as a common stock to men, it follows that land is the common property of all, and to reduce the soil to private ownership is to rob of their birthright those who are excluded from the division. It is this exclusion of the masses from their right to the land that lies at the bottom of all social ills; for once inequality originates in a society, the operation of inexorable economic laws tends to render it greater and greater. "For whosoever hath, to him shall be given, and he shall have more abundance; but whosoever hath not, from him shall be taken away even that he hath."

The method George proposes to use in confiscating land for the public good—the "single tax," or levy on land to full extent of its value, or economic rent—is immaterial for our purposes. Enough has been said to show how closely he conforms to the premises of the Jeffersonian political philosophy, and what conclusions he draws from them. The equality of men presupposes, for Henry George, an equal right to the bounties of nature: that is, to the fruits of the soil; and he turns the democratic tradition, for the first time consciously, to a consideration of the problem of the distribution of wealth.

III

Under the industrial conditions of latter nineteenth-century America, the comparatively simple machinery of the Jeffer-

[14] To Madison, Sept. 16, 1789, *Writings*, VII, 454 ff.; cf. above, chap. 7, v; chap. 8, i.

sonian state had broken down, and the capitalistic class, whose development Jefferson had feared and fought against with all the prophetic fervor of his nature, had secured political as well as economic control. For Jefferson the remedy had lain in the good sense and ingenuity of the common man, and it was to the common man that those who sought social justice turned, calling themselves Populist or Progressive, and demanding a New Nationalism, a New Freedom, or a New Deal.

The unequal distribution of wealth which inspired the single tax theory of Henry George was also the motivation for the other diverse movements which were brought together in the People's Party. It was in 1886 that George ran for mayor of New York on a reform ticket; and in the same year the Farmers' Alliance of Texas, emulating the Granger movement of the seventies, brought the agrarian demands into politics, with a platform calling for more adequate taxation of the railroads and higher taxes on land held for speculative purposes, the prevention of dealing in futures in the case of agricultural products, new issues of paper money, an interstate commerce law, and other political novelties.[15] The move was premature, but though it wrought a temporary split in the Texas Alliance, it served to define the issues and to prepare the ground for a united effort on the political front.

Like the Jeffersonian "revolution" of nearly a century earlier, the populist revolt was basically agrarian and proletarian. It was a movement of western and southern farmers and eastern workers; and its main theme was the right of every man to earn a decent living. Falling prices for farm products, a rising cost of living, a mountainous burden of debt, and extortionate railroad rates were the original grievances, while the unemployment and poverty of the lower classes, contrasted with the vast fortunes of a few industrialists, bankers and speculators served to fix the lines along which the struggle was to be fought out. Many reforms were included at various times in the populist programs, all of them designed to place government more

[15] John D. Hicks, *The Populist Revolt* (Minneapolis, 1931), p. 106.

directly in the hands of the people, and to restrain for the common good the tyranny of unbridled individualism as it manifested itself in the practices of corporate business and finance. The principal focal points of agitation, however, were the currency system and the restraint of monopolies. The efforts to secure more direct popular control in matters of government were more as means of securing other reforms than as ends in themselves.

The demands were crystallized in 1889, when the Southern and Northern Farmers' Alliances and the Knights of Labor met jointly in St. Louis. All three groups sought government ownership and operation of the railroads, to which the Southern Alliance added all means of transportation and communication, and all wished the abolition of the national banks, for which some system of direct treasury notes was to be substituted. The Southern Alliance and the Knights of Labor agreed on free and unlimited coinage of silver, on the prevention of dealing in futures of all agricultural and mechanical productions, and in the Jeffersonian demand that taxation, national or state, "shall not be used to build up one interest or class at the expense of another." The Northern Alliance added a demand for a graduated income tax and a tax on real estate mortgages, and wrote in a plank favoring the Australian ballot.[16] At the same convention, C. W. Macune, leader of the Southern Alliance, proposed the subtreasury plan as a substitute for the national banking system, calling for warehouses where farmers could "deposit" nonperishable crops, drawing against them paper money up to eighty per cent of the local value of the crops, at one per cent interest.[17]

Under the imposing name of National Farmers' Alliance and Industrial Union, representatives of the same groups met at Ocala, Florida, in December, 1890, where the subtreasury plan became the first plank in their platform. The earlier demands were reiterated, with a further proposal for a constitutional amendment providing for direct election of United States Sen-

[16] *Ibid.*, Appendix A.   [17] *Ibid.*, pp. 186 ff.

ators, and a recommendation that the circulating medium be increased to fifty dollars per capita.[18] The Omaha resolutions of January, 1891, included in a brief outline of a similar program a call for a national convention; and in May of the same year the People's Party was born. The platforms of 1889 and 1890 were summarized, and declared to be the program of the new party, the demand for direct election of senators being expanded to include also president and vice-president of the United States; and a set of resolutions was added, recommending to favorable consideration the question of universal suffrage, and proposing an eight-hour day. As the program developed over the period between 1886 and 1892, it came also to include demands for postal savings banks, for direct loans from the government to the people at low interest, the prohibition of alien ownership of land, the preservation of all natural resources as the common heritage of the people, and opposition to the subsidizing of private business for any purpose or in any form. The nominating convention of the People's Party met in July, repeated substantially the same platform, and put a full national ticket in the field.[19]

The Populists, for all their social-democratic liberalism, were not as successful as they had hoped, largely because of inexperience in practical politics; but in the elections of 1892 they far outstripped the record of any previous third party, polling over a million popular votes with twenty-two votes in the electoral college, and gaining partial or complete control of the state offices in Kansas, Nebraska, North Dakota, Minnesota, and Colorado. Returns showed also the election of five United States senators and ten congressmen, to which the party added in the off-year elections of 1894 six more senators and seven congressmen, the total Populist vote having increased forty-two per cent in two years.[20]

In the states under Populist control, the record was unim-

---

[18] *Ibid.*, Appendix B.

[19] *Ibid.*, pp. 205 ff.; and Edward Stanwood, *History of the Presidency* (2nd ed. 2 vols. New York, 1924), I, 509 ff.

[20] Fred E. Haynes, *Third Party Movements Since the Civil War* (Iowa City, 1916), p. 281.

pressive. Reform legislation either failed to reach the statute books through combined opposition of the older parties, or was repudiated by the courts; while the administrative inexperience of officials bred confusion and disorder. It was in the national government, where the most able of the third party leaders had been sent, that the principal achievement of Populism was recorded, in the form of a gradual permeation of the older parties with the ideas of the radical minority. In 1894 the Democrats accepted the graduated income tax, which was added to the tariff act of that year; and from that time on for two decades Populist principles found their way with increasing ease into Democratic platforms.

Given a fair field, the essential features of the program might, in time, have become realities through third party action alone. By 1896, however, with the hardships of lean depression years uppermost in all minds, the inflationary demand for free silver became the paramount issue. On the strength of Democratic championship of bimetalism, the Populists endorsed the candidacy of William Jennings Bryan, and lost irrecoverably their identity as a separate party. It is the more ironical because the silver issue, on which Populism fell, was not only a mere by-product of a constructive social program: it was not even the most important feature of Populist monetary policy. It was not bimetalism as an end that the Populists sought, but temporary inflation, as a step toward a "commodity dollar." Senator Allen of Nebraska outlines concisely his party's objective on the currency question: "We believe it is possible so to regulate the issue of money as to make it approximately the same value at all times. The value of money ought to bear as nearly as possible a fixed relation to the value of commodities. If a man should borrow a thousand dollars on five years' time today, when it would take two bushels of wheat to pay each dollar, it is clear that it ought not to take any more wheat to pay that debt at the time of its maturity, except for the accrued interest."[21]

The Populist platform of 1896 was even more specific in its

---

[21] Hicks, *op. cit.*, pp. 316-17.

demands for social reform than the earlier documents had been. In addition to the older planks calling for a managed currency, government ownership of means of transportation and communication, a graduated income tax by constitutional amendment, the abolition of speculation in land, and the direct election of president, vice-president, and senators, the party favored also the initiative and referendum, and a program of public works to absorb idle labor in times of industrial depression; and protested against the use of injunctions in labor disputes.[22] As a whole, the program resembled that of the Socialists as closely as it did the Democratic credo; but the silver bloc won the convention, and on that issue alone Bryan was named standard bearer. To avoid embarrassing questions relative to the Populist platform, the nomination went by default, Bryan neither accepting nor rejecting the doubtful honor.

By fusing with Democracy on the silver issue, Populism signed its own death warrant. The party lingered on until 1908, but its own members knew it was dead. Its statutory accomplishments were slight, but its influence was vast, and in the end its principles were recognized. For Populism, with its emphasis on the social responsibilities of the state toward the common man, was instrumental in splitting the older parties, and in forcing them to face the problems of an industrial society. The party was dead, but the principles gained ever wider acceptance, finding their way into the new state constitutions, and at last into the White House itself. As one delegate to the last Populist convention put it, Theodore Roosevelt's messages "read like the preamble to the Populist platform."[23] By the turn of the century, individualism in the old laissez-faire sense was doomed; and though Populism passed off the stage, the progressive movement carried on.

IV

There were actually two progressive movements, one stemming from each of the old historical parties, and though in the

[22] Stanwood, *op. cit.*, I, 551 ff.   [23] Hicks, *op. cit.*, pp. 402-3.

main there was agreement as to program, there was less fusion than might have been expected. It was in the Democratic party, where the impact of Populism had been felt most strongly, that the body of doctrine known as "progressive" found its earliest widely accepted expression. Basically, its intent was to wrest the control of the machinery of government and the direction of the economic life of the nation from the hands of a capitalistic class, placing the welfare of the masses above the vested interests of an industrial oligarchy. The first steps were taken, hesitantly but with crusading zeal, in the Democratic platform of 1896, which condemned the action of the Supreme Court in invalidating the income tax law, and denounced government by injunction. Other significant proposals were for improvement at the expense of the federal government of the Mississippi river, and for enlargement of the powers of the Interstate Commerce Commission, giving it more direct control over railroads.[24]   Yet the radical leaders were willing to go only half way. The demand for free silver, though its inflationary effect would doubtless have been of some benefit to the debtor classes, was none the less a subsidy to a vested interest as surely as any Republican tariff had been.

Though the party lost the 1896 election, it gained enormously in strength; and its radical leadership endured. Bryan was renominated in 1900, and again in 1908, after a conservative bid in 1904 had resulted only in marked losses at the polls. During this period, the constructive social features of the Democratic program developed, partly through internal growth, and partly through contact with the insurgent Republicans and the Socialist agitators. Bryan returned in 1906 from an extended tour in Europe to announce that "public ownership is necessary where competition is impossible," and to declare for ultimate public ownership of railroads.[25]   He took pains not to commit his party to this view, but it is significant for its evidence of the increasing social emphasis in democratic theory. So far had the party of Jefferson gone in this direction that the Republican

²⁴ Stanwood, *op. cit.*, I, 542 ff.   ²⁵ Haynes, *op. cit.*, p. 383.

platform of 1908 could charge that the "trend of Democracy is toward socialism."[26]

The trend was, at least, toward greater governmental control over private interests, to be balanced by increasing the sphere of activity of the common man, and by greater responsiveness in high places to the popular will. The Democratic creed of 1908 sought full preëlection publicity for campaign contributions, and would prohibit altogether the acceptance of campaign funds from corporations. The platform had much to say, first and last, on the question of corporations, which it sought to control through prosecutions for monopoly practices, the withdrawal of tariff subsidies, the enlargement of the powers of the Interstate Commerce Commission, and a law "preventing a duplication of directors among competing corporations." A constitutional amendment specifically granting the power to tax incomes was advocated, together with such social reforms as an eight-hour day for government employees, the restriction of the use of injunctions in labor disputes, an employer's liability act, a separate department of labor with cabinet rank, direct election of United States Senators, regulation of telegraph and telephone rates under the Interstate Commerce Commission, and the improvement by the federal government of all inland waterways which might profitably be used for commercial navigation.

Again the Democratic vote increased, but again the party lost. The Progressive movement, however, had long since made its way into the Republican party also. Wisconsin had sent Robert M. LaFollette to the Senate in 1906, and Theodore Roosevelt, president at last in his own right, showed more than a little interest in a similar program. The whole attitude of the American public had, in fact, changed. The ideas that were revolutionary when Populism advanced them had become commonplace, and the common man was no longer disposed to accept calmly the rule of the "robber barons." By means of Chautauqua lectures, La Follette and Bryan had carried the gospel of social reform up and down the land, and President

[26] Stanwood, *op. cit.*, II, 179.

Roosevelt himself lost no opportunity to appeal directly to the people in support of his policies. Government by the people for the best interests of the whole, or government by corporate business for the economic advantage of the small group which controlled it—such was the issue, defined again and again in party documents, on the stump, in the vast literature of exposure: an issue which had been gaining impetus for a quarter of a century, and which came to a head in the campaign of 1912.

The Democratic party, still under the radical leadership of Bryan, nominated a progressive in Governor Woodrow Wilson of New Jersey; but the Republicans, for a generation allied with the corporate interests, were not prepared to accept the challenge. The progressive wing of the party had made important gains in the states, notably in Wisconsin, where LaFollette had secured the direct primary, railroad taxation proportionate to holdings, and a commission empowered to determine railroad rates on the basis of property valuation. The Wisconsin achievements made LaFollette the logical progressive candidate for the Republican presidential nomination; but he was regarded as too radical, and was deserted by his followers when Roosevelt entered the lists. The conservative Taft, however, by adroit manipulation of the convention delegates, secured his own renomination, and Roosevelt bolted to run on a separate "Progressive" ticket.

The contest was between Roosevelt and Wilson, with Taft a poor third; and so far as platforms and campaign promises went, the two progressive leaders were not far apart. Roosevelt outlined his principles in 1910, after his return from Europe and before there was any move for a third party. "The man who wrongly holds that every human right is secondary to his profit must now give way to the advocate of human welfare, who rightly maintains that every man holds his property subject to the general right of the community to regulate its use to whatever degree the public welfare may require it." And in another passage: "We are for the liberty of the individual up to, and not beyond, the point where it becomes inconsistent with the welfare of the community."[27] The platform on which the ex-president sought election was a thoroughgoing social document, including practically every device then discussed for popular control of government and for regulation of industry. On the tariff, however, it was vague; and there was an unpalatable distinction between "good trusts" and "bad trusts."[28]

Wilson saw in the protective tariff what Jefferson had seen in it—a means of building up and maintaining vested interests; and through an elaborate system of interlocking directorates, these vested interests had come to control, through the control of credit, the entire economic life of the country.[29] Mere regulation of monopolies was not enough for Wilson. With such necessary exceptions as railroads and communication systems, he would eliminate them altogether. The age demanded reform. Its abuses had been flaunted before the public by the muck-raking journalists, and by a host of official and semiofficial investigations, and they could no longer be evaded or concealed. Everywhere people awoke to the menace of an economic system grown out of hand, and to the threat of a democracy no longer responsive to the popular will. Wilson was the leader chosen to carry out the progressive program; but the change must have come, sooner or later. It had behind it the whole force of public opinion. It was the inevitable next step in the development of American institutions; and though it meant more government than ever before, it was a step essentially Jeffersonian, for it had as its purpose the welfare of the great mass of the people, and for its objective social justice.

Going back to the turn of the century, when the progressive movement first made its bid for national power, let us see what laws were actually passed in its name. To give to the individual citizen a greater share in carrying on the affairs of his government, the direct election of senators, and later woman's suffrage have become law through constitutional amendment; while di-

---

[27] T. Roosevelt, *The New Nationalism* (New York, 1910), pp. 23-24, 53-54.

[28] Stanwood, *op. cit.*, II, 281 ff.

[29] See W. Wilson, *The New Freedom* (New York, 1913), *passim;* and Louis D. Brandeis, *Other People's Money* (New York, 1914).

rect primaries, and the initiative, referendum and recall have been adopted widely by the states. The real issue of the progressive movement, however, was the economic issue; and while many significant changes were made, the problem was not solved. To cope with the situation, the federal government was gradually forced to assume an increasingly important rôle in relation to business, industry, and agriculture. The powers of the Interstate Commerce Commission were successively enlarged, giving more complete control over all forms of interstate transportation and communication. Laws governing hours, wages, conditions of labor, age, and liability for industrial accident found their way on to the statute books, federal or state. The Supreme Court upheld state legislation for compulsory insurance; a workman's compensation law applicable to all federal employees was passed; and the civil service was greatly extended. A separate Department of Labor with cabinet rank was formed; and the government took various steps looking to the arbitration of industrial disputes. Under Theodore Roosevelt a vast policy of land reclamation was inaugurated, while coal, oil, timber, and mineral lands were withdrawn from entry and added to the public domain.

Under President Wilson the protective principle in tariff legislation was abandoned; and the currency system was thoroughly renovated by the establishment of Federal Reserve Banks throughout the country, provision being made for expanding or contracting the circulating medium when necessary, and for concentrating resources quickly at any desired place. A Federal Trade Commission came into being, with wide powers over business in general, and new rules were made for the regulation of trusts. The government itself built and operated the Panama Canal and the Alaskan railways; and in 1916 launched also on a career of shipbuilding and operation. Altogether, the entire character of the government, federal and state, had altered by the time American entry into the World War forced a temporary change in emphasis by presenting new problems.

After the war, reconstruction and readjustment took precedence, and the progressive movement as such ceased to exist. Only LaFollette of the old leaders remained actively in the field, running as an independent candidate for president in 1924 with socialist support. But the problems which gave rise to the movement were only intensified by the prosperous decade of the 1920's. The old evils in business and government—interlocking directorates, higher and ever higher tariffs, and government in the interests of a class—returned; and when, after three years of the worst depression in our history, the New Deal was proclaimed on March 4, 1933, it was the old solutions, modified and brought up to date, which formed the basis of the program.

v

The tremendous industrial expansion necessitated by the war emergency, together with greatly increased commercial activity, served further to concentrate and solidify the power of corporate and financial interests. In a sense, therefore, the exigencies of Wilson's second term undid the constructive legislation of his first four years in office. The capitalistic interests were able to regain control of the machinery of government immediately after the war. A period of unparalleled prosperity lulled any murmurs of discontent; there were few voices raised in warning, and they were disregarded; and the decade culminated in an era of crazy speculation. Late in 1929 the crash came, with depression growing deeper month after month, until at the time of the presidential election in 1932, there were estimated to be more than twelve millions unemployed.

During the boom years, the Democratic party had been almost as conservative as the Republican; but with the coming of hard times the more radical elements dominated. In nominating and electing Franklin D. Roosevelt the party returned to the essential policies of its pre-war period, Roosevelt soon showing himself to be the inheritor of Bryan. The Democratic program, backed by insurgent Republicans, Progressives, and a few Socialists, has come to be called, in the President's phrase, the "New Deal"; and while it will be many years before any adequate evaluation of it can be made, the main features will be briefly sketched, in the light of the movements which preceded it.

The New Deal is characterized by the President as a "changed concept of the duty and responsibility of government toward economic life."[30] A change, that is, from the attitude of more recent administrations. It goes back for its inspiration to the Populist and Progressive platforms, only expanding its program to meet the contemporary situation. All these elements in the democratic tradition derive from the Jeffersonian formula of the right of every man to life, liberty, and the pursuit of happiness—a formula which, under the conditions of modern industrialism, must include the right of every man to earn by his own labor a decent living.[31] "We know that individual liberty and individual happiness mean nothing unless both are ordered in the sense that one man's meat is not another man's poison."[32] The objective of the state must be more than mere restriction: it must be to provide for every man, woman, and child an opportunity to achieve a more abundant life.[33]

In the introduction to the volume covering speeches and acts of his first year in office, President Roosevelt cites the three steps involved in building what he terms "a new order": The elimination of special privilege; a war on crime and graft; and an effort to bring about "a return of the swing of the pendulum, which for three generations had been sweeping toward a constantly increasing concentration of wealth in fewer and fewer hands—a swing back in the direction of wider distribution of the wealth and property of the nation."[34] The problem attacked is the same as that which has occupied the democratic tradition since the Civil War; and the ends sought are substantially those desired by every reform movement in the last

---

[30] F. D. Roosevelt, *Looking Forward* (New York, 1933), p. 241.
[31] *Ibid.*, p. 35.
[32] *Ibid.*, p. 36.
[33] F. D. Roosevelt, *On Our Way* (New York, 1924), pp. 194-95.
[34] *Ibid.*, pp. xi-xii.

half century. Only the method is more sweeping and the program more highly integrated.

Broadly speaking, the New Deal is being carried out on
three fronts—the agricultural, the industrial, and the financial,
—the program in each case calling for a large measure of government control, and for long time planning. The Agricultural
Adjustment Act seeks to raise the purchasing power of the
farmer by control of crop surpluses, the method being voluntary reduction of acreage in staple crops in return for a government subsidy. Technically, the government "rents" the acreage
withheld, the money being raised by a processing tax on the
crop in question. To head off possible opposition from distributors, the secretary of agriculture has been invested with a
licensing power which gives him wide control over markets.[35]
For meeting the immediate emergency, a Farm Credit Administration has been created, empowered to take up farm mortgages
on liberal terms; and for the future, the program contemplates
a vast project for withdrawing marginal lands from agricultural
use. In conjunction with this, reforestation, flood control,
drainage, irrigation, and soil erosion control are being carried on.

On the industrial front, the aim of the New Deal is to make
the business leader responsible to the public, on the principle
that private office, no less than public office, is a public trust.[36]
Under the National Industrial Recovery Act, the antitrust laws
were suspended to allow common action within an industry. All
the members of a given industrial group were then enjoined to
operate under the terms of a "code of fair competition," drawn
up by themselves and approved by the Administrator, which
aimed at eliminating abuses, which fixed hours, wages and working conditions, and which had power also to fix prices. By bringing competing firms under the same code, the NRA sought to
shorten hours and increase wages—essential factors in reducing
unemployment, while increasing purchasing power. "If all em-
ployers in each competitive group agree to pay their workers

[35] C. A. Beard and G. H. E. Smith, *The Future Comes* (New York, 1933), pp. 78 ff.
See also, Henry A. Wallace, *America Must Choose* (New York and Boston, 1934).
[36] F. D. Roosevelt, *On Our Way*, p. 250.

the same wages—reasonable wages—and require the same hours —reasonable hours—then higher wages and shorter hours will hurt no one. Moreover, such action is better for the employer than unemployment and low wages, because it makes more buyers for his product. This is the simple idea which is the very heart of the Industrial Recovery Act."[37] It amounts simply to an agreement between the members of a given industry and the government, representing the public, as to how the industry shall be conducted; and its goal "is the assurance of a reasonable profit to industry and living wages for labor with the elimination of the piratical methods and practices which have not only harassed honest business but also contributed to the ills of labor."[38] Though the act itself has been invalidated by the Supreme Court, the idea of voluntary coöperation within an industry has taken firmer root. It seems likely that the ultimate gain will be greater than it would have been had the codes retained their mandatory features.

The New Deal recognizes the right of every community to set up and operate as public ventures utility plants to compete with those believed to be charging extortionate rates; and a similar right on the part of the federal government to compete with private enterprize for the purpose of compelling fair treatment. The great power development at Muscle Shoals is thus intended primarily as a club to hold over private distributors of power, as are the plants under construction or contemplated on the Colorado, Columbia, and St. Lawrence rivers.[39] In general, public utilities are to be regulated in the interest of the public, being forced to give adequate service at fair rates; and any business dealing with the public may be regarded as a public utility. Overcapitalization—the sale of "watered" stock—will no longer pay, if the increased financial burden cannot be passed along to the consumer.[40] A Federal Coördinator of Transportation has been given sweeping authority over the railroads; while railroad holding companies have been brought under the

[37] *Ibid.*, p. 148.   [38] *Ibid.*, p. 97.
[39] F. D. Roosevelt, *Looking Forward*, pp. 152 ff.
[40] *Ibid.*, pp. 139 ff.

I. C. C., and numerous other bureaus and commissions have been created to carry out the regulatory program.

In line with the new responsibilities placed upon the shoulders of business is the Securities Act, designed to protect the public from false statements made by those who issue and sell stocks. "Those who manage banks, corporations and other agencies handling or using other people's money are trustees acting for others."[41] On the tariff question—another feature of all reform agitation for three generations—the New Deal takes the traditional Democratic position. The tariff as a subsidy to industry must go. It has raised domestic prices to unreasonable levels, and has operated to close foreign markets to our agricultural products, as well as to give to powerful economic groups an incentive for interfering in governmental matters. The President has been empowered by Congress to adjust the tariff for negotiating reciprocal commercial treaties with other nations.

The emergency provisions of the program include the employment of some 600,000 young men in a civilian conservation corps, engaged in reforestation and flood control work; large appropriations for useful public works; direct loans through the Reconstruction Finance Corporation to commercial and industrial groups, and through other agencies to the owners of urban and suburban homes; and temporary direct relief for the needy. At the same time, under the direction of the Tennessee Valley Authority, a vast experiment in regional planning is being conducted, in an effort to develop methods which will eliminate the necessity of relief in the future.[42] Unemployment insurance is also advocated by the President as a means to the same end.[43]

The financial policy of the New Deal, like its other leading policies, goes back to the Populist agitation of the nineties. Looking toward a more equitable distribution of wealth, and to a managed currency, the gold content of the dollar has been rendered flexible within certain limits by authorizing the Treas-

[41] F. D. Roosevelt, *On Our Way*, pp. 45-46.
[42] *Ibid.*, pp. 53 ff.
[43] F. D. Roosevelt, *Looking Forward*, p. 46.

ury to buy gold at a price fixed by the secretary on consultation with the President. Mr. Roosevelt's statement on the currency question would sound remarkably familiar to the Populist of a generation ago. "The United States seeks the kind of a dollar which a generation hence will have the same purchasing power as the dollar value we hope to achieve in the near future."[44] Silver, too, has been remonetized to the extent of authorizing the treasury to keep twenty-five per cent of its reserve in that metal. In the taxation policy, the social democratic emphasis speaks again. "Not only must government income meet prospective expenditures, but this income must be secured on the principle of ability to pay. This is a declaration in favor of graduated income, inheritance and profits taxes, and against taxes on food and clothing, whose burden is actually shifted to the consumers of these necessities of life on a per capita basis rather than on the basis of the relative size of personal incomes."[45]

Like all programs of social reform, the New Deal has not consistently followed its declared policy, and its failures and compromises afford ample room for criticism. In its broad outlines, however, the philosophy behind the program is fairly clear, and it is a philosophy essentially Jeffersonian. It is merely selecting for emphasis the social rather than the individualistic side of the tradition. One emphasis is as necessary as the other if a working balance between liberty and equality, the basic concepts of democracy, is to be effected. The times may stress now one and now the other, but in historical perspective the two have advanced and will advance together.

Perhaps the most significant feature of the socialized democracy of today is the acceptance by the state of the responsibility for keeping the economic machinery in operation. The one perfectly clear fact of modern civilization seems to be that political power and economic power must and will be identified. The individualistic theory of democracy tended to concentrate polit-

---

[44] F. D. Roosevelt, *On Our Way*, p. 125.
[45] F. D. Roosevelt, *Looking Forward*, p. 105.

ical power in the hands of the dominant economic groups, while social democracy seeks to work out the problem by arrogating to the state the direction of the economic life of the nation. In the process, it is inevitable that individual liberty will in certain particulars be curtailed as the activities of government are extended: only by some such means can the welfare of the group as a whole be secured, and the welfare of the group is the ultimate end of the state. To balance the potential danger inherent in this growing power of government in individual affairs, there has been a continuous extension of the means of expressing public opinion. The common man, although he tends in a sense to be submerged in the state, has found means of making his will articulate, and he is more widely appealed to than ever before. In the Democratic convention of 1912, for example, Bryan's anti-Wall Street resolutions were adopted by overwhelming vote in the face of a hostile majority, solely in response to thousands of telegrams which poured in on the delegates from the people back home. President Roosevelt's adroit use of the radio is another instance of the way in which public opinion may be brought to bear on national questions, and pressure exerted on elected representatives. The future of democracy will depend largely on the extent to which these two tendencies can be brought to keep pace with each other.

In a world resorting on every hand for the solution of its political and economic problems to dictatorships—of military force, of the proletariat, of the colored shirt—American democracy has shown tremendous vitality. Because it is not rigid, or beyond the reach of change; because its principles are broad enough to permit of alteration and adjustment within the lines of the traditional governmental structure; because it has maintained the ideal of a free people coöperating under free institutions, American democracy has survived and prospered, justifying again and again the faith of Jefferson that an informed and intelligent people can and will work out their own salvation.

INDEX

AMERICAN CENTURY SERIES

Distinguished paperback books in the fields of literature and history.